I enjoy sharing my books as I do my friends, asking only that you treat them well and see them safely home

Mary Ellen James

D1566948

KNOWING AND THE KNOWN

Knowing *and*
the Known

JOHN DEWEY

and

ARTHUR F. BENTLEY

GREENWOOD PRESS, PUBLISHERS
WESTPORT, CONNECTICUT

Library of Congress Cataloging in Publication Data
Dewey, John, 1859-1952.
    Knowing and the known.

    Reprint of the 1960 issue of the ed. first published
in 1949 by Beacon Press, Boston.
    Includes index.
    1. Knowledge, Theory of. I. Bentley, Arthur Fisher,
1870-1957, joint author. II. Title.
BD161.D38 1975   121   75-31432
ISBN 0-8371-8498-3

PREFACE

THE difficulties attending dependability of communication and mutual intelligibility in connection with problems of knowledge are notoriously great. They are so numerous and acute that disagreement, controversy, and misunderstanding are almost taken to be matters of course. The studies upon which report is made in this volume are the outgrowth of a conviction that a greater degree of dependability, and hence of mutual understanding, and of ability to turn differences to mutual advantage, is as practicable as it is essential. This conviction has gained steadily in force as we have proceeded. We hold that it is practicable to employ in the study of problems of knowing and knowledge the postulational method now generally used in subjectmatters scientifically developed. The scientific method neither presupposes nor implies any set, rigid, theoretical position. We are too well aware of the futility of efforts to achieve greater dependability of communication and consequent mutual understanding by methods of imposition. In advancing fields of research, inquirers proceed by doing all they can to make clear to themselves and to others the points of view and the hypotheses by means of which their work is carried on. When those who disagree with one another in their conclusions join in a common demand for such clarification, their difficulties usually turn out to increase command of the subject.

Accordingly we stress that our experiment is one of co-operative research. Our confidence is placed in this method; it is placed in the particular conclusions presented as far as they are found to be results of this method.

Our belief that future advance in knowledge about knowings requires dependability of communication is integrally connected with the transactional point of view and frame of reference we employ. Emphasis upon the transactional grew steadily as our studies proceeded. We believe the tenor of our development will be grasped most readily when the distinction of the transactional from the interactional and self-actional points of view is systematically borne in mind. The transactional is in fact that point of view which systematically proceeds upon the ground that knowing is co-operative and as such is integral with communication. By its own processes it is allied with the postulational. It demands that statements be made as descriptions of events in terms of durations in time and areas in space. It excludes assertions of fixity and attempts to impose them. It installs openness and flexibility in the very process of knowing. It treats knowledge as itself inquiry — as a goal *within* inquiry, not as a terminus outside or beyond inquiry. We wish the tests of openness and flexibility to be applied to our work; any attempts to impose fixity would be a denial — a rupture — of the very method we employ. Our requirement of openness in our own work, nevertheless, does not mean we disregard or reject criticisms from absolute points of view. It does, however, require of such criticisms that the particular absolute point of view be itself frankly, explicitly, stated in its bearing upon the views that are presented.

We trust that if these studies initiate a co-operative movement of this sort, the outcome will be progress in firmness and dependability in communication which is an indispensable condition of progress in knowledge of fact.

The inquiry has covered a period of four years and the material has had preliminary publication in one or other of the philosophical journals. We have not undertaken to remove from our pages the overlappings arising out of the protracted inquiry and of the varied manners of presentation. Since new points of approach are involved, along with progress in grasp of the problems, even the repetitions, we may hope, will at times be beneficial. We have taken advantage of this opportunity to make a number of small changes, mostly in phrasings, and in the style and scope of inter-chapter references. Some additional citations from recent discussions have been made. In only one case, we believe, has a substantive change in formulation been made, and that is exhibited in a footnote.

As continuance of our present work we hope the future will see the completion of papers on the transactional construction of psychology; on the presentation of language as human behavior; on the application of mathematical symbolism to linguistic namings and to perceivings; and on the significance of the wide range of employment, both philosophically and in practical life, of the word "sign" in recent generations.

The reader's attention is called to the Appendix containing a letter from John Dewey to a philosopher friend. He who fails to grasp the viewpoint therein expressed may find himself in the shadow as respects all else we have to say.

We owe our thanks to Joseph Ratner and Jules Altman for their many suggestions in the course of this study, and to the latter particularly for his careful work in preparing the Index.

June, 1948

CONTENTS

INTRODUCTION

A SEARCH FOR FIRM NAMES

A YEAR or so ago we decided that the time had come to undertake a postponed task: the attempt to fix a set of leading words capable of firm use in the discussion of "knowings" and "existings" in that specialized region of research called the theory of knowledge. The undertaking proved to be of the kind that grows. Firm words for our own use had to be based on well-founded observation. Such observation had to be sound enough, and well enough labeled, to be used with definiteness, not only between ourselves, but also in intercourse with other workers, including even those who might be at far extremes from us in their manner of interpretation and construction. It is clear, we think, that without some such agreement on the simpler fact-names, no progress of the kind the modern world knows as scientific will be probable; and, further, that so long as man, the organism, is viewed naturalistically within the cosmos, research of the scientific type into his "knowings" is a worth-while objective. The results of our inquiry are to be reported in a series of papers, some individually signed, some over our joint names,[1] depending on the extent to which problems set up and investigations undertaken become specialized or consolidated as we proceed. We shall examine such words as fact, existence, event; designation, experience, agency; situation, object, subjectmatter; interaction, transaction; definition, description, specification, characterization; signal, sign, symbol; centering, of course, on those regions of application in which phrasings in the vaguely allusive form of "subject" and "object" conventionally appear.

---

[1] References are to the notes at the end of each chapter.

The opening chapter arose from the accumulation of many illustrations, which we first segregated and then advanced to introductory position because we found they yielded a startling diagnosis of linguistic disease not only in the general epistemological field, where everyone would anticipate it, but also in the specialized logical field, which ought to be reasonably immune. This diagnosis furnishes the strongest evidence that there is a need for the type of terminological inquiry we are engaged in, whether it is done at our hands and from our manner of approach, or at the hands and under the differing approach of others. We are in full agreement as to the general development of the chapter and as to the demonstration of the extent of the evil in the logics, its roots and the steps that should be taken to cure it.

One point needs stress at once. In seeking firm names, we do not assume that any name may be wholly right, nor any wholly wrong. We introduce into language no melodrama of villains all black, nor of heroes all white. We take names always as namings: as living behaviors in an evolving world of men and things. Thus taken, the poorest and feeblest name has its place in living and its work to do, whether we can today trace backward or forecast ahead its capabilities; and the best and strongest name gains nowhere over us completed dominance.[2]

It should be plain enough that the discussions in the first chapter, as well as in those that are to follow, are not designed primarily for criticizing individual logicians. In view of the competence of the writers who are discussed, the great variety of the confusions that are found can be attributed only to something defective in the underlying assumptions that influence the writers' approach. The nature of these underlying defects will, we trust, become evident as we proceed; and we hope the specific criticisms we are compelled to make in order to exhibit the difficulty will be taken as concerned solely with the situation of inquiry, and not with personalities.[3]

1 Of the papers chosen for incorporation in this book, those forming Chapters I, VIII, and IX are written by Bentley. That forming Chapter X is written by Dewey. The rest were signed jointly. The original titles of some of the papers have been altered for the present use. Places of original publication are noted in an appended comment.

2 In later development we shall grade the poorer namings as Cues and Characterizations; and the better and best as Specifications.

3 As a preliminary to further appraisal, one may profitably examine Max Wertheimer's discussion of the vague uses of leading terms in the traditional deductive and inductive logics, due to piecemeal dealings with "words" and "things" in blind disregard of structures. *Productive Thinking*, (New York, 1945) , pp. 204-205.

October, 1944

KNOWING AND THE KNOWN

CHAPTER ONE

VAGUENESS IN LOGIC[1]

I

LOGICIANS largely eschew epistemology. Thereby they save themselves much illogicality. They do not, however, eschew the assumed cosmic pattern within which the standardized epistemologies operate. They accept that pattern practically and work within it. They accept it, indeed, in such simple faith that they neglect to turn their professional skills upon it. They tolerate thereby a basic vagueness in their work. Sometimes they sense such defects in their fellow logicians, but rarely do they look closely at home, or try to locate the source of the defects found in others. Perhaps a tour of inspection by inquirers who use a different approach may indicate the source from which the trouble proceeds and suggest a different and more coherent construction.

The logical texts to which we shall give especial attention are the work of Carnap, Cohen and Nagel, Ducasse, Lewis, Morris, and Tarski. To economize space citations in our text will be made by use of initials of the authors, respectively, C, CN, D, L, M, and T.[2]

The cosmic pattern to which we have referred is one used by Peirce as an aid to many of his explorations, and commonly accepted as characteristic of him, although it does not at all represent his basic envisionment. It introduces for logical purposes three kinds of materials: (1) men; (2) things; (3) an intervening interpretative activity, product, or medium — linguistic, symbolic, mental, ra-

---

[1] References are to the notes at the end of each chapter.

tional, logical, or other — such as language, sign, sentence, proposition, meaning, truth, or thought. Its very appearance in so many variations seems of itself to suggest a vagueness in grasp of fundamentals. A crude form of it is well known in Ogden and Richard's triangle (*The Meaning of Meaning*, p. 14) presenting "thought or reference," "symbol," and "referent." Similarly we find Cohen and Nagel remarking (*CN*, p. 16) that "it seems impossible that there should be any confusion between a physical object, our 'idea' or image of it, and the word that denotes it. . . ." Lewis, claiming the authority of Peirce, holds that "the essentials of the meaning-situation are found wherever there is anything which, for some mind, stands as sign of something else" (*L*, p. 236). Carnap sets up "the speaker, the expression uttered, and the designatum of the expression," altering this at once into "the speaker, the expression, and what is referred to" (*C*, pp. 8-9), a change of phrasing which is not in the interest of clarity, more particularly as the "what is referred to" is also spoken of as that to which the speaker "intends" to refer. Morris introduces officially a "triadic relation of semiosis" correlating sign vehicle, designatum and interpreter (*M*, p. 6), sometimes substituting interpretant for interpreter (*M*, p. 3), sometimes using both interpreter and interpretant to yield what is apparently a "quadratic" instead of a "triadic" form, and always tolerating scattered meanings for his leading words.

We view all the above arrangements as varieties of a single cosmic pattern — an ancient patchwork cobbling, at times a crazy quilt. The components shift unconscionably. Anyone who has ever tried to make them lie still long enough for matter-of-fact classification has quickly found this out.

We may not take time to show in detail here how radically different all this is from Peirce's basic procedure — our attention will be given to that at another time[3] — but since Peirce is continually quoted, and misquoted, by all

parties involved, we shall pause just long enough to illuminate the issue slightly. Such words as Lewis takes from
Peirce do *not* mean that minds, signs and things should be
established in credal separations sharper than those of
levers, fulcrums, and weights; Peirce was probing a linguistic disorder and learning fifty years ago how to avoid
the type of chaos Lewis's development shows. Similarly
Cohen and Nagel (*CN*, p. 117) quote a sentence from Peirce
as if in their own support, when actually they depart not
merely from Peirce's intent but from the very wording
they quote. In his *Syllabus of Certain Topics of Logic*
(1903) Peirce wrote:

The woof and warp of all thought and all research is symbols, and the life of thought and science is the life inherent
in symbols; so that it is wrong to say that a good language
is *important* to good thought, merely; for it is of the essence
of it.[4]

Peirce here makes flat denial of that separation of word,
idea and object which Cohen and Nagel employ, and
which they believe "impossible" to confuse. The two
world-views are in radical contrast.

Consider again what Peirce, cutting still more deeply,
wrote about the *sign* "lithium" in its scientific use:

The peculiarity of this definition — or rather this precept
that is more serviceable than a definition — is that it tells you
what the word "lithium" denotes by prescribing what you are
to *do* in order to gain a perceptual acquaintance with the object of the word.[5]

Notice the "perceptual"; notice the "object" of the
"word." There is nothing here that implies a pattern of
two orders or realms brought into connection by a third
intervening thing or sign. This is the real Peirce: Peirce
on the advance — not bedded down in the ancient swamp.

The cosmic pattern we shall employ, and by the aid of
which we shall make our tests, differs sharply from the
current conventional one and is in line with what Peirce
persistently sought. It will treat the talking and talk-
products or effects of man (the namings, thinkings, argu-

ings, reasonings, etc.) as the men themselves in action, not as some third type of entity to be inserted between the men and the things they deal with. *To this extent* it will be not three-realm, but two-realm: men and things. The difference in the treatment of language is radical. Nevertheless it is not of the type called "theoretical," nor does it transmute the men from organisms into putative "psyches." It rests in the simplest, most direct, matter-of-fact, everyday, common sense observation. Talking-organisms and things — there they are; if there, let us study them as they come: the men talking. To make this observation and retain it in memory while we proceed are the only requirements we place upon readers of this first chapter. When, however, we undertake hereafter a changed form of construction, we must strengthen the formulation under this observation, and secure a still broader observation. The revelatory value of our present report nevertheless remains, whether such further construction is attempted or not.

In the current logics, probably the commonest third-realm insertion between men and things is "proposition," though among other insertions "meaning" and "thought" are at times most active rivals for that position. In the first two logics we examine, those of Cohen and Nagel, and of Carnap, we shall give attention primarily to "proposition." Our aim will be to find out what in logic — in these logics, particularly — a proposition *is*, where by "is" we intend just some plain, matter-of-fact characterization such as any man may reasonably well be expected to offer to establish that he *knows what he is talking about* when he names the subjectmatter of his discussion. We shall ask, in other words, what sort of fact a proposition **is** taken to be.

In the logics, in place of an endeavor to find out whether the propositions in question are facts, we shall find a marked tendency to reverse the procedure and to declare that facts are propositions. Sometimes this is asserted openly and above board; at other times it is covert, or implied. Cohen and Nagel flatly tell us that facts are propositions — "true" propositions, this is to say. Their book (*CN*) is divided between formal logic and scientific method. Under the circumstances we shall feel at liberty to bring together passages from the two portions of the work, and we shall not apologize — formal logic or no formal logic — for a treatment of the issues of fact and proposition in common. Following this we shall examine the manner in which Carnap (*C*), though always seeming to be pushing fact behind him with the flat of his hand, makes his most critical, and possibly his most incoherent, decision — that concerning sentence and proposition — with an eye upon the very "fact" he disguises behind a tangle of meanings and designations.

The issue between proposition and fact is not minor, even though it enters as a detail in logical systematization. It is apparently an incidental manifestation of the determined effort of logicians during the past generation to supply mathematics with "foundations" through which they could dominate it and make further pretense to authority over science and fact as well. (The whole tendency might be shown to be a survival from antiquity, but we shall not go that far afield at this time.) We shall simply stress here that if fact is important to the modern world, and if logic has reached the point where it declares facts to be propositions, then it is high time to reverse the operation, and find out whether *propositions* themselves, as the logicians present them, are facts—and if so, what kind.

II

Cohen and Nagel's *Logic* (*CN*) is outstanding, not only for its pedagogical clarity but for the wide-ranging competence of its authors going far beyond the immediate requirements of a collegiate textbook. The index of their book does not list "fact," *as* "fact," but does list "facts," directing us among other things to a six-page discussion of facts and hypotheses. We are frequently told that a "fact" *is* a "proposition" that is "true." Thus (*CN*, p. 392): "The 'facts' for which every inquiry reaches out are propositions for whose truth there is considerable evidence." Notice that it is their own direct choice of expression, not some inference from it or interpretation of it, that sets our problem. If they had said, as some logicians do, that "fact" is truth, or propositional truth, that might have led us on a different course, but they make "true" the adjective and "proposition" the noun, and thus guide us to our present form of inquiry.

As the case stands, it is very much easier in their work to find out what a "proposition" is *not*, than to find out what it *is*. Propositions are:

> *not* sentences (*CN*, p. 27, No. 1)
> *not* mental acts (*CN*, p. 28, No. 4)
> *not* concrete objects, things, or events (*CN*, p. 28, No. 5) .[6]

What, now, are propositions, if they are neither physical, mental, nor linguistic? It takes more ingenuity than we have to make sure; it is a strain even to make the attempt. A form of definition is, indeed, offered thus: "a *proposition* may be defined as anything which can be said to be true or false" (*CN*, p. 27). This is fairly loose language, to start with, and how it operates without involving either the mental or the linguistic is difficult to see. A variant, but not equivalent, phrasing is that a proposition is "something concerning which questions of truth and falsity are significant" (*CN*, p. 28, No. 3). Unfortunately the words "something," "anything," "said" and "significant" in these citations — just dictionary words here, and nothing more — are hard to apply in the face of all the negations. We are no better off from incidental phrasings such as that a proposition is "information conveyed by sentences" (*CN*, p. 17), or that it is "objective meaning" (*CN*, p. 28, No. 4), or that it is what a sentence "signifies" (*CN*, p. 27). If sentences are actually, as they tell us, just marks or sounds having a "physical existence" on surfaces or in air waves (*CN*, p. 27), just how such marks "convey" or "signify" anything needs elucidation; as for "objective meaning," the words rumble in the deepest bowels of epistemology. We also note other difficulties when we take their language literally, not impressionistically. While the proposition "must not be confused with the symbols which state it," it cannot be "*expressed or conveyed* without symbols" (*CN*, p. 27) ; while it is not "object, thing, or event," it may be "relation," though relations are "objects of our thought," and, as such, "elements or aspects of actual, concrete situations" (*CN*, pp. 28-29) ; while a proposition is what is "true or false," there is no requirement that anyone, living or dead, "*know* which of these alternatives is the case" (*CN*, p. 29, No. 6).[7]

Literally and with straight-faced attention we are asked by Cohen and Nagel to concern ourselves with propositions that are not physical, not mental, not linguistic, and not even something in process of being expressed or conveyed, but that nevertheless have a tremendous actuality wherein they possess truth and falsity on their own account, regardless of all human participation and of any trace of human knowing. All of which is very difficult to accomplish in the Year of Our Lord, 1944. It is even more troublesome factually, since everything we are logically authorized to know about *facts* (apart from certain "sensations" and other dubieties residing on the far side of the logical tracks) must be acquired from such "propositions." Our "knowledge," even, the authors tell us, "is *of* propositions" (*CN*, p. 29); and what a proposition *that* is, unless the "of" by some strange choice is a synonym of "through" or "by means of." [8]

Supplementing their position that facts are propositions — while propositions are, at the same time, stripped of all the characteristics research workers since Galileo would accept as factual — Cohen and Nagel offer a free account of "facts" (*CN*, pp. 217-218). This, however, clears up nothing. They note "different senses" of "fact" which they pro-

ceed at once to render as "distinct things" "denoted" by
the word. Apparently they do not intend either four different dictionary meanings of the word, as "senses" would
imply, or four distinct "classes of objects," as "denotes"
would require (*CN*, p. 31), but something uncertainly between the two. The passage in question reads:

> We must, obviously, distinguish between the different senses
> of "fact." It denotes at least four distinct things.
> 1 . . . certain discriminated elements in sense percep-
> tion. . . .
> 2 . . . the propositions which *interpret* what is given to us
> in sense experience.
> 3 . . . propositions which truly assert an invariable se-
> quence or conjunction of characters. . . .
> 4 . . . those things existing in space or time, together with
> the relations between them, in virtue of which a proposition
> is true.

Two of these four do not enter as propositions at all.
The other two use the word "propositions" but involve interpretations and technical assertion of types which evidently run far into the "mental" region from which
"proposition" is excluded. Whether we have here "senses"
or "classes of objects," some kind of organization of the
"things" should be offered if the passage is to have any
logical relevance whatever. Such organization is conspicu-
ously lacking,[9] and the total effect of the passage is to take
advantage of the very confusion that so greatly needs to be
cleared away.

We get no help by going back to the word "meaning,"
for meaning is as badly off as "proposition" is. Some logicians employ the word heavily — we shall note one of them
later — but in the present work, so far as the index indicates, the word merely yields a change of phrasing. The
"meaning of a proposition" is something we must know
before deciding whether it is "true" (*CN*, p. 9) ; no matter
how formal our implication, it must not ignore "the entire
meaning" (*CN*, p. 12); universal propositions have mean-

ings that require "at least *possible* matters of fact" (*CN*, p. 43).

Nor do we get any help when we try the words "true" and "false." No direct discussion of "true" has been observed by us in the book. It enters as the essential "is-ness" of propositions: "if a proposition is true it must always be true" (*CN*, p. 29). Apparently neither truth nor proposition can survive without an eye on the other, but when emphasis is desired we hear of "true in fact" (as *CN*, p. 7, p. 76), so that even the axioms must have their truth empirically established (*CN*, p. 132). This is the only variety of "true" we have noticed, even though we are told that "truths" may be proved out of other "truths." We have the curious situation (1) that facts are propositions; (2) that propositions are truth (or falsity) assertions; (3) that under pressure "true" turns out to be "true in fact" — just like that, no more, no less — and "false," no doubt, the same.

We are about half through with our exhibit, but we shall omit the rest of it. It all comes to the same thing. A word is officially introduced and assigned a task. Turn around once, and when you look back it is doing something else. You do not even need to turn around; just let your direct gaze slip, and the word is off on the bias. Cohen and Nagel believe their logic to be in tune with the infinite, this being a standard convention among logicians. "Its principles," they say, "are inherently applicable because they are concerned with ontological [10] traits of utmost generality" (*CN*, p. v). We, on the contrary, believe their "principles" are inherently defective because they are concerned with verbal traits of the utmost triviality. The practical work of discussing evidence and proof is admirably done in their work. Theoretical construction defaults altogether. But the very deficiencies are valuable — if one will but look at them — as clues to the kind of research that, under our present manner of examination, is most important for the immediate future.

III

When Professor Nagel reviewed Carnap's *Introduction to Semantics* (*C*) and came to its "propositions," he felt impelled to shake his head sadly at such "hypostatic Platonic entities." [11] Now Carnap's "propositions" may be more *spirituelles* than Cohen-Nagel's — which are hopefully of the earth earthy, even though nothing of the physical, mental, linguistic or communicative is allowed them — but what little difference there is between the two types is one of philosophical convention rather than of character. Nevertheless, such is logic that we are not greatly surprised, while Nagel is grieving over Carnap, to find Carnap placing Cohen-Nagel in the lead among his fellow-travelers, with evidence attached (*C*, p. 236).

Fact, in Carnap's work, is farther away around the corner than it is in Cohen-Nagel's. It is something logic is supposed never quite to reach, but only to skim past at the edges, with perhaps a little thought-transference on the way. It has a sort of surrogate in "absolute concepts" which are to be recognized as being present when all words agree, and which therefore, somewhat surprisingly, are said to be totally unaffected by language (*C*, pp. 41-42; p. 89, Convention 17-1). Nevertheless, when Carnap distinguishes proposition from sentence he does it with a hazy eye upon a certain unity of organization which must some way or other, some time or other, be secured between the formal and the factual.

In his thirteen-page terminological appendix which cries "Peace, peace" where there is no peace, Carnap notes two main uses — two "different concepts," he says — for the word "proposition" (*C*, p. 235). He distills these out of a welter of logical confusions he finds well illustrated in Bertrand Russell. These outstanding uses are first "for certain expressions" and then "for their designata." His elaboration — we cite meticulously, and in full, since this is the only way to make the exhibit plain — runs:

'Proposition'. The term is used for two different concepts, namely for certain expressions (I) and for their designata (II).

I: As 'declarative sentence'. Other terms: 'sentence'*, 'statement' (Quine), 'formula' (Bernays).

II*: As "that which is expressed (signified, formulated, represented, designated) by a (declarative) sentence" (§§ 6 and 18). Other terms: 'Satz an sich' (Bolzano), 'Objectiv' (A. Meinong), 'state of affairs' (Wittgenstein), 'condition'.

The asterisks are used by Carnap to mark the terminology he himself adopts. In I, he states he will use the word "sentence" for what others might call declarative sentence, statement, or formula. In II*, he adopts the word "proposition" for whatever it is he there sets forth. 'Sentence' (I) and 'Proposition' (II) together make up what the man in the street would call a sentence: roughly, this is to say, an expression of meaning in words. A reader who merely wants a whiff of characterization while the semantic march proceeds may be satisfied with the passage as we have cited it. It offers, however, serious difficulty to the man who wants to grasp what is involved before he goes farther. We propose to take this passage apart and find out what is in it; for nothing of the semantic construction is safe if this is defective. Since Carnap offers us "pure" semantics — free from all outer influence, practical or other — *we shall give it "pure" linguistic analysis, staying right among its sentences,* and dragging nothing in from the outside. He is meticulous about his definitions, his theorems and his conventions; we shall be meticulous about the verbal materials out of which he builds them. This will take much space, but no other course is possible. One great hindrance is the way he slips one word into the place of another, presumably in synonymic substitution, but usually with so much wavering of allusion that delivery becomes uncertain. Such shifting verbal sands make progress slow. For our immediate purposes, we shall employ *italics* to display precisely the wordings we quote as we dissect them.

The word "proposition," if used without quotation

marks, would be an "expression (sign, word)." Supplied
with single quotation marks — thus 'Proposition' — it becomes "a name for that expression . . . in the metalanguage for that language" (C, p. 237). Having written
down 'Proposition', he then proceeds: The term is used for
. . . . Here "term" is an evasive word, unindexed, un-
specified and undiscussed in his text. (It, together with certain other evasive words, will be given separate attention
later.)   In the present passage it represents either "proposition" or 'proposition' or possibly a mixture of both. Look
at it, and it should represent the latter. Read it, and you
will think it represents the former. We shall risk no
opinion, more particularly because of the vagueness of
what follows.[12] Taking the is used for, however, we may
venture to guess we have here a substitute for "names" (as
the word "names" is used in C, p. 237), with an implication
of variety in namings, and this evasively with respect to
"current" uses on the one side, and names as they "ought
to be" used on the other. Our criticism here may look
finical, but it is not. When the word "term" is used in a
vital passage in a logic, we have a right to know exactly
how it is being used.

If we add the next three words, the declaration thus far
seems to be to the effect that the name of the expression, or
perhaps the expression itself, names variously, for various
people, two different concepts.

The word "concept" dominates this sentence and produces its flight from simplicity and its distortion. What follows is worse. We face something undecipherable and
without clue. Balanced against "concept" in some unknown form of organization we find certain expressions
(I) and . . . their designata (II). Here concept introduces (presents? represents? applies to? names? designates?
includes? covers?) certain expressions and their (certain)
designata. If he had said in simple words that "proposition" is currently used in two ways, one of which he proposes to call 'sentence,' and the other, 'proposition,' the

reader's attention might have been directed to certain features of his account, in which something factually defective
would have been noted.[13] What concerns us, however, is
not this defect but his elaborate apparatus of terminological obscurity, and to this we shall restrict ourselves. Holding for the moment to the three words "concept," "expression" and "designatum," and noting that the "certain"
designata here in question are "propositions," we turn to
his introductory table (C, p. 18) in which he offers his
"terminology of designata." Applying our attention to this
we are led to report that for Carnap:

1. concepts are one variety of designata, the other varieties being individuals and propositions;

2. designata enter as entities, with which, so far as we
are told, they coincide in extension;

3. expressions (signs, terms), in the functions they perform in the *Semantics*, are not entities, but are balanced
theoretically over against entities; they live their lives in a
separate column of the table, the whole distinction between syntactics and semantics resting in this separation of
the columns;

4. propositions, though entities, are most emphatically
not a variety of concept; they are collateral to the whole
group of concepts;

5. despite (3) and (4) the important terminological passage before us (from C, p. 235) reads: *for . . . concepts,
namely, for certain expressions . . . and* [14] *for their designata . . . ;*

6. there is a curious shift of phrasing between the paragraphs of our citation (C, p. 235), where "the term" is the
expressed or implied subject for each sentence: in the introductory statement it is used "for" concepts, in I "as" an
expression, and in II "as" a designatum; in loose colloquial
phrasing such shifts are familiar, but where the whole technique of a logic is at stake they make one wonder what is
being done.[15]

There is a marked difference in allusion and in verbal

"feel" between "entity" and "designatum" in the above procedure, so that a report on the extension and intension of these two words would be helpful. Such a report, however, would require adjustments to the word "object," which is one of the vaguest in Carnap's text — an adjustment that we may well believe would be wholly impracticabie for him under his present methods. It would be helpful also, as we shall see, if we could distinguish the cases in which a concept enters as an "entity" from those in which it is used as a sign or expression. In the present instance we have already found much room for suspicion that it is used, in part, "as" a sign and not "for" a designatum.[16] It seems to have never occurred to him that the "concept" that runs trippingly throughout the text requires terminological stability with respect to the "concept" that enters among the materials, objects or objectives, of his inquiry.

The case being as it is, our report on the nineteen-word sentence comprising the first paragraph of the citation must be that it tells us that a certain expression, or its name, is used to name concepts which in their turn either are or name certain expressions *and* their designata, although neither the expressions nor their designata are officially concepts.

Having thus made his approach to "proposition" in a characteristic mixture of allusions, he now turns to the distinctions he himself intends to display. Earlier (*C*, p. 14), and as a legitimate labor-saving device, he had said that the word "sentence" was to stand for "declarative sentence" throughout his treatise. His desire and aim is to study the coherence of certain types of connective signs (calculus) in such declarative sentences in separation from the substance of the declaration (semantics). To do this he splits the common or vulgar "sentence" of the man in the street into two separate "things." This sort of "thing-production" is, of course, the outstanding feature of his entire logical attitude. The coherence-aspect now presents itself as the first "thing" (I), even though under his preliminary tabulation (as we have already seen) it is not listed among the "entities." The "meaning" portion, or substance of the declaration (II), is no longer to be called "sentence" under any circumstance whatever,[17] but is to be named 'proposition.' These names, it is to be understood, themselves belong in the metalanguage as it applies to the object language. As before, we shall not argue about the merits of the position he takes but confine ourselves to the question: how well, how coherently, does he develop it?

Since the sentence in question is a declarative sentence, one might reasonably expect that any "proposition" carved out of it would be described as "that which is declared." It is not so described. Carnap shifts from the word "declare" to the word "express," and characterizes *proposition* as *that which is expressed.* "Expressions" (inclusive of "sentences") had previously, however, been separated from meaningfulness, when "meaning" was closely identified as "proposition." (We shall later display this in connection with "language" and with "meaning.") Despite this, the verb "expressed" is now used to establish that very meaningfulness of which the noun "expression" has been denied the benefit. Thus the word "express" openly indulges in double-talk between its noun and verb forms.[18] For any logic such a procedure would rate as incoherent. Yet before we recover from it, whether to make outcry or to forgive, we find ourselves in worse. We at once face four synonymic (or are they?) substitutes for *expressed,* namely: *signified, formulated, represented, designated.* Each of these words breathes a different atmosphere. "Signified" has an internally mentalistic feel, sucking up the "signs," so to speak, into the "significance"; "formulated" wavers between linguistic embodiment and rationalistic authority; "designated" has its origins, at least, among physical things, no matter how it wanders; "represented" holds up its face for any passing bee to kiss that is not satisfied with the other pretty word-flowers in the bouquet.[19]

At this point we should probably pause for a discussion

of "designation." Designation is not a chance visitor, but a prominent inmate of the system. As such it certainly ought not to be tossed around as one among several casual words. Neither it nor any of its derivatives, however, has gained place in the terminological appendix. Full discussion would take much time and space. We shall here confine ourselves to a few hints. At its original entrance (*C*, p. 9) the status of designatum is so low that it is merely "what is referred to," possibly something outside the logic altogether. We have seen it gain the status of "what is expressed" in substitution for "what is declared" in a fast company of "meanings" that run far beyond the range of the usual official identification of meaning with designatum. Designation is sometimes a "relation" of a type that can "apply" (*C*, p. 49) to expressions; again "having a certain designatum" may be " a semantical property of an expression"; [20] still again it tells what the speaker *intends* to refer to (*C*, p. 8); and there are times when Carnap inspects an open question as to whether the designata of sentences may not be "possible facts . . . or rather thoughts" (*C*, p. 53). *Officially* he decides that the designatum of a sentence (I) is a proposition (II*), much as the designatum of an object-name is an object (*C*, p. 45; p. 50 Des-Prop; p. 54; p. 99). Suppose the proposition is the designatum of the sentence; suppose the proposition (as we shall note later) may be called "true" as well as the sentence (which latter is officially what is "true" or "false") (*C*, p. 26, p. 90, p. 240); and suppose that "true" is built up around designation. It would then appear that the proposition which "is" the designatum of its own sentence must have somewhere beyond it certain sub-designata which it sub-designates directly instead of by way of its master (or is it servant?) sentence. This is far too intricately imaginative for any probing here. It looks plausible, but whether it makes sense or not we would not know.

The three-realm pattern of organization Carnap uses includes speakers (I), expressions (II) and designata (III).

It is now in desperate state. We are not here arguing its
falsity — we shall take care of that in another place — but
only showing the *incoherence it itself achieves*. Expressions (II) are meaningful or not, but on any show-down
they presumptively take speakers (I) to operate them. The
meaning of an expression (II) is a designatum (III), but
soon it becomes in a special case an expression-meaning
that has not moved out of realm II. This designatum (as
object) in II is presumptively given justification by comparison with an object in III, although the object in III is
so void of status of its own in the logic (other than "intuitively" nominal) that it itself might do better by seeking
its own justification through comparison with the proposi-
tion-object in II.

The soil in which such vegetation grows is "language" as
Carnap sees it. Here he seems to have become progressively vaguer in recent years.[21] We found Cohen-Nagel
asserting flatly that language consists of physical things
called "signs." Carnap proceeds to similar intent part of
the time, but differently the rest of the time, and always
avoids plain statement. Consider the first sentence of his
first chapter (*C*, p. 3):

A *language,* as it is usually understood, is a system of sounds,
or rather of the habits of producing them by the speaking
organs, for the purpose of communicating with other persons,
i.e., of influencing their actions, decisions, thoughts, etc.

Does "usually" give *his* understanding? If the sounds are
physical, in what sense are they in system? Can physics set
up and discuss such a "system"? How do "habits" [22] of producing differ from "producing," especially when "speaking organs" are specified as the producers? Does the "i.e."
mean that "communicating" is always an "influencing"?
What range have the words "purpose," "actions," "decisions," "thoughts"? Sounds are perhaps physical, habits
physiological, communications and influencings broadly
behavioral, and the other items narrowly "psychical." May

not, perhaps, any one of these words — or, indeed, still more dangerously, the word "person" under some specialized stress its user gives it — destroy the presumable import of many of the others?

Even if we accept the cited sentence as a permissible opening, surely better development should at once follow. Instead we find nothing but wavering words. We are told (C, pp. 4-5) that utterances may be analyzed into "smaller and smaller parts," that "ultimate units" of expressions are called "signs," that expressions are finite sequences of signs and that expressions may be "meaningful or not." We are not told whether signs are strictly physical sounds or marks, or whether they are products, habits or purposes. Later on (C, p. 18) we find sign, term and expression used as equivalents. We suspect as the work proceeds that the word "sign" is used mostly where physical implications are desired, and the word "term" mostly for the logical, while the word "expression" is waveringly intermediate — the precision-status being more that of campaign oratory than of careful inquiry. When the accent mark on a French é is viewed as a separate sign from the e without the accent (C, p. 5), "sign" seems clearly physical. When expression is "any finite sequence of signs," "sign" is certainly physical if the word "physical" means anything at all. Still, an expression may be a name, a compound or a sentence (C, p. 25, p. 50). And when an expression expresses a proposition, what are we to say? Again the issue is evaded. We get no answer, and surely we are not unreasonable in wanting to find out before we get too far along. Not knowing, not being able to find out — this is why we have here to search into the text so painfully.

All in all, the best that we are able to report of Carnap's procedure is that 'proposition' or proposition appears as or names an entity, this entity being the certain meaning or designatum that is meant or designated by a non-designating and meaningless, though nevertheless declarative, sentence, representing, whether internally or externally, cer-

tain other designata besides itself, and manipulated
through a terminology of "concepts" under which it at
times is, and at times is not, itself a concept.

It is difficult to tell just where the most vicious center of
terminological evil lies in Carnap's procedure. Probably,
however, the dubious honor should go to "concept," a
word that is all things to all sentences. We shall exhibit
a few samples of his dealings with this word, and then quote
what he once said in a moment when he stopped to think
about it — which is not the case in the book in hand. The
word, as he uses it, derives, of course, from *Begriff*, which
among its addicts on its native soil can without fatigue insert itself a dozen times on a page for any number of pages.
In the present book (*C*) "concept" is employed in thirteen
of the thirty headings of the constructive sections lying
between the introductory chapter and the appendix, without in any case having determinable significance. The
appendix (*C*, p. 230) lists three types of current uses for
the word "concept": (1) psychological; (2) logical; (3)
"as term or expression." The first and last of these uses he
rejects. Among variations in the logical use he accepts the
"widest," using asterisks (see *C*, p. 229 n.) to make the
word "concept" cover properties, relations, functions, all
three.

One could show without difficulty that Carnap's own
practical use of "concept" is heavily infected with the psychological quality, despite his disavowal of this use; one
can likewise show that he frequently uses the word for
"term" or "expression," and this perhaps as often as he
uses it for some form of "entity." We find him (*C*, p. 41)
treating concepts as being "applicable" to certain attributes in almost precisely the same way that in another passage (*C*, p. 88) he makes terms "apply." [23] On pages 88 and
89 all semantical concepts are based on relations; some concepts are relations, and some are attributed to expressions
only, not to designata. We get glimpses of such things as
"intuitive concepts" (*C*, p. 119) and heavy use of "absolute

concepts" of which a word later. Endless illustrations of incoherent use could be given, but no instance in which he has made any attempt to orient this word-of-all-work either to language, to thing, or to mind.

The passage in which he once stopped for an instant to think about the word may be found in his paper "Logical Foundations of the Unity of Science," [24] published a few years before the present book. He wrote:

> Instead of the word 'term' the word 'concept' could be taken, which is more frequently used by logicians. But the word 'term' is more clear, since it shows that we mean signs, e.g., words, expressions consisting of words, artificial symbols, etc., of course with the meaning they have in the language in question.

The vagueness of his position could hardly be more vividly revealed. It is as if a microscopist could not tell his slide from the section he mounted on it, and went through a lot of abracadabra about metaslides to hide his confusion. Not until the words "concept" and "term" are clarified will a metalanguage be able to yield clear results.

"Term" runs "concept" a close second. One finds an interesting illustration (C, p. 89) where Carnap finds it convenient to use "the same term" for a certain "semantical concept" and for its corresponding "absolute concept." He goes on to remark, though without correcting his text, that what he really meant was "the same word," not "the same term," but in Convention 17-1 he goes back to "term" again. Thus a single "term" is authorized by convention to designate (if "designate" is the proper word) two meanings (if "meanings" is the proper word) at a critical stage of inquiry. Carnap considers the ambiguity harmless. Indeed he says "there is no ambiguity." The use of an admittedly wrong word in his convention was apparently the lesser of two evils he was facing, since if one takes the trouble to insert what he says is the right word (viz., word) for what he says is the wrong word (viz., term) in the convention and then skeletonizes the assertion, one will somewhat surprisingly find oneself told that "a word . . . will be applied . . . without reference to a language system." [25] Similarly a term may apply both to attributes and to predicates that designate attributes, i.e., both to designata and to expressions (C, p. 42).

For a mixture of terms and concepts his defense of his "multiple use" of term (C, p. 238) is worth study. A "radical term" may "designate" relations between propositions or relations between attributes (both cases being of "absolute concepts"), or between sentences or between predicates (these cases being "semantical"). In other words every possible opening is left for evasive manipulation.

"Definition" gets into trouble along with "term" and "concept." It enters, not by positive assertion, but by suggestion, as a matter of abbreviations, equalities and equivalences (C, p. 17). However, we find concepts that are entities being defined as liberally as terms that are expressions (C, p. 33). The absolute concepts are heavily favored in this way (C, p. 41, p. 90). One may even seek definitions to be in agreement with intuitive concepts for which only vague explanations have been given (C, p. 119). So many experiences has definition had en route that, when the calculus is reached, the assurance (C, p. 157) that definition may be employed there also seems almost apologetic. [26]

An excellent illustration of the status of many of the confusions we have been noting — involving also the mystery of "object" in the logic — is found in the case of Function (C, pp. 232-233) a brief notice of which is given in footnote 23 on page 43. Here a certain designatum is referred to as "strictly speaking, the entity determined by the expression." The word "determined" interests us, but is difficult to trace back to its den. The "entity" is what gets determined. Surely the "expression," taken *physically* as a sign, cannot be the determiner, nor can it, as a word of record, label, or tag, have initiative assigned it. Designation appears frequently as a "relation" between entity and expression, but we are told nothing to indicate that the expression is the active, and the entity the passive, member of the "relation." Back in its hide-out a "determiner" doubtless lurks, as soul, or intellect, or mind, or will — it can make little difference which, so long as something can be summoned for the task. Our objection at the moment is not to such a soul — that issue lying beyond our immediate range — but to the bad job it does; for if the *expression*, with or without such a proxy, determines the *entity*, it gives the lie to the whole third-realm scheme of relational construction for expression, sentence, proposition and designatum.

We have written at length about expression and concept, and briefly about term, designation, definition and object. The word "relation" (presumptively entitative) is found in suspicious circumstances, similar to those of concept and the others. Thus (*C*, p. 49) you can "apply" a relation to a system. The word "meaning" deserves further mention as it is involved with all the rest. Most frequently "meaning" stands for designatum (*C*, p. 245); wherever a "sentence," as in the calculus, appears as meaningless, it is because designation (as "meaning") is there excluded from consideration. However, if one examines the passages in which meaning is casually spoken of, and those in which sense or meaning is brought into contact with truth-conditions (*C*, p. 10, p. 22, p. 232), the case is not so simple. In *The Formalization of Logic* (p. 6) it occurs to Carnap that he might let pure semantics abstract from "the meaning of descriptive signs" and then let syntax abstract from "the meaning of all signs, including the logical ones." This manner of observation could be carried much farther, and with profit, since one of the first practical observations one makes on his work is that six or eight layers of "meaning" could be peeled apart in his materials, and that he is highly arbitrary in establishing the two or three sharp lines he does.

We have said nothing about "true" in Carnap's procedure, for there is almost nothing that can be said de-

pendably. He introduces it for "sentences" (and for classes
of sentences), but takes the privilege at times of talking of
the truth of "propositions," despite the sharp distinctions
he has drawn between the two on the lines we have so
elaborately examined (C, p. 26, p. 90; and compare p. 240
on "deliberate ambiguity"). He has C-true, L-true, F-true,
and 'true,' distinguished (and legitimately so, if consistently
organized and presented) ; he might have many more.

The situation may be fairly appraised in connection with
"interpretation," an important word in the treatise. Leaving pragmatics for others, Carnap considers syntax and
semantics as separate, with an additional "indispensable"
disinction between factual and logical truth *inside* the latter (C, p. vii). A semantical system is a system of rules; it
is an interpreted system ("interpreted by rules," p. 22);
and it may be an interpretation of a calculus (p. 202). It
also turns out, though, that interpretation is not a semantical system but a "relation" between semantical systems
and calculi, belonging "neither to semantics nor to syntax" (C, p. 202, p. 240).

Fact does not enter by name until the work is more than
half finished (C, p. 140), except for slight references to
"factual knowledge" (C, p. 33, p. 81) and possibly for a few
rare cases of presumptively positive use of "object" such as
we have already mentioned (C, p. 54). However, it has a
vociferous surrogate in "absolute concepts," the ones that
are "not dependent upon language" and merely require
"certain conditions with respect to truth-values" (C, p. 35)
— "conveniences" (C, p. 90) — which are able to be *much
less important* than the L- and C-concepts and, at the same
time, to serve chiefly as *a basis* for them (C, p. 35).

We repeat once more that the significance we stress in
our inquiry lies entirely in the interior incoherence of current logical statement it exhibits. While (as we have intimated) we believe the source of such incoherence is visible
behind its smoke-screens, the weight of our argument does
not rest upon our opinion in this respect.

We find it further only fair to say of Carnap that in many respects he is becoming less assertive and more open to the influence of observation than he has been in the past. He recognizes now, for example (*C*, p. 18), something "not quite satisfactory" in his namings for his designata. He is aware that his basic distinction between logical and descriptive signs (*C*, p. vii, p. 56, p. 59, p. 87) needs further inquiry. He sees an *open* problem as to extensional and intensional language systems (*C*, p. 101, p. 118). He notes the "obviously rather vague" entry of his L-terms (*C*, p. 62). At one point he remarks that his whole structure (and with it all his terminology) may have to change (*C*, p. 229). More significant still, he has a moment when he notes that "even the nature of propositions" is still controversial (*C*, p. 101).

If he should come to question similarly his entitative concentrations he might have a better outlook, but in his latest publication he still feels assured that certain critical semantical terms can be "exactly defined on the basis of the concept of entities satisfying a sentential function," and that "having a certain designatum is a semantical property of an expression,"[27] though just how he would build those two remarks together into a coherent whole we do not know. His confidence that his own semantics is "the fulfillment of the old search for a logic of meaning which had not been fulfilled before in any precise and satisfactory way" (*C*, p. 249) needs modification, it would thus appear, under the various qualifications we have considered.

IV

Let us next glance at three specialized treatments of proposition, meaning and designation: those of Morris, Ducasse and Lewis.[28]

Morris attaches himself to Carnap. His contribution (apart from the verbal chaos of his semiotic) lies in the "pragmatics" he has added to the earlier "semantics" and "syntactics" (*M*, p. 6, p. 8) to yield the three "irreducibles," the "equally legitimates" (*M*, p. 53) that form his rotund trinity. Carnap gratefully accepts this offering with qualifications (*C*, p. 9). It enables him to toss all such uncomfortable issues as "gaining and communicating knowledge" to the garbage bucket of pragmatics, while himself pursuing unhampered his "logical analysis" (*C*, p. 250) in the ivory tower of syntactics and in the straggling mud huts of semantics scattered around its base. Neither Carnap nor Morris seems to be aware — or, if aware, neither of them is bothered by the fact — that pragmatism, in every forward step that has been taken in the central line from Peirce,[29] has concentrated on "meanings" — in other words, on the very field of semantics from which Carnap and Morris now exclude it. To tear semantics and pragmatics thus apart is to leap from Peirce back towards the medieval.[30]

As for the "semiotic" which he offers as a "science among the sciences" (*M*, p. 2), as underlying syntactics, semantics and pragmatics, and as being designed to "supply a language . . . to improve the language of science" (*M*, p. 3) , we need give only a few illustrations of the extent to which its own language falls below the most ordinary standards of everyday coherence. He employs a "triadic relation" possessing "three correlates": sign vehicle, designatum and interpreter (*M*, p. 6). These, however, had entered three pages earlier as "three (or four) factors" where "interpretant" was listed with the parenthetic comment that "interpreter" may be a fourth. Concerning each of these three (or four) factors in his "triadic relations," he writes so many varying sentences it is safe to say that in simple addition all would cancel out and nothing be left.

Consider the dramatic case of the birth of an interpretant.[31] You take a certain "that which" that *acts* as a sign and make it produce an *effect* (called interpretant) on an interpreter, *in virtue of which* the "that which" becomes, or "is," a sign (*M*, p. 3, lines 23-25). Four pages later the sign may *express* its interpreter. The words are incoherent when checked one against another. As for the signs themselves, they are "simply the objects" (*M*, p. 2); they are "things or properties . . . in their function" (*M*, p. 2); they are something "denoting the objects" (*M*, p. 2) ; they are something to be determined for certain cases by "semantical rule" (*M*, pp. 23-24); they are something of which (for other cases) one can say that "the sign vehicle is only that aspect of the apparent sign vehicle in virtue of which semiosis takes place" (*M*, p. 49) etc., etc. Some signs designate without denoting (*M*, p. 5); [32] others indicate without designating (*M*, p. 29). Some objects exist without semiosis (*M*, p. 5), and sometimes the designatum of a sign need not be an "actual existent object" (*M*, p. 5) . Comparably a man may "point without pointing to anything" (*M*, p. 5), which is as neat a survival of medieval mentality in the modern age as one would wish to see.[33]

In Morris' procedure language is one thing, and "using it" is another. He may talk behaviorally about it for a paragraph or two, but his boldest advance in that direction would be to develop its "relation" to the "interpreter" ("dog" or "person") who uses it. Sometimes, for him, science *is* a language; at other times science *has* a language, although semiotic has a better one. A "dual control of linguistic structure" is set up (*M*, pp. 12-13) requiring both events and behaviors, but independently physical signs and objects that are not actual find their way in. Similarly, in the more expansive generalizations, at one time we find (as *M*, p. 29) that syntactic or semantic rules are only verbal formulations within semiotic, while at other times (as *M*, p. 33) we learn that syntactics must be established before we can relate signs to interpreters or to things. The net result is such a complete blank that we find it almost exciting when such a venturesome conclusion is reached as marked an earlier paper by Morris: that "signs which constitute scientific treatises have, to some extent at least, a correlation with objects." [34]

V

Ducasse has labored industriously to discover what a proposition actually "is," if it is the sort of thing he and Cohen-Nagel believe it to be. We do not need to follow him through his long studies since, fortunately, he has recently provided a compact statement. Rearranging somewhat his recipe for the hunting of his snark (D, p. 134), though taking pains to preserve its purity, we get:

Catch an assertion (such as "the dog is red"). Note it is "the verbal symbol of an opinion." Pin it securely on the operating table.

Peel off all that is "verbal" and throw away. Peel off all "epistemic attitude" (here "belief") and throw away also.

The remainder will be a *proposition*.

Dissect carefully. The proposition will be found to have two components, both "physical entities": the first, a "physical object"; the second, a "physical property."

Distill away from these components all traces of conscious process — in especial, as to "object," all that is perceptual; as to "property," all that is conceptual.

When this has been skilfully done you will have remaining the pure components of the pure proposition, with all that is verbal or mental removed.

Further contemplation of the pure proposition will reveal that it has the following peculiarities: (a) if its two components cleave together in intimate union, the first "possessing" the second, then the proposition is "true," and the "true proposition" is "fact"; (b) if the second component vanishes, then what remains (despite the lack of one of its two essential components) is still a proposition, but this time a "false proposition," and a false proposition is "not a fact," or perhaps more accurately, since it is still an important something, it might be called a "not-fact."

This is no comfortable outcome. The only way it can "make" sense, so far as one can see is by continuous implied orientation towards a concealed mental operator, for whom one would have more respect if he came out in front and did business in his own name.[35]

VI

Lewis illustrates what happens when words as physical facts are sharply severed from meanings as psychical facts, with the former employed by a superior agency — a "mind" — to "convey" the latter (*L*, p. 236). He makes so sharp a split between ink-marks and meanings that he at once faces a "which comes first?" puzzler of the "chicken or egg" type, his sympathies giving priority to the meanings over the wordings.

He tells us (*L*, p. 237) that "a linguistic expression is constituted by the association of a verbal symbol and a fixed meaning." Here the original ink-spot-verbal is allotted symbolic quality (surely it must be "psychic") while the meaning is allegedly "fixed" (which sounds very "physical"). Our bigamist is thus unfaithful in both houses. He is doubly and triply unfaithful, at that, for the last part of the cited sentence reads: "but the linguistic expression cannot be identified with the symbol alone nor with the meaning alone." First we had physical words and mental meanings; then we had verbal symbols and fixed meanings; now we have symbol alone and meaning alone, neither of them being expressive. He uses, it is true, a purportedly vitalizing word — or, rather, a word that might vitalize if it had any vitality left in it. This word is "association," outcast of both philosophy and psychology, a thorough ne'er-do-well, that at best points a dirty finger at a region in which research is required.

So slippery are the above phrasings that no matter how sternly one pursues them they can not be held fast. The signs are physical, but they become verbal symbols. A verbal symbol is a pattern of marks; it is a "recognizable pattern"; it becomes a pattern even when apart from its "instances"; it winds up as an "abstract entity" (all in *L*, pp. 236-237). Expression goes the same route from ink-spots on up (or down), so that finally, when the symbol becomes an abstract entity, the expression (originally a physical "thing") becomes a "correlative abstraction" (*L*, p. 237).

A term is an expression that "names or applies to" (one would like to clear up the difference or the identity here) "a thing or things, of some kind, actual or thought of" (again plenty of room for clarification); it changes into something that is "capable" of naming, where naming is at times used as a synonym for "speaking of" (*L*, p. 237); in the case of the "abstract term," however, the term "names what it signifies" (*L*, p. 239). One would like to understand the status of proposition as "assertable content" (*L*, p. 242) ; of a "sense-meaning" that is "intension in the mode of a criterion in mind" (*L*, p. 247); of signification as "comprehensive essential character" (*L*, p. 239). One could even endure a little information about the way in which "denote" is to be maintained as different from "denotation," and how one can avoid "the awkward consequences" of this difference by adopting the word "designation" (apparently from Carnap and Morris, and apparently in a sense different from either of theirs) — an effort which Lewis himself does not find it worth his while to make (*L*, p. 237). Finally, if "meaning" and "physical sign" cannot be better held apart than Lewis succeeds in doing, one would like to know why he tries so elaborately.[36]

VII

We shall discuss Bertrand Russell's logical setting in Chapter VIII. His terminology, as previously noted, appears confused, even to Carnap, who finds Russell's explanations of his various uses of the word "proposition" very difficult to understand" (*C*, pp. 235-236). The voluminous interchanges Russell has had with others result in ever renewed complaints by him that he is not properly understood. Despite his great initiative in symbolic formulation in the border regions between logic and mathematics, and despite the many specializations of inquiry he has carried through, no progress in basic organization has resulted from his work. This seems to be the main lesson from logical inquiry in general as it has thus far been carried on. We may stress this highly unsatisfactory status by quoting a few other remarks by logicians on the work of their fellows.

Carnap, in his latest volume,[37] regrets that most logicians still leave "the understanding and use of [semantical] terms . . . to common sense and instinct," and feels that the work of Hilbert and Bernays would be clearer "if the distinction between expressions and their designata were observed more strictly" — and this despite his own chaos in that respect.

Cohen and Nagel in their preface pay their compliments to their fellows thus:

> Florence Nightingale transformed modern hospital practice by the motto: Whatever hospitals do, they should not spread disease. Similarly, logic should not infect students with fallacies and confusions as to the fundamental nature of valid or scientific reasoning.

Tarski, whose procedure is the next and last we shall examine, writes (*T,* p. 345):

> It is perhaps worth-while saying that semantics as it is conceived in this paper (and in former papers of the author) is a sober and modest discipline which has no pretensions of being a universal patent medicine for all the ills and diseases of mankind whether imaginary or real. You will not find in semantics any remedy for decayed teeth or illusions of grandeur or class conflicts. Nor is semantics a device for establishing that every one except the speaker and his friends is speaking nonsense.

VIII

Tarski's work is indeed like a breath of fresh air after the murky atmosphere we have been in. It is not that he has undertaken positive construction or given concentrated attention to the old abuses of terminology, but he is on the way — shaking himself, one might say, to get free. His procedure is simple, unpretentious, and cleared of many of the ancient verbal unintelligibilities. He does not formally abandon the three-realm background and he occasionally, though not often, lapses into using it — speaking of "terms," for example, as "indispensable means for conveying human thoughts" [38] — but he seems free from that persistent, malignant orientation towards the kind of fictive mental operator which the preceding logicians examined in this chapter have implicitly or explicitly relied upon. He sets "sentences" (as expressions) over against "objects referred to" (*T*, p. 345) in a matter-of-fact way, and goes to work. He employs a metalanguage to control object-languages, not as an esoteric, facultative mystery, but as a simple technical device, such as any good research man might seek in a form appropriate to his field, to fixate the materials under his examination.[39]

In his latest appraisal of "true" under the title "The Semantic Conception of Truth," Tarski concludes that for a given object-language and for such other formalized languages as are now known (*T*, p. 371, n. 14) — and he believes he can generalize for a comprehensive class of object-languages (*T*, p. 355) — "a sentence is true if it is satisfied by all objects, and false otherwise" (*T*, p. 353). The development, as we appraise it, informs us that if we assume (*a*) isolable things (here we make explicit his implicit assumption of the "thing") and (*b*) human assertions about them, then this use can be consistently maintained. In his demonstration Tarski discards "propositions," beloved of Cohen-Nagel, Carnap and Ducasse, saying they are too often "ideal entities" of which the "meaning . . . seems never to have been made quite clear and unambiguous" (*T*, p. 342). He establishes "sentences" with the characteristics of "assertions," and then considers such a sentence on the one hand as in active assertion, and on the other hand as designated or named, and thus identified, so that it can be more accurately handled and dealt with by the inquirer. After establishing certain "equivalences of the form (*T*)" which assure us that the sentence is well-named

(x is true if, and only if, p) (T, p. 344), he sharpens an earlier formulation for "adequacy," the requirement now becoming that "all equivalences of the form (T) can be asserted" (T, p. 344). (For all of this we are, of course, employing our own free phrasing, which we are able to do because his work, unlike the others, is substantial enough to tolerate it.) "A definition of truth is 'adequate' if all these equivalences follow from it." Given such adequacy we have a "semantic" conception of truth, although the expression (T) itself is not yet a definition.

To demonstrate his conclusion Tarski identifies as primarily semantic: (1) designation (denoting), (2) satisfaction (for conditions), (3) definition (unique determining); he calls them "relations" between "sentences" and "objects." "True," however, he says, is not such a "relation"; instead it expresses a property (or denotes a class) of sentences (T, p. 345). Nevertheless it is to be called "semantic" because the best way of defining it is by aid of the semantic relations (T, p. 345). His outcome, he thinks, is "formally correct" and "materially adequate," the conditions for material adequacy being such as to determine uniquely the extension of the term "true" (T, p. 353). *What he has done is to make plain to himself at the start what he believes truth to be in everyday use, after which by prolonged study he advances from a poorer and less reliable to a richer and more reliable formulation of it.* We do not say this in deprecation, but rather as high praise of the extent of progress in his standpoint. We may quote his saying that his aim is "to catch hold of the actual meaning of an old notion" (T, p. 341; compare also p. 361, bottom paragraph), where, if one strikes out any remaining sentimentality from the word "actual" and treats it rigorously, the sense becomes close to what we have expressed.

We must nevertheless, to make his status clear, list some of the flaws. He does not tell us clearly what he intends by the words "concept," "word," "term," "meaning" and "object." His applications of them are frequently mixed.[40]

"Word" shades into "term," and "term" into "concept," and "concept" retains much of its traditional vagueness. Designation and satisfaction, as "relations," enter as running between expression and thing (the "semantic" requirement), but definition, also a relation, runs largely between expressions (a very different matter).[41] "True," while not offered as a "relation," is at one stage said to "denote," although denoting has been presented as a relating. The word "meaning" remains two-faced throughout, sometimes running from word (expression) to word, and sometimes from word to thing.[42] Lacking still is all endeavor to organize men's talkings to men's perceivings and manipulatings in the cultural world of their evolution. The ancient non-cultural verbal implications block the path.

IX

Along with proposition, truth, meaning and language, "fact" has been in difficulties in all the logics we have examined. We displayed this in Section II through the development of a curious contrast as to whether a fact is a proposition or a proposition a fact. The answer seemed to be "Neither." In various other ways the puzzle has appeared on the sidelines of the logics throughout.

Now, "fact" is not in trouble with the logics alone; the philosophies and epistemologies are equally chary of looking at it straight. Since direct construction in this field will occupy us later on, we shall here exhibit the character of this philosophical confusion by a few simple illustrations from the philosophical dictionaries and from current periodical essays.[43] Consider first what the dictionaries report.

The recently published *Dictionary of Philosophy* [44] limits itself to three lines as follows:

Fact (Lat. factus, p.p. of facio, do) : Actual individual occurrence. An indubitable truth of actuality. A brute event. Synonymous with actual event.

Any high-school condensation of a dictionary should do better than that. This is supplemented, however, by another entry, allotted three times the space, and entitled "Fact: in Husserl" (whatever that may literally mean). Here unblinking use is made of such locutions as "categorical-syntactical structure," "simply is" and "regardless of value."

Baldwin's definition of a generation ago is well known. Fact is "objective datum of experience," by which is to be understood "datum of experience considered as abstracted from the experience of which it is a datum." This, of course, was well enough among specialists of its day, but the words it uses are hardly information-giving in our time.

Eisler's *Wörterbuch* (1930 edition) makes *Tatsache* out to be whatever we are convinced has objective or real *Bestand* — whatever is firmly established through thought as content of experience, as *Bestandteil* of the ordering under law of things and events. These again are words but are not helps.

Lalande's *Vocabulaire* (1928 edition) does better. It discusses fact to the extent of two pages, settling upon the wording of Seignobos and Langlois that "La notion de *fait,* quand on la précise, se ramène à un jugement d'affirmation sur la réalité extérieure." This at least sounds clear, and will satisfy anyone who accepts its neat psychology and overlooks the difficulties that lie in *jugement,* as we have just been surveying them.

Turning to current discussions in the journals for further illustration we select three specimens, all appearing during the past year (1944). Where mere illustration is involved and all are alike in the dark, there is no need to be invidious, and we therefore omit names and references, all the better to attend to the astonishing things we are told.

1. "Fact: a situation having reality in its own right independent of cognition." Here the word "situation" evi-

dently enters because of its indefiniteness; "reality in its own right" follows with assertion of the most tremendous possible definiteness; and "independent of cognition," if it means anything, means "about which we know nothing at all." The whole statement is that fact is something very vague, yet most tremendously certain, about which we know nothing.

2. "There is something ultimately unprovable in a fact." Here a rapturous intellectualism entertains itself, forgetting that there has been something eventually uncertain about every "truth" man has thus far uncovered, and discrediting fact before trying to identify it.

3. "A fact can be an item of knowledge only because the *factual* is a character of reality. . . . Factual knowledge means the awareness of the occurrence of events felt, believed, or known to be independent of the volitional self. . . . The sense of fact is the sense of the self confronting the not-self." The outcome of this set of warring assertions is a four-fold universe, containing: (*a*) reality; (*b*) truth; (*c*) a sort of factuality that is quasi-real; (*d*) another sort of factuality that is quasi-true. Poor "fact" is slaughtered from all four quarters of the heavens at once.

The citations above have been given not because they are exceptional, but because they are standard. You find this sort of thing wherever you go. No stronger challenge could be given for research than the continuance of such a state of affairs in this scientific era.

X

Enough evidence of linguistic chaos has been presented in this paper to justify an overhauling of the entire background of recent logical construction. This chaos is due to logicians' accepting ancient popular phrasings about life and conduct as if such phrasings were valid, apart from inquiry into their factual status within modern knowledge. As a result, not only is logic disreputable from the point of view of fact, but the status of "fact" is wretched within the logics. The involvement both of logic and fact with language is manifest. Some logics, as anyone can quickly discover, look upon language only to deny it. Some allot it incidental attention. Even where it is more formally introduced, it is in the main merely tacked on to the older logical materials, without entering into them in full function.

Our understanding thus far has been gained by refusing to accept the words man utters as independent beings — logicians' playthings akin to magicians' vipers or children's fairies — and by insisting that language is veritably man himself in action, and thus observable. The "propositions" of Cohen and Nagel, of Ducasse and of Carnap, the "meanings" of Lewis, the "sign vehicles" and "interpretants" of Morris and the "truth" of Tarski all tell the same tale, though in varying degree. What is "man in action" gets distorted when manipulated as if detached; what is "other than man" gets plenty of crude assumption, but no fair factual treatment.

We said at the start that in closing we would indicate a still wider observation that must be made if better construction is to be achieved. The locus of such widened observation is where "object," "entity," "thing" or "designatum" is introduced. "Things" appear and are named, or they appear as named, or they appear through namings. Logics of the types we have been examining flutter and evade, but never attack directly the problem of sorting out and organizing words to things, and things to words, for their needs of research. They proceed as though some sort of oracle could be issued to settle all puzzles at once, with logicians as the priests presiding over the mysteries.

This problem, we believe, should be faced naturalistically. Passage should be made from the older half-light to such fuller light as modern science offers. In this fuller light the man who talks and thinks and knows belongs to the world in which he has been evolved in all his talkings, thinkings and knowings; while at the same time this world in which he has been evolved is the world of his knowing. Not even in his latest and most complex activities is it well to survey this natural man as magically "emergent" into something new and strange. Logic, we believe, must learn to accept him simply and naturally, if it is to begin the progress the future demands.

---

1 This chapter is written by Bentley.

2 The titles in full of the books or papers specially examined are:
C: Rudolf Carnap, *Introduction to Semantics*, Cambridge, 1942.
CN: Morris R. Cohen and Ernest Nagel, *An Introduction to Logic and Scientific Method*, New York, 1934. (References are to the fourth printing, 1937.)
D: C. J. Ducasse. "Is a Fact a True Proposition? — a Reply." *Journal of Philosophy*, XXXIX (1942), 132-136.
L: C. I. Lewis, "The Modes of Meaning," *Philosophy and Phenomenological Research*, IV (1943), 236-249.
M: Charles W. Morris, *Foundations of the Theory of Signs*, Chicago, 1938. (*International Encyclopedia of Unified Science* I, No. 2.)
T: Alfred Tarski, "The Semantic Conception of Truth and the Foundations of Semantics," *Philosophy and Phenomenological Research*, IV (1944), 341-376.
Other writings of these logicians will be cited in footnotes. To show the scope of these materials as a basis for judgment, it may be added that the seven logicians examined represent, respectively, The University of Chicago, The College of the City of New York, Columbia University, Brown University, Harvard University, The University of Chicago and The University of California.

3 Peirce experimented with many forms of expression. Anyone can, at will, select one of these forms. We believe the proper understanding is that which is consonant with his life-growth, from the essays of 1868-1869 through his logic of relatives, his pragmatic exposition of 1878, his theory of signs, and his endeavors to secure a functional logic. Recent papers to examine are: John Dewey, "Ethical Subjectmatter and Language," *The Journal of Philosophy*, XLII (1945) and "Peirce's Theory of Linguistic Signs, Thought, and Meaning" *Ibid.*, XLIII (1946), 85; Justus Buchler, review of James Feibleman's *An Introduction to Peirce's Philosophy Interpreted as a System, Ibid.*, XLIV (1947), 306; Thomas A. Goudge, "The Conflict of Naturalism and Transcendentalism in Peirce" *Ibid.*, XLIV (1947), 365. See also Chapter II, note 5, and Chapter IX, notes 61 and 62 of this volume.

It is of much interest with respect to this issue to note that in a late publication (October, 1944) Otto Neurath, the editor-in-chief of the *International Encyclopedia of Unified Science*, of which Carnap and Morris are associate editors, expressly disavows the threefold position the others have taken and thus makes an opening step towards a different development. "There is always," he writes, "a certain danger of looking at 'speaker,' 'speech,' and 'objects' as three actors . . . who may be separated. . . . I treat them as items of one aggregation. . . . The difference may be essential." ("Foundations of the Social Sciences," *International Encyclopedia of Unified Science*, II, No. 1, 11.)

4 *Collected Papers of Charles Sanders Peirce*, ed. by Charles Hartshorne and Paul Weiss (Cambridge, 1931) 2.220. See also footnote 31 in Section IV of this chapter.

5 *Ibid.*, 2.330.

6 The Cohen-Nagel indexing differs here from the text. It distinguishes propositions from sentences, judgments, resolutions, commands and things. Compare the old "laws of thought" which (*CN*, p. 182) take modernistic dress as laws of propositions.

7 Note that a proposition is first "not an object," then that it is an "object of thought," finally that it is an "aspect of the concrete," and that the first assertion and its dyadic belying all occur in a single paragraph. What the writers "really mean" is much less important logically than what they say (what they are able to say under their manner of approach) when they are manifestly *doing their best to say what they mean.*

8 The word "knowledge," incidentally, is unindexed, but we learn that it "involves abstraction" (*CN*, p. 371); that it does not cover merely the collecting of facts (*CN*, p. 215); that true knowledge cannot be restricted to objects actually existing (*CN*, p. 21); and that many open questions remain as to immediate knowings (*CN*, p. 5) — nothing of which is significantly treated.

9 Casual comments do not organize. As to the first item, we learn: "All observation appeals ultimately to certain *isolable* elements in sense experience. We search for such elements because concerning them *universal agreement among all people* is obtainable" (italics for "isolable" are theirs, the others ours). Again, a fact in the second or third sense "states" a fact in the fourth. And a fact in the fourth sense is not "true"; it just "is" (*CN*, p. 218). Separately such comments are plausible. Together they scatter like birdshot.

10 More recently, however, Professor Nagel has written a paper, "Logic without Ontology," which will be found in the volume *Naturalism and the Human Spirit* (1944), edited by Y. H. Krikorian. Here he advances to an operational position approximating that of the instrumental logic of the nineteen twenties, which he at that time assailed in a paper en-

titled "Can Logic Be Divorced from Ontology?" (*Journal of Philosophy,* XXVI [1929], 705-712) , written in confidence that "nature must contain the prototype of the logical" and that "relations are discovered as an integral factor in nature." Also of great interest for comparison is his paper "Truth and Knowledge of the Truth" (*Philosophy and Phenomenological Research,* V [1944], 50-68) , especially the distinction as it is sharply drawn (p. 68) .

11 *The Journal of Philosophy,* XXXIX (1942) , 471.

12 A competent critic, well acquainted with Carnap, and wholly unsympathetic to our procedure, attacks the above interpretation as follows: Since Carnap (*C*, p. 230, line 16) writes "Concept. The word is. . . . ," it is evident that to Carnap '*concept*' is here a word, not a name for a word; it is evident further that under even a half-way co-operative approach the reader should be able to carry this treatment forward five pages to the case of '*proposition*,' accepting this latter frankly as "word" not "term," and ceasing to bother. Unfortunately for our critic this course would make Carnap's treatment in both instances violate his prescription and thus strengthen our case. All we have done is to exhibit an instance of vagueness, drawing no inference here, and leaving further discussion to follow. To consider and adjust are (1) proposition-as-fact; (2) "proposition" as a current logical word; (3) 'proposition' in the metalanguage; (I) Carnap's prescription for 'sentence'; (II) Carnap's prescription for 'proposition'; (*a*) factual adequacy for 'sentence'; (*b*) factual adequacy for 'proposition'; (*c*) general coherence of the textual development within. the full syntactic-semantic-pragmatic construction. It is this last with which we are now concerned. Partial or impressionistically opinionative analyses are not likely to be pertinent.

13 Carnap reports his distinctions I and II as appearing in the literature along with mixed cases (*C*, p. 235) . His illustrations of his II, and of the mixed cases, fit fairly well. However, the wordings of Baldwin, Lalande, Eisler, Bosanquet, etc., cited for I, though they have some superficial verbal similarity, would not come out as at all "the same," if expanded in their full expressive settings, *viz.:* American, French, German and British. Certainly none would come out "the same as" Carnap's completely meaningless "expression" which, nevertheless, expresses all that men take it to express.

14 Carnap, if memory is correct, once displayed five varieties of "and," to which Bühler added two more. One wonders whether this "and" is one of them. Another illustration, an unforgettable one, of his libertine way with little connectives is his impressive advance from "not" to "especially not" in setting up the status of "formal" definition (*International Encyclopedia of Unified Science,* I, No. 3, 16) .

15 Again, the welcome comment of a critic unsympathetic to our procedure is of interest. As to (3) he asserts that since expressions consist of sign-events and sign-designs, the former being individuals and the

latter properties, and since both individuals and properties are entities, therefore expressions are themselves entities. We have no breath of objection to such a treatment; only if this *is* the view of the *Semantics*, why does the classification (p. 18) conflict? Or, alternatively, if the great technical advance rests on separating expressions from entities, what does it mean when we are told in answer to a first simple question that, *of course*, expressions *are* entities too? As to (4) and (5) our critic in a similar vein asserts that for Carnap propositions are properties of expressions, that properties are concepts, and hence that propositions *are* concepts. Here again, one asks: If so, why does Carnap classify them differently in his table? Dissecting our critic's development of his thesis we find it to contain the following assertions:

1. *Being a proposition* is a property of entities.
2. *Being a proposition* is therefore a concept.
3. The *property* (being a proposition) is named 'proposition.'
4. The *property* (being a proposition) is not a proposition.

From which we can hardly avoid concluding:

5. That which is named 'proposition' is not a proposition.

We leave these to the reader's private consideration, our own attention being occupied with the one central question of whether double-talk, rather than straight-talk, is sanitary in logic.

[16] Our phraseology in the text above is appalling to us, but since we here are reflecting Carnap it seems irremedial. The indicated reform would be to abandon the radical split between sign-user and sign with respect to object, as we shall do in our further development.

[17] However, before he concludes his terminological treatment he introduces (C, p. 236) certain sentences that he says are "in our terminology sentences in semantics, not in syntax." This is not so much a contradictory usage as it is an illustration of the come-easy, go-easy dealing with words.

[18] The source of tolerance for such contradictions is well enough known to us. It lies in the reference of the "meanings" to a mental actor behind the scenes. This is apart, however, from the immediate purpose of discussion at the present stage. Consider "adequacy" as intention (C, p. 53); also "sign" as involving intent (*International Encyclopedia of Unified Science*, I, No. 3, p. 4; and similarly C, p. 8).

[19] Alonzo Church, referring to this passage in its original magazine appearance, holds that the charge of inconsistency against Carnap's switch from "designation" to "expression" fails because the various alternatives Carnap suggests for "expression" refer, partially at least, to the views of others. This, at any rate, is the way we understand him. Church's words are: "The charge of inconsistency to Carnap because he says "officially" that a sentence *designates* a proposition but on page 235 writes of sentences as *expressing* propositions (along with a list of alternatives to the verb 'express') fails, because it is obvious that in the latter passage Carnap is describing the varied views of others as well as his own" (*The Journal of Symbolic Logic*, X (1945), p. 132). The situation here seems to be

about as follows: (1) Carnap's "designate" and "express" do not separate into an earlier official and a later casual or descriptive use, but both appear in a single passage of eight lines (*C*, p. 235) which is as "official" as anything in his text, and which we have already cited in full. (2) The pseudosynonyms for "express" are not attributed to other writers, but are run in without comment apparently as current usages. (3) In the succeeding page and a half of discussion he gives to other writers only one of these words, namely "represent," enters as employed by a specific other writer — in this case by Bosanquet (Compare Note 13 above). (4) The alternatives for "express" do not appear in the portion of the passage dealing with 'sentence,' but strangely enough in that portion dealing with 'proposition,' that is to say with "that which is expressed by a sentence." (5) Even if Church were correct in identifying here "the varied views of others," the point would be irrelevant for use as keystone in a charge of default in proof; our passage in question might be called irrelevant or flippant, but certainly never a determining factor. (6) The charge in our text is one of abundant chaos in Carnap's linguistic foundations, and never of a particular inconsistency. We strongly recommend the careful examination of the texts of Carnap and Church alongside our own in this particular disagreement, and equally of the other positions Church attributes to us in comparison with the positions we actually take in our examination. Only through hard, close work in this field can the full extent of the linguistic chaos involved become evident.

[20] Rudolf Carnap, *The Formalization of Logic* (Cambridge, 1943), pp. 3-4.

[21] However, to his credit, he seems to have largely dropped or smoothed over the older jargon of physical language, physical thing-language, and observable thing-predicates (as in *International Encyclopedia of Unified Science*, I, No. 1, 52).

[22] In an earlier paper (*Ibid.*, I, No. 3, 3) such "habits" were called "dispositions," and we were told both that language is a system of dispositions and that its elements are sounds or written marks. Whether Carnap regards dispositions as sounds, or sounds as dispositions, he does not make clear.

[23] An interesting case of comparable confusion (superficial, however, rather than malignant) appears in the word "function," which is listed (*C*, p. 18) among the "entities," although "expressional function" and "sentential function" (both non-entitative) appear in the accompanying text. Terminological discussion (*C*, pp. 232-233) strongly favors the entitative use but still fails to star it as Carnap's own. The starring gives endorsement to the expressive uses cited above. In place of expression and entity consider, for comparison's sake, inorganic and organic. Then in place of a function among entities we might take a rooster among organisms. Carnap's "expressional function" can now be compared to something like "inorganic rooster."

[24] *International Encyclopedia of Unified Science*, I, No. 1 (1938), 49.

25 Carnap has, as is well known, a standing alibi in all such cases as this. It is that he is not talking about an actual language, but about an abstract system of signs with meanings. In the present case there would seem to be all the less excuse for vacillating between word and term. If the distinctions are valid, and are intended to be adhered to, exact statement should not be difficult. It is, of course, understood that the general problem of the use of "word" and "term" is not being raised by us here; no more is the general problem of the entry of "fact," whether by "convention" or not, into a logic. For further comparison, and to avoid misinterpretation, the text of Convention 17-1 follows: "A term used for a radical semantical property of expressions will be applied in an absolute way (i.e. without reference to a language system) to an entity u if and only if every expression $\mathfrak{A}$, which designates u in any semantical system S has that semantical property in S. Analogously with a semantical relation between two or more expressions."

26 Again, we are not assailing Carnap's actual research into linguistic connectivities. The point is the importance of talking coherently about them.

27 *The Formalization of Logic*, p. xi, p. 3.

28 Procedure should be like that of entomologists, who gather specimen bugs by the thousands to make sure of their results. It should also be like that of engineers getting the "bugs" (another kind, it is true) out of machinery. Space considerations permit the exhibit of only a few specimens. But we believe these specimens are significant. We trust they may stimulate other "naturalists" to do field work of their own. Compare the comment of Karl Menger when in a somewhat similar difficulty over what the "intuitionists" stood for in mathematics. "Naturally," he wrote, "a sober critic can do nothing but stick to their external communications." "The New Logic," *Philosophy of Science*, IV (1937), 320. Compare also our further comment on this phase of inquiry in Chapter III, note 48.

29 In "How to Make our Ideas Clear" (1878) where "practical" bearings and effects are introduced, and where it is asserted that "our conception of these effects is the whole of our conception of the object" (*Collected Papers*, 5.402).

30 That even Morris himself has now become troubled appears from a later discussion in which — under the stimulus of a marvelously succulent, syllabic synthesis applied to "linguistic signs," namely, that they are "transsituationally intersubjective" — he votes in favor of a "wider use of 'semantics'" and a "narrower use of 'pragmatics'" hereafter (*Philosophy of Science*, X [1943], 248-249). Indeed, Morris' whole tone in this new paper is apologetic, though falling far short of hinting at a much-needed thorough-going house-cleaning. No effect of this suggested change in viewpoint is, however, manifested in his subsequent book, *Signs, Language, and Behavior* (New York, 1946), nor is his paper of 1943 as much as listed in the bibliography therein provided.

31 Where Morris allots a possible four components to his "triadic relation" he employs the evasive phrase-device "commonly regarded as," itself as common in logic as outside. (*Cf.* Carnap's "language as it is usually understood," which we have discussed previously.) The word "interpretant" is of course lifted verbally, though not meaningfully, from Peirce, who used it for the operational outcome of sets of ordered signs (*Collected Papers*, 2.92 to 2.94, and *cf.* also 2.646). The effect (outcome or consequences) of which Peirce speaks is definitely *not* an effect upon an interpreter. There is no ground in Peirce's writings for identifying "interpretant" with "interpreter."

32 A demonstration of the meaninglessness of Morris' treatment of denotation and designation — of objects, classes and entities — has been published by George V. Gentry since this paper was prepared. (*The Journal of Philosophy*, XLI [1944], 376-384).

33 For Morris' later development of "sign" (1946) see Chapter IX.

34 *International Encyclopedia of Unified Science*, I, No. 1 (1938), p. 69.

35 A later attempt by Ducasse is found in a paper, "Propositions, Truth, and the Ultimate Criterion of Truth" (*Philosophy and Phenomenological Research*, IV [1944], 317-340), which became available after the above was written. In it the confusion heightens. For Ducasse, now, no proposition has either a subject or a predicate (p. 321). Many varieties of "things" or "somethings" are introduced, and there is complete absence of information as to what we are to understand by "thing" or "something." Thus: "the sort of thing, and the only sort of thing, which either is true or is false is a proposition" (p. 318); it is to be sharply discriminated from "other sorts of things called respectively statements, opinions, and judgments . . ." (p. 318); "the ultimate . . . constituents of a proposition are some *ubi* and some *quid* — some *locus* and some *quale*" (p. 323); "a fact is not something to which true propositions 'correspond' in some sense . . . a fact *is* a true proposition" (p. 320). Incidentally a proposition is also the *content* of an opinion (p. 320) from which we may infer that a fact, being a true proposition, is likewise the content of an opinion. It is very discouraging.

36 Professor Baylis finds some of the same difficulties we have found in Lewis' procedure, and several more, and regards portions of it as "cagey" (*Philosophy and Phenomenological Research*, V [1944], 80-88). He does not, however, draw the conclusion we draw as to the radical deficiency in the whole scheme of terminology. Professor Lewis, replying to Professor Baylis (*ibid.*, 94-96), finds as much uncertainty in the latter as the latter finds in him.

37 *Formalization of Logic* pp. xii, xiii.

38 Alfred Tarski, *Introduction to Logic and to the Methodology of Deductive Sciences* (New York, 1941), p. 18. Compare also his remark about "innate or acquired capacity," *ibid.*, p. 134.

³⁹ In the preface to the original (Polish) edition of his *Logic* he had held that "the concepts of logic permeate the whole of mathematics," considering the specifically mathematical concepts "special cases," and had gone so far as to assert that "logical laws are constantly applied — be it consciously or unconsciously — in mathematical reasonings" (*ibid.*, p. xvii). In his new preface (*ibid.*, p. xi, p. xiii) he reduces this to the assurance that logic "seeks to create . . . apparatus" and that it "analyzes the meaning" and "establishes the general laws." Even more significantly he remarks (*ibid.*, p. 140) that "meta-logic and meta-mathematics" means about the same as "the science of logic and mathematics." (Compare also *ibid.*, p. 134.)

⁴⁰ Thus *Logic*, p. 18, p. 139. For "object" see *T*, p. 374, n. 35. He recognizes the vagueness in the word "concept" (*T*, p. 370) but continues to use it. His employment of it on page 108 of the *Logic* and his phrasing about "laws . . . concerning concepts" are of interest. His abuses of this word, however, are so slight compared with the naïve specimens we have previously examined that complaint is not severe.

⁴¹ For "definition," consider the stipulating convention (*Logic*, p. 33) and the equivalence (p. 150) and compare these with the use of "relation" (*T*, p. 345) and with the comments (*T*, p. 374, n. 35). It is not the use of the single word "definition" for different processes that is objectionable, but the confusion in the uses.

⁴² Thus *Logic*, p. 133; one can discard first of all "independent meanings," and then the customary meanings of "logical concepts," and finally, apparently, "the meanings of all expressions encountered in the given discipline . . . without exception." The word "meaning" is, of course, one of the most unreliable in the dictionary, but that is no reason for playing fast and loose with it in logic.

⁴³ The only considerable discussion of fact we have noted is the volume *Studies in the Nature of Facts* (*University of California Publications in Philosophy*, XIV [1932]), a series of eight lectures by men of different specializations. An examination of the points of view represented will reward anyone interested in further development of this field.

⁴⁴ D. D. Runes, editor (New York, 1942).

CHAPTER TWO

THE TERMINOLOGICAL PROBLEM

SCIENCE uses its technical names efficiently. Such names serve to mark off certain portions of the scientific subjectmatter as provisionally acceptable, thereby freeing the worker's attention for closer consideration of other portions that remain problematic. The efficiency lies in the ability given the worker to hold such names steady — to know what he properly names with them — first at different stages of his own procedure and then in interchange with his associates.

Theories of knowledge provide their investigators with no such dependable aids. The traditional namings they employ have primitive cultural origins and the supplemental "terms" they evolve have frequently no ascertainable application as names at all.

We have asserted that the time has come when a few leading names for knowings and knowns can be established and put to use. We hold further that this undertaking should be placed upon a scientific basis; where by "scientific" we understand very simply a form of "factual" inquiry, in which the knowing man is accepted as a factual component of the factual cosmos, as he is elsewhere in modern research. We know of no other basis on which to anticipate dependable results — more particularly since the past history of "epistemology" is filled with danger-signs.

What we advocate is in very simple statement a passage from loose to firm namings. Some purported names do little more than indicate fields of inquiry — some, even, do hardly that. Others specify with a high degree of firmness. The word "knowledge," as a name, is a loose name. We do not employ it in the titles of our chapters and shall not use it in any significant way as we proceed. It is often a convenience, and it is probably not objectionable — at least it may be kept from being dangerous — where there is no stress upon its accurate application and no great probability that a reader will assume there is; at any rate we shall thus occasionally risk it. We shall rate it as No. 1 on a list of "vague words"[1] to which we shall call attention and add from time to time in footnotes. Only through prolonged factual inquiry, of which little has been undertaken as yet, can the word "knowledge" be given determinable status with respect to such questions as: (1) the range of its application to human or animal behaviors; (2) the types of its distribution between knowers, knowns, and presumptive intermediaries; (3) the possible localizations implied for knowledges as present in space and time. In place of examining such a vague generality as the word "knowledge" offers, we shall speak of and concern ourselves directly with knowings and knowns — and, moreover, in each instance, with those particular forms of knowings and knowns in respect to which we may hope for reasonably definite identifications.

I

The conditions that the sort of namings we seek must satisfy, positively and negatively, include the following:

1. The names are to be based on such observations as are accessible to and attainable by everybody. This condition excludes, as being negligible to knowledge, any report of purported observation which the reporter avows to be radically and exclusively private.

2. The status of observation and the use of reports upon it are to be tentative, postulational, hypothetical.[2] This condition excludes all purported materials and all alleged

fixed principles that are offered as providing original and necessary "foundations" for either the knowings or the knowns.

3. The aim of the observation and naming adopted is to promote further observation and naming which in turn will advance and improve. This condition excludes all namings that are asserted to give, or that claim to be, finished reports on "reality."

The above conditions amount to saying that the names we need have to do with knowings and knowns in and by means of continuous operation and test in work, where any knowing or known establishes itself or fails to establish itself through continued search and research solely, never on the ground of any alleged outside "foundation," " premise," "axiom" or *ipse dixit*. In line with this attitude we do not assert that the conditions stated above are "true"; we are not even arguing in their behalf. We advance them as the conditions which, we hold, should be satisfied by the kind of names that are needed by us here and now if we are to advance knowledge of knowledge. Our procedure, then, does not stand in the way of inquiry into knowledge by other workers on the basis either of established creeds or tenets, or of alternative hypotheses; we but state the ground upon which we ourselves wish to work, in the belief that others are prepared to co-operate. The postulates and methods we wish to use are, we believe, akin to those of the sciences which have so greatly advanced knowledge in other fields.

The difficulties in our way are serious, but we believe these difficulties have their chief source in the control exercised over men by traditional phrasings originating when observation was relatively primitive and lacked the many important materials that are now easily available. Cultural conditions (such as ethnological research reveals) favored in earlier days the introduction of factors that have now been shown to be irrelevant to the operations of inquiry and to stand in the way of the formation of a straightforward theory of knowledge — straightforward in the sense of setting forth conclusions reached through inquiry into knowings as themselves facts.

The basic postulate of our procedure is that knowings are observable facts in exactly the same sense as are the subjectmatters that are known. A glance at any collection of books and periodicals discloses the immense number of subjectmatters that have been studied and the various grades of their establishment in the outcome. No great argument is required to' warrant the statement that this wide field of knowledge (possessed of varying depths in its different portions) can be studied not only in terms of things [3] known, but also in terms of the knowings.

In the previous chapter we pointed out instances, in the works of prominent contemporary logicians, of an extraordinary confusion arising from an uncritical use in logic, as theory of knowledge, of forms of primitive observation; sometimes to the utter neglect of the fuller and keener observation now available, and in other cases producing such a mixture of two incompatible types of observation as inevitably wrecks achievement. It was affirmed in that chapter that further advance will require complete abandonment of the customary isolation of the word from the man speaking, and likewise of the word from the thing spoken of or named. In effect, and often overtly, words are dealt with in the logics as if they were a new and third kind of fact lying between man as speaker and things as spoken of. The net result is to erect a new barrier in human behavior between the things that are involved and the operating organisms. While the logical writers in question have professedly departed from the earlier epistemological theories framed in terms of a mind basic as subject and an external world as object, competent analysis shows that the surviving separation their writings exhibit is the ghost of the seventeenth-century epistemological separation of knowing subject and object known, as that in turn was the ghost of the medieval separation of the "spiritual" essence from the "material" nature and body, often with an intervening "soul" of mixed or alternating activities.

Sometimes the intervening realm of names as a new and third kind of fact lying between man as speaker and things as spoken of takes the strange appearance of a denial not only of language as essential in logic, but even of names as essential in language. Thus Quine in a recent discussion of the issue of "universals" as "entities" tells us that "names generally . . . are inessential to language" and that his "suppression of names is a superficial revision of language." The world in which he operates would thus seem comparable with that of Whitehead in which "language" (including apparently that which he himself is using) is "always ambiguous," and in which "spoken language is merely a series of squeaks." [4] One may admire the skill with which Quine uses his method of abstraction to secure a unified field for symbolic logic in which "all names are abstract," and in which the bound variables of quantification become "the sole vehicle of direct objective reference," and still feel that the more he detaches his symbolic construction from the language he is referring to through the agency of the language he is using, the more he assimilates his construction to the other instances of "intervening" language, however less subtly these latter are deployed.

The importance we allot to the introduction of firm names is very quickly felt when one begins to make observation of knowledge as a going fact of behavioral activity. Observation not only separates but also brings together in combination in a single sweep matters which at other times have been treated as isolated and hence as requiring to be forced into organization ("synthesized" is the traditional word) by some outside agency. To see language, with all its speakings and writings, as man-himself-in-action-dealing-with-things is observation of the combining type. Meaningful conveyance is, of course, included, as itself of the very texture of language. The full event is before us thus in durational spread. The observation is no longer made in terms of "isolates" requiring to be "synthesized." Such procedure is common enough in all science. The extension as observation in our case is that we make it cover the speaker or knower along with the spoken of or known as being one common durational event. Here primary speaking is as observable as is a bird in flight. The inclusion of books and periodicals as a case of observable man-in-action is no different in kind from the observation of the steel girders of a bridge connecting the mining and smelting of ores with the operations of a steel mill, and with the building of bridges, in turn, out of the products. For that matter, it is no different from observation extended far enough to take in not just a bird while in flight but bird nest-building, egg-laying and hatching. Observation of this general type sees man-in-action, not as something radically set over against an environing world, nor yet as something merely acting "in" a world, but as action *of* and *in* the world in which the man belongs as an integral constituent.

To see an event filling a certain duration of time as a description across a full duration, rather than as composed of an addition or other kind of combination of separate, instantaneous, or short-span events is another aspect of such observation. Procedure of this type was continuously used by Peirce, though he had no favorable opportunity for developing it, and it was basic to him from the time when in one of his earliest papers he stressed that all thought is in signs and requires a time.[5] The "immediate" or "neutral" experience of William James was definitely an effort at such a form of direct observation in the field of knowings. Dewey's development in use of interaction and transaction, and in presentation of experience as neither subjective nor objective but as a method or system of organization, is strongly of this form; his psychological studies have made special contributions in this line, and in his *Logic, The Theory of Inquiry* (1938), following

upon his logical essays of 1903 and 1916, he has developed
the processes of inquiry in a situational setting. Bentley's
Process of Government in 1908 developed political description in a manner approaching what we would here call
"transactional," and his later analysis of mathematics as
language, his situational treatment of behavior and his
factual development of behavioral space-time belong in
this line of research.

If there should be difficulty in understanding this use of
the word "observation," the difficulty illustrates the point
earlier made as to the influence of materials introduced
from inadequate sources. The current philosophical notion
of observation is derived from a psychology of "consciousness" (or some version of the "mental" as an isolate), and
it endeavors to reduce what is observed either to some
single sensory quality or to some other "content" of such
short time-span as to have no connections — except what
may be provided through inference as an operation outside
of observation. As against such a method of obtaining a description of observation, the procedure we adopt reports
and describes observation on the same basis the worker
in knowledge — astronomer, physicist, psychologist, etc. —
employs when he makes use of a test observation in arriving at conclusions to be accepted as known. We proceed upon the postulate that *knowings* are always and
everywhere inseparable from *the knowns* — that the two
are twin aspects of common fact.

II

"Fact" is a name of central position in the material we
propose to use in forming a terminology. If there are such
things as facts, and if they are of such importance that they
have a vital status in questions of knowledge, then in any
theory of knowings and knowns we should be able to characterize fact — we should be able to say, that is, that we
know what we are talking *about* "in fact" when we apply

the word "fact" to the fact of Fact.[6] The primary consideration in fulfilling the desired condition with respect to Fact
is that the activity by which it is identified and the *what*
that is identified are both required, and are required in
such a way that each is taken along with the other, and in
no sense as separable. Our terminology is involved in fact,
and equally "fact" is involved in our terminology. This
repeats in effect the statement that knowledge requires and
includes both knowings and knowns. Anything named
"fact" is such both with respect to the knowing operation
and with respect to what is known.[7] We establish for our
use, with respect to both fact and knowledge, that we have
no "something known" and no "something identified"
apart from its know*ing* and identify*ing,* and that we have
no know*ing* and identify*ing* apart from the somewhats and
somethings that are being known and identified. Again
we do not put forth this statement as a truth about "reality," but as the only position we find it possible to take on
the ground of that reference to the observed which we regard as an essential condition of our inquiry. The statement is one about ourselves observed in action in the
world. From the standpoint of what is observable, it is
of the same straightforward kind as is the statement that
when chopping occurs something is chopped and that when
seeing takes place something is seen. We select the name
"fact" because we believe that it carries and suggests this
"double-barrelled" sense (to borrow a word from William
James), while such words as "object" and "entity" have
acquired from traditional philosophical use the signification of something set over against the doing or acting.
That Fact is literally or etymologically *something done or
made* has also the advantage of suggesting that the knowing and identifying, as ways of acting, are as much ways
of doing, of making (just as much "behaviors," we may
say), as are chopping wood, singing songs, seeing sights or
making hay.

In what follows we shall continue the devices we have in

a manner employed in the preceding paragraph, namely the use of quotation marks, italics, and capitalized initials as aids to presentation, the two former holding close to common usage, while the third has a more specialized application. We shall also freely employ hyphenization in a specialized way, and this perhaps even more frequently than the others. Thus the use of the word "fact" without quotation marks will be in a general or even casual manner. With quotation marks "fact" will indicate the verbal aspect, the word, sometimes impartially, and sometimes as held off at arm's length where the responsibility for its application is not the writer's. With initial capitalization Fact may be taken to stand for the full word-and-thing subjectmatter into which we are inquiring. Italicising in either form, whether as *"fact"* or as *Fact* will indicate stress of attention. Hyphenization will indicate attention directed to the importance which the components of the word hyphenized have for the present consideration. The words *inter-action* and *trans-action* will enter shortly in this way, and will receive a considerable amount of hyphenizing for emphasis throughout. No use of single quotation marks will be made to distinguish the name of a thing from the thing, for the evident reason that expectantly rigid fixations of this type are just what we most need to avoid. All the devices mentioned are conveniences in their way, but only safe if used cautiously. Thus in the third preceding sentence (as in several others) its most stressed words, there inspected as words, should have quotation marks, but to use such marks would in this case destroy the intended assertion. Rather than being rigorous our own use will be casually variable. This last is best at our present stage of inquiry.

For the purpose of facilitating further inquiry what has been said will be restated in negative terms. We shall *not* proceed as if we were concerned with "existent things" or "objects" entirely apart from men, nor with men entirely apart from things. Accordingly, we do not have on our hands the problem of forcing them into some kind of organization or connection. We shall proceed by taking for granted human organisms developed, living, carrying on, of and in the cosmos. They are there in such system that their operations and transactions can be viewed directly — including those that constitute knowings. When they are so viewed, knowings and knowns come before us differentiated within the factual cosmos, not as if they were there provided in advance so that out of them cosmos — system — fact — knowledge — have to be produced. Fact, language, knowledge have on this procedure cosmic status; they are not taken as if they existed originally in irreconcilably hostile camps. This, again, is but to say that we shall inquire into knowings, both as to materials and workmanship, in the sense of ordinary science.[8]

The reader will note (that is, observe, give heed to) the superiority of our position with respect to observation over that of the older epistemological constructions. Who would assert he can properly and in a worth-while manner *observe* a "mind" *in addition to* the organism that is engaged in the transactions pertinent to it in an observable world? An attempt to answer this question in the affirmative results in regarding observation as private introspection — and this is sufficient evidence of departure from procedures having scientific standing.[9] Likewise, the assertion or belief that things considered as "objects" outside of and apart from human operations are observed, or are observable, is equally absurd when carefully guarded statement is demanded of it. Observation is operation; it is human operation. If attributed to a "mind" it itself becomes unobservable. If surveyed in an observable world — in what we call cosmos or nature — the object observed is as much a part of the operation as is the observing organism.

This statement about observation, in name and fact, is necessary to avoid misinterpretation. It is not "observation," however, to which we are here giving inquiry; we shall not even attempt to make the word "firm" at a later stage. In the range in which we shall work — the seeking of sound names for processes involving naming — observation is always involved and such observation in this range is in fusion with name-application, so that neither takes place except in and through the other, whatever further applications of the word "observation" (comparable to applications of "naming" and of "knowing") may in widened inquiries be required.

If we have succeeded in making clear our position with respect to the type of name for which we are in search, it will be clear also that this type of name comes in clusters. "Fact" will for us be a central name with other names clustering around it. If "observation" should be taken as central, it in its turn could be made firm only in orientation to its companionate cluster. In any case much serious co-operative inquiry is involved. In no case can we hope to succeed by first setting up separated names and then putting them in pigeonholes or bundling them together with wire provided from without. Names are, indeed, to be differentiated from one another, but the differentiation takes place with respect to other names in clusters; and the same thing holds for clusters that are differentiated from one another. This procedure has its well-established precedents in scientific procedure. The genera and species of botany and zoology are excellent examples — provided they are taken as determinations in process and not as taxonomic rigidities.[10]

III

In certain important respects we have placed limitations on the range of our inquiry and on the methods we use. The purpose is to increase the efficiency of what we do. These decisions have been made only after much experimentation in manners of organization and presentation. The main points should be kept steadily in mind as we now stress them.

As already said, we do not propose to issue any flat de-
crees as to the names others should adopt. Moreover, at
the start we shall in some cases not even declare our permanent choices, but instead will deliberately introduce provisional "second-string" names. For this we have two sound
reasons. First, our task requires us to locate the regions
(some now very largely ignored) that are most in need of
firm observation. Second, we must draw upon a dictionary
stock of words that have multiple, and often confusedly
tangled, applications. We run the risk that the name first
introduced may, on these accounts, become involved in
misapprehensions on the reader's part, sufficient to ruin it
for the future. Hence the value of attempting to establish
the regions to be named by provisional namings, in the
hope we shall secure stepping stones to better concentration
of procedure at the end.

We do not propose in this inquiry to cover the entire
range of "knowledge"; that is, the entire range of life and
behavior to which the word "knowledge," at one time or
another and in one way or another can be applied. We
have already listed "knowledge" as a vague word and said
we shall specify "knowings" and "knowns" for our attention. Throughout our entire treatment, "knowledge" will
remain a word referring roughly to the general field within
which we select subjectmatters for closer examination.
Even for the words "knowings" and "knowns" the range of
common application runs all the way from infusoria approaching food to mathematicians operating with their
most recondite dimensions. We shall confine ourselves to
a central region: that of identifications under namings, of
knowing-by-naming — of "specified existence," if one will.
Time will take care of the passage of inquiry across the
border regions from naming-knowing to the simpler and
to the more complex forms.

We shall regard these naming-knowings directly as a
form of knowings. *Take this statement literally as it is
written.* It means we do not regard namings as primarily

instrumental or specifically ancillary to something else called knowings (or knowledge) except as any behavior may enter as ancillary to any other. We do not split a corporeal naming from a presumptively non-corporeal or "mental" knowing, nor do we permit a mentaloid "brain" to make pretense of being a substitute for a "mind" thus maintaining a split between knowings and namings. This is postulation on our part; but surely the exhibits we secured in the preceding chapter of what happens in the logics under the separation of spoken word from speaking man should be enough to justify any postulate that offers hope of relief. The acceptance of this postulate, even strictly during working hours, may be difficult. We do not expect assent at the start, and we do not here argue the case. We expect to display the value in further action.

IV

Thus far we have been discussing the conditions under which a search for firm names for knowings and knowns must be carried on. In summary our procedure is to be as follows: Working under hypothesis we concentrate upon a special region of knowings and knowns; we seek to spotlight aspects of that region that today are but dimly observed; we suggest tentative namings; through the development of these names in a cluster we hope advance can be made towards construction under dependable naming in the future.

1. *Fact, Event, Designation.* We start with the cosmos of knowledge — with nature as known and as in process of being better known — ourselves and our knowings included. We establish this cosmos as *fact,* and name it "fact" with all its knowings and its knowns included. We do *not* introduce, either by hypothesis or by dogma, knowers and knowns as prerequisites to fact. Instead we observe both knowers and knowns as factual, as cosmic; and never — either of them — as extra-cosmic accessories.

We specialize our studies in the region of naming-knowings, of knowings through namings, wherein we identify two great *factual aspects* to be examined. We name these *event* and *designation*. The application of the word "fact" may perhaps in the end need to be extended beyond the behavioral processes of event-designation. Fact, in other words, as it may be presumed to be present for animal life prior to (or below) linguistic and proto-linguistic behaviors, or as it may be presumed to be attainable by mathematical behaviors developed later than (or above) the ranges of the language behavior that names, is no affair of ours at this immediate time and place. We note the locus of such contingent extensions, leave the way open for the future, and proceed to cultivate the garden of our choice, namely, the characteristic Fact we have before us.

Upon these namings the following comments will, for the present, suffice:

(*a*) In Fact-Event-Designation we do not have a three-fold organization, or a two-fold; we have instead one system.

(*b*) Given the language and knowledge we now possess, the use of the word "fact" imposes upon its users the necessity of selection and acceptance. This manifest status is recognized terminologically by our adoption of the name "designation."

(*c*) The word "aspect" as used here is not stressed as information-giving. It must be taken to register — register, and nothing more — the duplex, aspectual observation and report that are required if we are to characterize Fact at all. The word "phase" may be expected to become available for comparable application when, under the development of the word "aspect," we are sufficiently advanced to consider time-alternations and rhythms of event and of designation in knowledge process.[11]

(*d*) "Event" involves in normal use the extensional and the durational. "Designation" for our purposes must likewise be so taken. The Designation we postulate and discuss is not of the nature of *a* sound or *a* mark applied *as* a name *to* an event. Instead of this it is the entire activity — the behavioral action and activity — of naming through which Event appears in our knowing as Fact.

(*e*) We expect the word "fact" to be able to maintain itself for terminological purposes, and we shall give reasons for this in a succeeding chapter, though still retaining freedom to alter it. As for the words "event" and "designation," their use here is provisional and replacement more probable. Should we, for example, adopt such words as "existence" and "name," both words (as the case stands at this stage) would carry with them to most readers many implications false to our intentions — the latter even more than the former; understanding of our procedure would then become distorted and ineffective.

(*f*) "Fact," in our use, is to be taken with a range of reference as extensive as is allotted to any other name for cosmos, universe or nature, where the context shows that knowledge, not poesy, is concerned. It is to be taken with its pasts and its futures, its growings-out-of and its growings-into; its transitions of report from poorer to richer, and from less to more. It is to be taken with as much solidity and substantiality as nature, universe or world, by any name whatsoever. It is to be taken, however, with the understanding that instead of inserting gratuitously an unknown something as foundation for the factually known, we are taking the knowledge in full — the knowings-knowns as they come: namely, both in one — without appeal to cosmic tortoise to hold up cosmic elephant to hold up cosmic pillar to hold up the factual cosmos we are considering.

(*g*) In a myopic and short-time view Event and Designation appear to be separates. The appearance does no harm if it is held where it belongs within narrow ranges of inquiry. For a general account of knowings and knowns the wider envisionment in system is proposed.

(*h*) Overlapping Fact, as we are postulating it within

the range of *namings,* are, on one side, perceptions, manipulations, habituations and other adaptations; on the other side, symbolic-knowledge procedures such as those of mathematics. We shall be taking these into account as events-designated, even though for the present we are not inquiring into them with respect to possible designatory, quasi-designatory or otherwise fact-presenting functions of their own along the evolutionary line. Our terminology will in no way be such as to restrict consideration of them, but rather to further it, when such consideration becomes practicable.

(*i*) If Designations, as we postulate them for our inquiry, are factually durational-extensional, then these Designations, as designat*ings, are* themselves Events. Similarly, the Events as events are designational. The two phases, designating and designated, lie within a full process of designation. It is not the subjectmatter before us, but the available language forms, that make this latter statement difficult.[12]

(*j*) Most generally, Fact, in our terminology, is not limited to what any one man knows, nor to what is known to any one human grouping, nor to any one span of time such as our own day and age. On the designatory side in our project of research it has the full range and spread that, as we said above, it has on the event side, with all the futures and the pasts, the betters and the poorers, comprised as they come. In our belief the Newtonian era has settled the status of fact definitely in this way, for our generation of research at least. First, Newtonian mechanics rose to credal strength in the shelter of its glorified absolutes. Then at the hands of Faraday, Clerk Maxwell and Einstein, it lost its absolutes, lost its credal claims, and emerged chastened and improved. It thus gained the high rating of a magnificent approximation as compared with its earlier trivial self-rating of eternal certainty. The coming years — fifty, or a thousand, whatever it takes — remain quite free for change. Any intelligent voice will say this;

the trouble is to get ears to hear. Our new assurance is better than the old assurance. Knowing and the known, event and designation — the full knowledge — go forward together. Eventuation is observed. Accept this in principle, not merely as a casual comment on an accidental happening: — you then have before you what our terminology recognizes when it places Fact-in-growth as a sound enough base for research with no need to bother over minuscular mentals or crepuscular reals alleged to be responsible for it.

2. *Circularity*. When we said above that designations are events and events designations, we adopted *circularity* — procedure in a circle — openly, explicitly, emphatically. Several ways of pretending to avoid such circularity are well known. Perhaps at one end everything is made tweedledum, and perhaps at the other everything is made tweedledee, or perhaps in between little tweedledums and little tweedledees, companionable but infertile, essential to each other but untouchable by each other, are reported all along the line. We have nothing to apologize for in the circularity we choose in preference to the old talk-ways. We observe world-being-known-to-man-in-it; we report the observation; we proceed to inquire into it, circularity or no circularity. This is all there is to it. And the circularity is not merely round the circle in one direction: the course is both ways round at once in full mutual function.

3. *The Differentiations That Follow*. Given fact, observed aspectually as Event and as Designation, our next indicated task is to develop further terminological organization for the two aspects separately. We shall undertake this shortly and leave the matter there so far as the present preliminary outline is concerned. To aid us, though, we shall require firm statement about certain tools to be used in the process. We must, that is, be able to name certain procedures so definitely that they will not be confounded with current procedures on a different basis. Events will be differentiated with respect to a certain range of plasticity

that is comparable in a general way to the physical differentiations of gaseous, liquid and solid. For these we shall use the names Situation, Occurrence and Object. As for Designation, we shall organize it in an evolutionary scheme of behavioral sign processes of which it is one form, the names we apply being Sign, Signal, Name and Symbol. The preliminary steps we find it necessary to take before presenting these differentiations are: first, steady maintenance of a distinction among the various branches of scientific inquiry in terms of selected subjectmatters of research, rather than in terms of materials assumed to be waiting for research in advance; second, a firm use of the word "specification" to designate the type of naming to be employed as contrasted with the myriad verbal processes that go by the name of "definition"; third, the establishment of our right to selective observational control of specific situations within subjectmatters by a competent distinction of *trans*-actions from *inter*-actions.

4. *Sciences as Subjectmatters*. The broad division of regions of scientific research commonly recognized today is that into the physical, the biological and the psychological. However mathematics, where inquiry attains maximum precision, lacks any generally accepted form of organization with these sciences; and sociology, where maximum imprecision is found, also fails of a distinctive manner of incorporation.[13] Fortunately this scheme of division is gradually losing its rigidities. A generation or two ago physics stood aloof from chemistry; today it has constructively incorporated it. In the biological range today, the most vivid and distinctive member is physiology, yet the name "biology" covers many gross adaptational studies not employing the physiological techniques; in addition, the name "biology" assuredly covers everything that is psychological, unless perchance some "psyche" is involved that is "non-" or "ultra-"human. The word "psychological" itself is a hold-over from an earlier era, in which such a material series as "*the* physical," "*the* vital" and "*the*

psychic" was still believed in and taken to offer three different realms of substance presented as raw material by Nature or by God for our perpetual puzzlement. If we are to establish knowings and knowns in a single system of Fact, we certainly must be free from addiction to a presumptive universe compounded out of three basically different kinds of materials. Better said, however, it is our present freedom from such material enthrallment, attained for us by the general advance of scientific research, that at long last has made us able to see all knowings and knowns, by hypothesis, as in one system.

Within Fact we shall recognize the distinctions of the scientific field as being those of subjectmatters, not those of materials,[14] unless one speaks of materials only in the sense that their differences themselves arise in and are vouched for strictly by the technological procedures that are available in the given stages of inquiry. Terminologically, we shall distinguish *physical, physiological* and *behavioral*[15] regions of science. We shall accept the word "biological" under our postulation as covering unquestionably both physiological and behavioral inquiries, but we find the range of its current applications much too broad to be safe for the purposes of the present distinctive terminology. The technical differentiation, in research, of physiological procedures from behavioral is of the greatest import in the state of inquiry today, and this would be pushed down out of sight by any heavy stress on the word "biological," which, as we have said, we emphatically believe *must* cover them both. We wish to stress most strongly that physical, physiological and behavioral inquiries in the present state of knowledge represent three great distinctive lines of technique; while any one of them may be brought to the aid of any other, *direct* positive extension of statement from the firm technical formulations of one into the information-stating requirements of another cannot be significantly made as knowledge today stands. Physical formulation does not directly yield heredity, nor does physiological formulation directly yield word-meanings, sentences and mathematical formulas. To complete the circle, behavioral process, while producing physical science, cannot directly in its own procedure yield report on the embodied physical event. This circularity, once again, is in the knowledge — in the knowings and the knowns — not in any easy-going choice we are free and competent to make in the hope we can cleave to it, evidence or no evidence.

5. *Specification.* The word "definition," as currently used, covers exact symbolic statements in mathematics; it covers procedures under Aristotelian logic; it covers all the collections of word-uses, old and new, that the dictionaries assemble, and many still more casual linguistic procedures. The word "definition" must manifestly be straightened out, if any sound presentation of knowings and knowns is to be secured.[16] We have fair reason to believe that most of the difficulty in what is called the "logic of mathematics" is due to an endeavor to force consolidation of two types of human behavior, both labeled "definition," (though one stresses heavily, while the other diverges from, the use of namings) without preliminary inquiry into the simpler facts of the life linguistic. In our terminology we shall assign the word "definition" to the region of mathematical and syntactical consistency, while for the lesser specimens of "dictionary definition" we shall employ the name "characterization." In our own work in this book we shall attempt no *definition* whatever in the formal sense we shall assign the word. We shall at times not succeed in getting beyond preliminary characterization. Our aim in the project, however, is to advance towards such an accuracy in naming as science ever increasingly achieves. Such accuracy in naming we shall call "specification." Consider what the word "heat" stood for in physics before Rumford and Joule, and what it tells us in physical specification today. Consider the changes the word "atom" has undergone in the past generation. Mod-

ern chemical terminology is a highly specialized form of specification of operations undertaken. However, the best illustration for our purposes is probably the terminology of genera and species. In the days when animals were theological specialities of creation, the naming level was that of characterization. After demonstration had been given that species had natural origins, scientific specification, as we understand it, developed. We still find it, of course, straining at times towards taxonomic rigidities, but over against this we find it forever rejuvenating itself by free inquiry up even to the risk of its own obliteration. Abandonment of the older magic of name-to-reality correspondence is one of the marks of specification. Another will be observed when specification has been clearly differentiated from symbolic definition. In both its aspects of Event and Designation we find Fact spread in "spectrum-like" form. We use "specification" to mark this scientific characteristic of efficient naming. Peirce's stress on the "precept that is more serviceable than a definition" [17] involves the attitude we are here indicating. Specification operates everywhere in that field of inquiry covered by affirmation and assertion, proposition and judgment, in Dewey's logical program. The defects of the traditional logics exhibited in Chapter I were connected with their lack of attention to the accurate specification of their own subjectmatters; at no point in our examination did we make our criticisms rest on consistency in definition in the sense of the word "consistency" which we shall develop as we proceed through the differentiation of symbol from name and of symbolic behavior from naming behavior.

6. *Transaction.* We have established Fact as involving both Designation and designated Event. We have inspected inquiry into Fact in terms of subjectmatters that are determinable under the techniques of inquiry, not in terms of materials presented from without. [18] Both treatments make selection under hypothesis a dominant phase of procedure. Selection under hypothesis, however, affects

all observation. We shall take this into account terminologically by contrasting events reported in interactions with events reported as transactions. Later chapters will follow dealing with this central issue in our procedure: the right, namely, to open our eyes to see. Here we can only touch broadly upon it. Pre-scientific procedure largely regarded "things" as possessing powers of their own, under or in which they acted. Galileo is the scientist whose name is most strongly identified with the change to modern procedure. We may take the word *"action"* as a most general characterization for events where their durational process is being stressed. Where the older approach had most commonly seen *self-action* in "the facts," the newer approach took form under Newton as a system of interaction, marked especially by the third "law of motion" — that action and reaction are equal and opposite. The classical mechanics is such a system of interaction involving particles, boundaries, and laws of effects. Before it was developed — before, apparently, it could develop — observation of a new type differing from the pre-Galilean was made in a manner essentially transactional. This enters in Galileo's report on inertia, appearing in the Newtonian formulation as the first "law of motion," namely, that any motion uninterfered with will continue in a straight line. This set up a motion, directly, factually, as event.[19] The field of knowings and knowns in which we are working requires transactional observation, and this is what we are giving it and what our terminology is designed to deal with. The epistemologies, logics, psychologies and sociologies today are still largely on a self-actional basis. In psychology a number of tentative efforts are being made towards an *interactional* presentation, with balanced components. Our position is that the traditional language currently used about knowings and knowns (and most other language about behaviors, as well) shatters the subjectmatter into fragments in advance of inquiry and thus destroys instead of furthering comprehensive observation for it. We hold that observation must be set free; and that, to advance this aim, a postulatory appraisal of the main historical patterns of observation should be made, and identifying namings should be provided. Our own procedure is the *transactional*, in which is asserted the right to see together, extensionally and durationally, much that is talked about conventionally as if it were composed of irreconcilable separates. We do not present this procedure as being more real or generally valid than any other, but as being the one now needed in the field where we work. In the same spirit in which physicists perforce use both particle and wave presentations we here employ both interactional and transactional observation.[20] Important specialized studies belong in this field in which the organism is made central to attention. This is always legitimate in all forms of inquiry within a transactional setting, so long as it is deliberately undertaken, not confusedly or with "self-actional" implications. As place-holders in this region of nomenclature we shall provisionally set down *behavior-agent* and *behavior-object*. They represent specialized interactional treatments within the wider transactional presentation, with organisms or persons or actors named uncertainly on the one hand and with environments named in variegated forms on the other.

7. *Situation, Occurrence, Object.* We may now proceed to distinguish Situation, Occurrence and Object as forms of Event. Event is durational-extensional; it is what "takes place," what is inspected as "*a* taking place." These names do not provide a "classification," unless classification is understood as a focusing of attention within subjectmatters rather than as an arrangement of materials. The word "situation" is used with increasing frequency today, but so waveringly that the more it is used the worse its own status seems to become. We insist that in simple honesty it should stand *either* for the environment of an object (interactionally), *or* for the full situation including whatever object may be selectively specified within it (transactionally),

and that there be no wavering. We shall establish our own use for the word *situation* in this latter form. When an event is of the type that is readily observable in transition within the ordinary spans of human discrimination of temporal and spatial changes, we shall call it *occurrence*. The ordinary use of "event" in daily life is close to this, and if we generalize the application of the word, as we have provisionally done, to cover situation and object as well as occurrence, then we require a substitute in the more limited place. Occurrence fairly fills the vacancy. *Object* [21] is chosen as the clearly indicated name for stabilized, enduring situations, for occurrences that need so long a span of time, or perhaps so minute a space-change, that the space and time changes are not themselves within the scope of ordinary, everyday perceptual attention. Thus any one of the three words Situation, Occurrence and Object may, if focusing of attention shifts, spread over the range of the others, all being equally held as Event. We have here a fair illustration of what we have previously called a word-cluster. The Parthenon is an object to a visitor, and has so been for all the centuries since its construction. It is nevertheless an occurrence across some thousands of years. While for certain purposes of inquiry it may be marked off as object-in-environment, for thoroughgoing investigation it must be seized as situation, of which the object-specification is at best one phase or feature. There is here no issue of reality, no absolute yes or no to assert, but only free determination under inquiry.

8. *Sign, Signal, Name, Symbol.* When we turn to Designation, our immediate problem is not that of distinguishing the variety of *its* forms. Specification, the form most immediately concerning us, has already been noted. What we have to do instead is to place designation itself among behavioral events. Circularity is again here strikingly involved. Our treatment must be in terms of Event as much as in terms of Designation, with full convertibility of the two. The event is behavioral. Designation (a behavioral

event) can be viewed as one stage in the range of behavioral evolution from the sensitive reactions of protozoa
to the most complex symbolic procedures of mathematics.
In this phase of the inquiry we shall alter the naming.
Viewing the behavioral event, we shall name it directly
Name instead of replacing "name" by "designation" as
seemed necessary for provisional practical reasons on the
obverse side of the inquiry. At a later stage we shall undertake to establish the characteristic behavioral process as
sign, a process not found in either physical or physiological
techniques of inquiry. We shall thus understand the name
"sign" to be used so as to cover the entire range of behavioral activity. There are many stages or levels of behaviors, but for the greater part of our needs a three-level
differentiation will furnish gross guidance. The lower
level, including perceptions, manipulations, habituations,
adaptations, etc., we shall name *signal* (adapting the word
from Pavlov's frequent usage). Where organized language
is employed as sign, we shall speak of *name*. In mathematical regions (for reasons to be discussed fully later)
we shall speak of *symbol*. Signal, Name and Symbol will
be the three differentiations of Sign, where "sign" indicates
most broadly the "knowledge-like" processes of behavior
in a long ascending series. Vital to this construction, even
though no development for the moment may be offered,
is the following statement: The name "Sign" and the
names adjusted to it *shall all be understood transactionally,*
which in this particular case is to say that they do not name
items or characteristics of organisms alone, nor do they
name items or characteristics of environments alone; in
every case, they name the *activity* that occurs *of both
together.*

V

By the use of Sign-Signal-Name-Symbol we indicate the
locus for the knowing-naming process and for other be-

havioral processes within cosmos. By the use of Fact-Event-Designation we specify the process of event-determination through which cosmos is presented as itself a locus for such loci. The two types of terminology set forth different phases of a common process. They can be so held, if we insist upon freedom for transactional observation in cases in which ancient word-forms have fractured fact and if we lose fear of circularity. It is our task in later chapters to develop this terminology and to test it in situations that arise.

For the present our terminological guide-posts, provisionally laid out, are as follows:

SUGGESTED EXPERIMENTAL NAMING

Fact: Our cosmos as it is before us progressively in knowings through namings.

Event: [22] "Fact" named as taking place.

Designation: Naming as taking place in "fact."

Physical,
Physiological,
Behavioral: Differentiations of the techniques of inquiry, marking off subjectmatters as sciences under development, and not constricted to conformity with primitive pre-views of "materials" of "reality."

Characterization: Linguistic procedure preliminary to developed specification, including much "dictionary-definition."

Specification: Accuracy of designation along the free lines through which modern sciences have developed.

Definition: [23] Symbolic procedure linguistically evolved, not directly employing designatory tests.

Action (Activity) : Event stressed with respect to durational transition.

Self-Action: Pre-scientific presentation in terms of presumptively independent "actors," "souls," "minds," "selves," "powers" or "forces," taken as activating events.

Interaction: Presentation of particles or other objects organized as operating upon one another.

Transaction: [24] Functional observation of full system, actively necessary to inquiry at some stages, held in reserve at other stages, frequently requiring the breaking down of older verbal impactions of naming.

Behavior-Agent: Behavioral organic action, interactionally inspected within transaction; agent in the sense of *re*-agent rather than of act*or*.

Behavior-Object: Environmental specialization of object with respect to agent within behavioral transaction.

Situation: Event as subjectmatter of inquiry, always transactionally viewed as the full subjectmatter; never to be taken as detachable "environment" over against object.

Occurrence: [25] Event designated as in process under transitions such as are most readily identifiable in everyday human-size contacts.

Object: Event in its more firmly stabilized forms — never, however, as in final fixations — always available as subjectmatter under transfer to situational inspection, should need arise as inquiry progresses.

Sign: Characteristic adaptational behavior of organism-environment; the "cognitive" in its broadest reaches when viewed transactionally as process (not in organic or environmental specialization).

Signal: Transactional sign in the perceptive-manipulative ranges.

Name: Specialized development of sign among hominidae; apparently not reaching the full designational stage (excepting, perhaps, on blocked evolutional lines) until *homo sapiens*.

Symbol: A later linguistic development of sign, forfeiting specific designatory applications to gain heightened efficiency in other ways.

The above terminology is offered as provisional only. Especially is further discussion needed in the cases of Event, Occurrence, and Definition. Later decisions, after further examination, are reported in Chapter XI, with several footnotes along the route serving as markers for progress being made.

We regard the following as common sense observation upon the manner of discourse about knowledge that we find current around us.

The knowledge of knowledge itself that we possess today is weak knowledge — perhaps as weak as any we have; it stands greatly in need of de-sentimentalized research.

Fact is notoriously two-faced. It is cosmos as noted by a speck of cosmos. Competent appraisal takes this into account.

What is beyond Fact — beyond the knowing and the known — is not worth bothering about in any inquiry undertaken into knowings and knowns.

Science as *inquiry* thrives within limits such as these, and science offers sound guidance. Scientific specification thrives in, and requires, such limits; why, then, should not also inquiry and specification for knowings and the known?

Knowings are behaviors. Neither inquiry into knowings nor inquiry into behaviors can expect satisfactory results unless the other goes with it hand in hand.[26]

---

1 Even the words "vague," "firm" and loose," as we at this stage are able to use them, are loosely used. We undertake development definitely and deliberately within an atmosphere (one might perhaps better call it a swamp) of vague language. We reject the alternative — the initial dependence on some schematism of verbal impactions — and propose to destroy the authoritarian claims of such impactions by means of distinctions to be introduced later, including particularly that between specification and definition.

2 The postulations we are using, their origin and status, will be discussed in a following chapter. See also Dewey, *Logic, the Theory of Inquiry* (New York, 1938), Chap. I, and Bentley, "Postulation for Behavioral Inquiry" (*The Journal of Philosophy*, XXXVI [1939], 405-413).

8 "Thing" is another vague word. It is in good standing, however, where general reference is intended, and it is safer in such cases than words like "entity" which carry too great a variety of philosophical and epistemological implications. We shall use it freely in this way, but for more determinate uses shall substitute "object" when we later have given this latter word sufficient definiteness.

4 Alfred North Whitehead: *Process and Reality* (New York, 1929), p. 403; W. V. Quine, "On Universals," *The Journal of Symbolic Logic*, XII (1947), p. 74. Compare also W. V. Quine, *Mathematical Logic*, Second Printing, (Cambridge, 1947), pp. 149-152 *et al.*

5 "The only cases of thought which we can find are of thought in signs" (*Collected Papers*, 5.251); "To say that thought cannot happen in an instant but requires a time is but another way of saying that every thought must be interpreted in another, or that all thought is in signs" (*ibid.*, 5.253). See also comment in our preceding chapter, pp. 3-5. For a survey of Peirce's development (the citations being to his *Collected Papers*) see "Questions Concerning Certain Faculties Claimed for Man" (1868), 5.213 to 5.263, "How to Make Our Ideas Clear" (1878), 5.388 to 5.410, "A Pragmatic Interpretation of the Logical Subject" (1902), 2.328 to 2.331, and "The Ethics of Terminology" (1903), 2.219 to 2.226. On his use of leading principles, see 3.154 to 3.171 and 5.365 to 5.369; on the open field of inquiry, 5.376n; on truth, 5.407, 5.565; on the social status of logic and knowledge, 2.220, 2.654, 5.311, 5.316, 5.331. 5.354, 5.421, 5.444, 6.610; on the duplex nature of "experience," 1.321, 5.51, 5.284, 5.613. For William James's development, see his essays in *Mind, a Quarterly Review of Psychology and Philosophy* in the early eighteen-eighties, Chapter X on "Self" in *The Principles of Psychology* (New York, 1890), the epilogue to the *Briefer Course* (New York, 1893) and *Essays in Radical Empiricism* (New York, 1912). For Dewey, see *Studies in Logical Theory* (Chicago, 1903), *How We Think* (Boston, 1910, revised 1933), *Essays in Experimental Logic* (Chicago, 1916), *Experience and Nature* (Chicago, 1925), *Logic, the Theory of Inquiry*, and three psychological papers reprinted in *Philosophy and Civilization* (New York, 1931) as follows: "The Reflex Arc Concept in Psychology" (1896, reprinted as "The Unit of Behavior"), "The Naturalistic Theory of Perception by the Senses" (1925) and "Conduct and Experience" (1930). See also "Context and Thought" (*University of California Publications in Philosophy* XII [1931], 203-224), "How Is Mind to Be Known?" (*The Journal of Philosophy*, XXXIX [1942], 29-35) and "By Nature and by Art" (*ibid.*, XLI [1944], 281-292). For Bentley, see *The Process of Government* (Chicago, 1908), *Relativity in Man and Society* (New York, 1926), *Linguistic Analysis of Mathematics* (Bloomington, Indiana, 1932), *Behavior, Knowledge, Fact* (Bloomington, Indiana, 1935), three papers on situational treatment of behavior (*The Journal of Philosophy*, XXXVI

[1939], 169-181, 309-323, 405-413) , "The Factual Space and Time of Behavior" (ibid., XXXVIII [1941], 477-485) , "The Human Skin: Philosophy's Last Line of Defense" (Philosophy of Science, VIII [1941], 1-19) , "Observable Behaviors" (Psychological Review, XLVII [1940], 230-253) , "The Behavioral Superfice" (ibid., XLVIII [1941], 39-59) and "The Jamesian Datum" (The Journal of Psychology, XVI [1943], 35-79) .

6 The wretched status of the word "fact" with respect to its "knowing" and its "known" (and in other respects as well) was illustrated in Chapter I, Section IX.

7 It may be well to repeat here what has already been said. In making the above statement we are not attempting to legislate concerning the proper use of a word, but are stating the procedure we are adopting.

8 It is practically impossible to guard against every form of misapprehension arising from prevalent dominance of language-attitudes holding over from a relatively pre-scientific period. There are probably readers who will translate what has been said about knowings-knowns into terms of epistemological idealism. Such a translation misses the main point — namely, that man and his doings and transactions have to be viewed as facts within the natural cosmos.

9 "Conceptions derived from . . . anything that is so occult as not to be open to public inspection and verification (such as the purely psychical, for example) are excluded" (Dewey, Logic, p. 19) .

10 Other defects in the language we must use, in addition to the tendency towards prematurely stiffened namings, offer continuous interference with communication such as we must attempt. Our language is not at present grammatically adapted to the statements we have to make. Especially is this true with respect to the prepositions which in toto we must list among the "vague words" against which we have given warning. Mention of special dangers will be made as occasion arises. We do the best we can, and discussion, we hope, should never turn on some particular man's personal rendering of some particular preposition in some particular passage. The "Cimmerian" effect that appears when one attempts to use conventional linguistic equipment to secure direct statement in this region will be readily recalled.

11 "Aspect" and "phase" may stand, therefore, as somewhat superior to the "vague words" against which we give warning, though not as yet presenting positive information in our field.

12 This paragraph replaces one noted in the Preface as deleted. As first written it read, after the opening sentence, as follows: "Similarly, the Events as designational, are Designations. It is not the subjectmatter before us, but the available language forms that make this latter statement difficult. The two uses of 'are' in the sentence 'Events are Designations' and 'Designations are Events' differ greatly, each 'are' representing one of the aspects within the broader presentation of Fact. To recognize events

as designated while refusing to call them designations in the activity sense, would be a limitation that would maintain a radical split between naming and named at the very time that their connective framework was being acknowledged. Our position is emphatic upon this point. It is clear enough that in the older sense events are not designations; it should be equally clear and definite that in our procedure and terminology they are designational — designation — or (with due caution in pluralizing) Designations. To control the two uses of the word 'are' in the two forms of statement, and to maintain the observation and report that 'Designations are Events,' while also 'Events are Designations' — this is the main strain our procedure will place upon the reader. Proceeding under hypothesis (and without habituation to hypothesis there will be no advance at all) this should not be too severe a requirement for one who recognizes the complexity of the situation and has an active interest in clearing it up."

13 We shall deal with the very important subject of mathematics elsewhere. Sociological inquiries, with the exception of anthropology, are hardly far enough advanced to justify any use of them as subjectmatters in our present inquiry.

14 An extended consideration of many phases of this issue and approaches to its treatment is given by Coleman R. Griffith in his *Principles of Systematic Psychology* (Urbana, Illinois, 1943). Compare the section on "The Scientific Use of Participles and Nouns" (pp. 489-497) and various passages indexed under "Science."

15 Our use of the word "behavioral" has no "behavioristic" implications. We are no more behavioristic than mentalistic, disavowing as we do, under hypothesis, "isms" and "istics" of all types. The word "behavior" is in frequent use by astronomers, physicists, physiologists and ecologists, as well as by psychologists and sociologists. Applied in the earlier days of its history to human conduct, it has drifted along to other uses, pausing for a time among animal-students, and having had much hopeful abuse by mechanistic enthusiasts. We believe it rightfully belongs, however, where we are placing it. Such a word as "conduct" has many more specialized implications than has "behavior" and would not serve at all well for the name for a great division of research. We shall be open to the adoption of any substitutes as our work proceeds, but thus far have failed to find a more efficient or safer word to use. In such a matter as this, long-term considerations are much more important than the verbal fashions of a decade or two.

16 The task of straightening out proved to be more complex, even, than we had estimated. It led us to drop the word "definition" altogether from technical terminology, thus reducing it for the time being to the status of a colloquialism. We nevertheless permit our text in this passage to appear unrevised, since we are more interested in the continuity of inquiry than we are in positive determinations of word-usage at this stage. *See* the introductory remarks to Chapter VII, and the summary in Chapter XI.

17 See Chapter I, Section I.

18 Again, a very vaguely used word.

19 In the psychological range the comparable fundamental laboratory experiments of import for our purposes are those of Max Wertheimer upon the direct visual observability of motions. See "Experimentelle Studien über das Sehen von Bewegung" (*Zeitschrift für Psychologie*, LXI [1912], 161-265). In a much weakened form his results are used in the type of psychology known as "Gestalt," but in principle they still await constructive development.

20 The word "field" is a strong candidate for use in the transactional region. However, it has not been fully clarified as yet for physics, and the way it has been employed in psychological and social studies has been impressionistic and often unscrupulous. "Field" must remain, therefore, on our list of vague words, candidates for improvement. When the physical status of the word is settled — and Einstein and his immediate associates have long concentrated on this problem — then if the terminology can be transferred to behavioral inquiry we shall know how to make the transfer with integrity. See Chapter V, note 17.

21 "The name *objects* will be reserved for subjectmatter so far as it has been produced and ordered in settled form by means of inquiry; proleptically, objects are the *objectives* of inquiry" (*Logic, the Theory of Inquiry*, p. 119). For "situation" see *ibid.*, pp. 66 ff. The word "occurrence" is, as has been indicated, provisionally placed.

22 The word "existence" was later substituted for "event" in this position. See Chapter XI.

23 The word "definition" later dropped from technical terminological use, so far as our present development goes.

24 For introductory uses of the word see John Dewey, "Conduct and Experience," in *Psychologies of 1930* (Worcester, Massachusetts). Compare also his *Logic, the Theory of Inquiry*, p. 458, where stress is placed on the *single continuous event*.

25 The word "event" was later substituted for "occurrence" in this usage. See Chapter XI.

26 Attention is called in summary to the "vague words" one is at times compelled to use. "Knowledge," "thing," "field," "within" and "without" have been so characterized in text or footnotes; also all prepositions and the use of "quotes" to distinguish names from the named; even the words "vague" and "firm" as we find them in use today. "Aspect" and "phase" have been indicated as vague for our purposes today, but as having definite possibilities of development as we proceed. It will be noticed that the word "experience" has not been used in the present text. No matter what efforts have heretofore been made to apply it definitely, it has been given conflicting renderings by readers who among them, one may almost say, have persisted in forcing vagueness upon it. We shall discuss it along with other abused words at a later place.

CHAPTER THREE

POSTULATIONS

I

IN the search to secure firm names for knowings and knowns, we have held, first, that man, inclusive of all his knowings, should be investigated as "natural" within a natural world;[1] and, secondly, that investigation can, and must, employ sustained observation akin in its standards — though not, of course, in all its techniques — to the direct observation through which science advances.

Scientific observation does not report by fiat; it is checked and rechecked by many observers upon their own work and the work of others until its report is assured. This is its great characteristic. From its simplest to its most far-reaching activities it holds itself open to revision in a degree made strikingly clear by what happened to the Newtonian account of gravitation after its quarter millennium of established "certainty." The more scientific and accurate observation becomes, the less does it claim ultimacy for the specific assertions it achieves.

Where observation remains open to revision, there is always a certain "if" about it. Its report is thus conditional, and the surrounding conditions, under careful formulation, become the postulation under which it holds place. In the case of problems of limited range, where conditions are familiar to the workers (as, for example, in a physical laboratory, for a particular experiment under way), an unqualified report of the verified results as "fact" is customary and meets no objection. Where, however, assertions that run far afield are involved, the postulational background must be kept steadily in view, and must be stated as conditional to the report itself; otherwise serious distortions may result.

This is emphatically required for a search such as ours in the case of knowings and knowns. Our procedure must rest on observation and must report under postulation. Simply and directly we say that the sciences work in nature, and that any inquiry into knowings and knowns must work in the same nature the sciences work in and, as far as possible, along the same general lines. We say observation is the great scientific stronghold. We say that all[2] observations belong in system, and that where their connections are not now known it is, by postulation, permissible to approach them as if connection could be established. We totally reject that ancient hindrance put upon inquiry such as ours by those who proclaim that the "knower" must be in some way superior to the nature he knows; and equally by those who give superiority to that which they call "the known." We recognize that as observers we are human organisms, limited to the positions on the globe from which we make our observations, and we accept this not as being a hindrance, but instead as a situation from which great gain may be secured. We let our postulations rise out of the observations, and we then use the postulations to increase efficiency of observation, never to restrain it. It is in this sense of circularity that we employ those very postulations of nature, of observation and of postulation itself, that our opening paragraphs have set down.[3]

The dictionaries allot to the word "postulate" two types of application. One presents something "taken for granted as the true basis for reasoning or belief"; the other, "a condition required for further operations." Our approach is manifestly of this second type.[4] We shall mark this by speaking of postulations rather than of postulates, so far as our own procedures are concerned. This phrasing is more reliable, even though at times it will seem a bit clumsy.

What we have said is equivalent to holding that postulations arise out of the field of inquiry, and maintain themselves strictly subject to the needs of that field.[5] They are always open to re-examination. The one thing they most emphatically *never* are is unexaminable.

To this must be added a further comment that postulation is double-fronted.[6] It must give as thorough a consideration to attitudes of approach in inquiry as it does to the subjectmatter examined, and to each always in conjunction with the other.[7]

It is very frequently said that no matter what form of inquiry one undertakes into life and mind one involves himself always in metaphysics and can never escape it. In contrast with this hoary adage, our position is that if one seeks with enough earnestness to identify his attitude of workmanship and the directions of his orientation, he can by-pass the metaphysics by the simple act of keeping observation and postulation hand-in-hand; the varied "ultimates" of metaphysics become chips that lie where they fall. Our postulations, accordingly, gain their rating, not by any peculiarity or priority they possess, but by the plainness and openness of their statement of the conditions under which work is, and will be, done. If this statement at times takes categorical verbal form, this is by way of endeavor at sharpness of expression, not through any desire to impose guidance on the work of others.

In the course of our preliminary studies for this series of reports we assembled a score or two of groups of postulations. These experiments taught us the complexity of the problem and the need for a steady eye upon all phases of inquiry. Instead of obtaining a single overall postulation, as we might have anticipated, we found that the more thorough the work became, the more it required specializations of postulations, and these in forms that are complementary. We shall display certain of these postulations, primarily as aids to our further discussion, but partly because of the interest such exhibits may have for workers in collateral fields. We further hope the display may stimulate co-operation leading to better formulation from other experimenters with similar manners of inquiry.

In approaching the examination let the reader recall, first, that we have previously selected namings as the species of knowings most directly open to observation, and thus as our best entry to inquiry; [8] and, secondly, that we have taken the named and the namings (being instances of the known and the knowings) as forming together one event for inquiry [9] — one transaction [10] — since, in any full observation, if one vanishes, the other vanishes also. These things we observe; we observe them under and through the attitudes expressed in our opening paragraphs; as such observations they form the core of the postulatory expansion to follow.[11]

II

In order to make plain the background against which our postulations can be appraised, we start by exhibiting certain frequently occurring programs for behavioral inquiry,[12] which are to be rated as postu*lates* rather than as postu*lations* under the differentiation we have drawn between the two words. Characteristic of them is that they evade, ignore, or strive to rid themselves of that "circularity"[13] in knowledge which we, in contrast, frankly accept as we find it. Characteristic, further, is that their proponents take them for granted so unhesitatingly in the form of "truths" that they rarely bring them out into clear expression. It is because of this latter characteristic that we cannot readily find well-organized specimens to cite but are compelled to construct them as best we can out of the scattered materials we find in works on epistemology, logic, and psychology. Because their type is so different from the postulations we shall develop for our own use, we label them with the letters X, Y, and Z in a series kept separate at the far end of the alphabet.

X. EPISTEMOLOGICAL IRRECONCILABLES

1. "Reals" exist and become known.
2. "Minds" exist and do the knowing.
3. "Reals" and "minds" inhabit irreconcilable "realms." [14]
4. Epistemological magic [15] is required to reveal how the one irreconcilable achieves its knowing and the other its being known.

Y. LOGICAL GO-BETWEENS

1. "Reals" exist ("objects," "entities," "substances," etc.) .
2. "Minds" exist ("thoughts," "meanings," "judgments," etc.) .
3. "Thirds" exist to intervene ("words," "terms," "sentences," "propositions," etc.) .
4. Logical exploration of "thirds" [16] will reconcile the irreconcilables.

Z. PHYSIOLOGIC-PSYCHOLOGIC STRAITJACKETS

1. "Reals" exist as matter, tactually or otherwise sensibly vouched for.
2. "Minds" exist as mentaloid manifestations of organically specialized "reals." [17]
3. Study of organically "real" matter (muscular, neural, or cortical) yields knowledge of matter, including the organic, the mentaloid, and the knowledges themselves.
4. The "certainty" of matter in some way survives all the "uncertainties" of growing knowledge about it.

These three groups of postulates all include non-observables; that is, through the retention of primitive namings surviving from early cultures they adopt or purport to adopt certain materials of inquiry that can not be identified as "objects" under any of the forms of observation modern research employs.[18] X is in notorious disrepute except among limited groups of epistemological specialists. Y works hopefully with linguistic devices that our preceding examination has shown to be radically deficient.[19] Z is serviceable for simple problems at the level of what used to be called "the senses," and at times for preliminary orderings of more complex subjectmatters, but it quickly shows itself unable to provide the all-essential direct descriptions these latter require. All three default not only in observability, but also in the characteristics of that manner of approach which we have here called "natural" (though Z has aspirations in this latter direction).[20] Beyond this, as already indicated, all three are employed rather as articles of faith than as postulations proper.

III

In contrast with the approaches X, Y, and Z, we shall now write down in simple introductory statement what we regard as the main features of the postulations which, inspired by and in sympathy with the progress modern sciences have made, are most broadly needed as guides to inquiry into behaviors as natural events in the world.

A. POSTULATIONS FOR BEHAVIORAL RESEARCH

1. **The cosmos:**   as system or field of factual inquiry.[21]
2. **Organisms:**   as cosmic components.
3. **Men:**   as organisms.
4. **Behavings of men:** as organic-environmental events.
5. Knowings (including the knowings of the cosmos and its postulation) : as such organic-environmental behavings.

The above postulations are to be taken literally and to be scrupulously so maintained in inquiry.

So important is the italicized sentence, and so common and vicious that manner of lip-service to which hands and eyes pay no attention, that we might well give this sentence place as a sixth postulation.

Entry No. 1 accepts positively the cosmos of science as the locus of behavioral inquiry. This acceptance is full and unqualified, though free, of course, from the expansive applications speculative scientists so often indulge in.

No. 2 and No. 3 are perhaps everywhere accepted, *except for inquiry into knowings and knowns.* No. 4 differs sharply from the common view in which the organism is taken as the locus of "the behavior" and as proceeding under its own powers in detachment from a comparably detachable environment, rather than as a phase of the full organic-environmental event.[22] No. 5, so far as we know, is not yet in explicit use in detailed research of the sort we are undertaking, and its introduction is here held to be required if firm names for knowings and knowns are to be achieved.

Following postulations *A* for behavioral events, as subjectmatters, we now set forth postulations *B* for inquiry into such behavioral subjectmatters. The type of inquiry we have before us is that which proceeds through Designation. Long ago we chose naming-events as the particular variety of knowings upon which to concentrate study.[23] Now we are selecting Designation[24] as the specialized method of inquiry we are to employ. Before proceeding to more detail with postulations *A*, we complement them with postulations *B*, as if we set a right hand over against a left somewhat in the manner we have already spoken of as "double-fronted." *A* and *B* together offer us instances of that "circularity" we find wherever we go, which by us is not merely recognized, but put to work — not deplored but seized upon as a key to observation, description, and controlled inquiry.[25] The procedure looks complex but we cannot help it any more than the physicists of three generations ago could "help it" when electricity (to say nothing of electromagnetic waves) refused to stay in locations or submit to a mathematics that had sufficed, until that time, for the mechanics of particles.

Given complementary postulations *A* and *B*, one may expect to find the components of one postulation reappearing in the other, but differently stressed, and under different development. Thus postulation *A*1 views Fact in the aspect of Event, whereas *B*1 views it in the aspect of inquiry under or through Designation ("event" being here understood with the range given in Chapter XI to the word "existence"). Similar cases appear frequently; they are typical and necessary.

B. POSTULATIONS FOR INQUIRY INTO SUBJECTMATTERS UNDER DESIGNATION [26]

1. A single system of subjectmatters is postulated, to be called cosmos or nature.

2. Distribution of subjectmatters of inquiry into departments varies [27] from era to era in accordance with variation in the technical stage of inquiry.

3. Postulations for each of the most commonly recognized present departments (physical, physiological, and behavioral) are separately practicable, free from the dictatorship of any one over another, yet holding all in system.[28]

4. The range of the knowings is coextensive with the range of the subjectmatters known.

5. Observation, such as modern technique of experiment has achieved, or fresh technique may achieve, is postulated for whatever is, or is to be, subjectmatter. Nothing enters inquiry as inherently non-observable nor as requiring an independent type of observation of its own. What is observed is linked with what is not then and there observed.

6. The subjectmatters of observation are durational and extensional.

7. Technical treatments of extensions and durations developed in one department of subjectmatter are to be accepted as aids for other subjectmatters, but never as controls beyond their direct value in operation.[29]

8. "Objects" in practical everyday identifications and namings prior to organized inquiry hold no permanent priority in such inquiry.[30] Inquiry is free and all "objects" are subject to examination whether as they thus practically come or with respect to components they may be found to contain, or under widened observation as transactional — in all cases retaining their extensional and durational status.[31]

9. Durationally and extensionally observable events suffice for inquiry. Nothing "more real" than the observable is se-

cured by using the word "real," or by peering for something behind or beyond the observable to which to apply the name.[32]

Having focussed postulations *B* upon the aspect of inquiry, we now return to the aspect of event in *A*.[33] Our declared purpose is to examine naming behaviors as knowings, and to hold the naming behaviors as events in contact with the signaling behaviors on one side and with the symboling behaviors on the other.[34] In expansion from *A* as events we shall therefore next present postulations *C* for knowings and *D* for namings, and shall follow these with indications of what will later be necessary as *E* for signalings and *F* for symbolings.

Postulations *C* are looser than the others, as will be evident at once by our permitting the vague word "knowledge" to creep in. There is sound reason for this. We secure an introductory background in the rough along the lines of ordinary discussion, against which to study namings as knowings. From future study of namings a better postulation for knowings should develop. A comment on the possible outcomes for *C* will follow.

C. Postulations for Knowings and Knowns as Behavioral Events [35]

1. Knowings and knowns (knowledge, knowledges, instances of knowledge) are natural events. A knowing is to be regarded as the same kind of an event *with respect to its being known* (i.e., just as much "extant") as an eclipse, a fossil, an earthquake, or any other subjectmatter of research.

2. Knowings and knowns are to be investigated by methods that have been elsewhere successful in the natural sciences.

3. Sufficient approach has already been made to knowledge about knowledge through cultural, psychological, and physiological investigations to make it practicable to begin today to use this program.[36]

4. As natural events, knowings and knowns are observable; as observable, they are enduring and extensive within enduring and extensive situations.[37]

5. Knowings and knowns are to be taken together as aspects of one event.[38] The outstanding need for inquiry into knowledge in its present stage is that the knowings and knowns be thus given transactional (as contrasted with interactional) observations.

6. The observable extensions of knowings and knowns run across the inhabited surface of the earth; the observable durations run across cultures,[39] backward into pre-history, forward into futures — all as subjectmatters of inquiry. Persistence (permanence and impermanence) characterize the knowings and the knowns alike.[40]

7. All actualities dealt with by knowledge have aspects of the knowing as well as of the known, with the knowings themselves among such actualities known.

Inspection of postulations C shows that the first two of the group provide for the development of A in accord with B2, while the third serves to make emphatic — against the denial everywhere prevalent — our assertion that inquiry *can* proceed on these lines. The fourth is in accord with B5, B6, and B7 as to observation, while the fifth states the type, and the sixth the range, of the observation needed. The seventh, in accord with B9, keeps in place the ever-needed bulwark against the traditional totalitarian hypostatizations.

D. POSTULATIONS FOR NAMINGS AND THE NAMED AS SPECIMENS OF KNOWINGS AND KNOWNS [41]

1. Namings may be segregated for special investigation within knowings much as any special region within scientific subjectmatter may be segregated for special consideration.

2. The namings thus segregated are taken as themselves the knowings to be investigated.[42]

3. The namings are directly observable in full behavioral durations and extensions.[43]

4. No instances of naming are observed that are not themselves directly knowings; and no instances of knowings within the range of naming-behaviors (we are not here postulating

for signal or symbol behaviors) that are not themselves namings.[44]

5. The namings and the named are one transaction. No instance of either is observable without the other.[45]

6. Namings and named develop and decline together, even though to myopic or close-up observation certain instances of either may appear to be established apart from the participation of the other.[46]

7. Warranted assertion, both in growth and in decline, both as to the warranty and the warranted, exhibits itself as a phase of situations in all degrees of development from indeterminate to determinate. The strongest warranted assertion is the hardest of hard fact, but with neither the determinacy, nor the warranty, nor the hardness, nor even the factuality itself ranging beyond the reach of inquiry — for what is "hard fact" at "one" time is not assuredly "hard" for "all" time.

8. The study of either naming or named in provisional severance as a phase of *the transaction* under the control of postulations $D4$ and $D5$, is always legitimate and useful — often an outstanding need. Apart from such controls it falsifies.[47]

9. The study of written texts (or their spoken equivalents) in provisional severance from the particular organisms engaged, but nevertheless as durational and extensional behaviors under cultural description, is legitimate and valuable.[48] The examination is comparable to that of species in life, of a slide under a microscope, or of a cadaver on the dissection table — directed strictly at what is present to observation, and not in search for non-observables presumed to underlie observation, though always in search for more observables ahead and beyond.[49]

10. Behavioral investigation of namings is to be correlated with the physiology of organism-in-environment rather than with the intra-dermal formulations which physiologists initially employed in reporting their earlier inquiries.[50]

Inspection of postulations D shows that the first four present definite subjectmatters for inquiry within the mistily presented regions of C. The fifth, sixth and seventh give further specifications to $C5$ and $C6$. The

eighth provides for legitimate interactional inquiry within
the transactional presentation, in sharp contrast with disruption of system, pseudo-interactions of mind-matter, and
the total default in results offered by the older procedures
for which X, Y, and Z stand as types. The ninth and tenth
present supplementary techniques of practical importance.

IV

It is evident from these comments, as well as from the
comments on postulations C, that although we are doing
our best to phrase each separate postulation as definitely
as the language available to us will permit, we are nevertheless allowing the selection and arrangement of the
postulations within each group to proceed informally,
since forced formality would be an artifice of little worth.

Two further comments are of special interest.

The first is that while we felt a strong need in our earlier
assemblage of B and of C for the protective postulations
B9 and C7, and while we shall later find it desirable to
re-enforce this protection with postulation H1, the program
of inquiry into namings as knowings represented by postulations D, in accord with B2, has already positively occupied the field, to fill which in older days the "reals" were
conjured from the depths.

The second comment is that the greatest requirement
for progressive observation in this field is freedom from
the limitations of the Newtonian space and time grille,
and the development of the more complete behavioral
space and time frame, for which indications have been
given in B7 and D3 and in the accompanying footnotes,
and upon which stress will be placed again in H4.

V

In the case of signalings and symbolings which, along
with namings, make up the broadest differentiation of

behaviors, both as evolutionary stages and as contemporary levels,[51] it would be a waste of time to attempt postulatory elaboration until much further preliminary description had been given. This will be developed elsewhere. For the present the following indications of the need must suffice.

E. Indicated Postulation For Signaling Behaviors

1. Signaling behaviors — the regions of perception-manipulation,[52] ranging from the earliest indirect cues for food-ingestion among protozoa and all the varied conditionings of animal life, to the most delicate human perceptional activities — require transactional observation.

2. The settings for such words as "stimulus" "reaction," and "response," furnished under postulations of the types X, Y, and Z, have resulted in such chaos as to show that this or some other alternative development is urgently required.

F. Indicated Postulation for Symboling Behaviors

1. Symboling behaviors — the regions of mathematical and syntactical consistency — require transactional observation.

2. In current inquiries "foundations" are sought for mathematics by the aid of logic which — if "foundations" are what is needed — is itself notoriously foundation-less.[53]

3. Differentiation of the naming procedures from the symboling procedures as to status (function), methods, and type of results secured — and always under progressive observation — is the indicated step.[54]

We have now postulations C and D and preparatory comments E and F focussed upon behaviors in their aspect as Event in expansion from postulations A. Over against all of these, but in accord with them, we have postulations B focussed upon the aspect of inquiry through designation — the region in which science develops. Postulations C, as has already been said, are of lower grade than D, as is marked by their employment of the vague word "knowledge," their purpose having been to furnish a rough background for the attempt in *D*, to present namings as knowings direct. Postulations *C* are in further danger of being misinterpreted by some, perhaps many, readers in the sense rather of *B* than of *A*, of designation rather than of event, of the knowing rather than of the known. With postulations *C* thus insecurely seated, what may we say of their probable future?

Of the three types of vagueness in the word "knowledge," [55] those of localization,[56] distribution, and range of application, the first two have been dealt with in preceding postulations. As for the third, the word bundles together such broadly different (or differently appearing) activities as "knowing how to say" and "knowing how to do"; and, further, from these as a center, has spreading applications or implications running as far down the scale as protozoan sign-behavior, and as far up as the most abstruse mathematical construction. Should future inquiry find it best to hold the word "knowledge" to a central range correlated with, or identified as, language-behaviors, then postulations *C* would merge with *D*. Should it be found preferable to extend the word, accompanied perhaps by the word "sign," over the entire behavioral range, then postulations *C* would return into *A* to find their home. We have no interest in sharp classification under rigid names — observable nature is not found yielding profitable results in that particular form. We do not expect to offer any prescription as to how the word "knowledge" should be used, being quite willing to have it either rehabilitate itself or, as the case may be, fall back into storage among the tattered blanket-wordings of the past. Whatever the future determination, narrow, wide, or medium, for the word "knowledge," postulations *C* keep the action provisionally open.

In the opening paragraphs of this chapter we held that man's knowings should be treated as natural, and should be studied through observation, under express recognition of the postulatory status of observation itself in the transi-

tions of both observations and postulations out of pasts
and into futures. We believe that we have not failed
throughout in proceeding in accordance therewith. These
opening attitudes might perhaps have been themselves set
forth as general postulations for the whole inquiry. The
objection to this procedure is that the three main words,
"nature," "observation," and "postulation," have such
varied possible readings that, put together, they make a
kite to which too many tails can be attached. From them,
however, may be extracted certain statements concerning
procedure with namings and things-named which may be
offered in postulational form. They present — still from
the designational approach as in postulations B — the cosmos as in action, the inquirers within it as themselves in
action, and the whole process as advancing through time
and across space. They are applicable to physical and physiological subjectmatters as well as to behaviorial. Whether
the aspect of inquiry B, as well as that of events D, E and
F, will permit broadening in the future is a question that
may be left for future discussion.

G. Postulational Orientation [57]

1. Subjectmatters of inquiry are to be taken in full durational spread as present through durations of time, comparable to that direct extensional observation they receive across
extensions of space.[58]

2. Namings of subjectmatters are to be taken as durational,
both as names and with respect to all that they name. Neither
instantaneities nor infinitesimalities, if taken as lacking durational or extensional spread, are to be set forth as within the
range of named Fact.

3. Secondary namings falling short of these requirements
are imperfections, often useful, but to be employed safely only
under express recognition at all critical stages of report that
they do not designate subjectmatters in full factuality.[59]

Still lacking in our development and not to be secured
until we have gained further knowledge of Signal and

Symbol is an efficient postulational organization of Symbol with Designation within modern research. Under Symbol the region of linguistic "consistency" is to be presented. Under Designation we consider, as repeatedly stressed, not some "real existence" in a corruptly ultrahuman extension of the words "real" and "exist," but instead an "existency" under thoroughgoing behavioral formulation. It is, we hope, not forcing words too far for the impressionistic statement of the moment if we say that this may be in a "persistency" of durations and extensions such as postulations G require.

It is practicable to postulate rejections as well as acceptances. Under postulations G we have in effect rejected all non-extensionals, non-durationals, and non-observables of whatever types, including all purported ultimate "isolates." To emphasize this for the present issues of inquiry into knowledge, we now set down the following cases as among the most harmful. Let it be understood that these rejections, like all the other postulations, are offered, not as matters of belief or disbelief, but for the aid they may give research.

H. POSTULATIONAL REJECTS

1. All "reals" beyond knowledge.
2. All "minds" as bearers of knowledge.
3. All assignments of behaviors to locations "within" an organism in disregard of the transactional phases of "outside" participation (and, of course, all similar assignments to "outsides" in similar disruption of transactional event).
4. All forcible applications of Newtonian space and time forms (or of the practical forms underlying the Newtonian) to behavioral events as frameworks or grilles of the checkerboard type, which are either (1) insisted upon as adequate for behavioral description, or (2) considered as so repugnant that behavior is divorced from them and expelled into some separate "realm" or "realms" of its own.

VI

One faces often the temptation to exhibit certain of the postulations as derived from others. We would advise against it, even when the durational postulation is used as source. We are impressed with the needlessness, under our approach, of "deriving" anything from anything else (except, of course, as may be convenient in propaedeutic display, where such a procedure perhaps properly belongs). The postulations present different stresses and offer different types of mutual aid, but no authoritarianism such as logics of ancient ancestry demand, including even (and sometimes peculiarly) those which strive to make their logicism look most positive. Many lines of ordering will suggest themselves as one works. If behaviors are durational, and knowings are behaviors, then the knowings become observable. If knowings and knowns are taken as in system, then one quickly arrives at a durational postulation in trying to report what one has observed; and from the durational one passes to the transactional. On the other hand, from this last, if arrived at first, one passes to the durational. This is, indeed, but a final reiteration of what was stressed in the opening paragraphs. Observation and postulation go hand in hand. The postulations hang together, not by grace of any one, or any two, or any three of them, but by organization in respect to the direction of approach, the points of entry, and the status of the audience — the status, that is, of the group of interested workers at the given time and place in history, and of that whole society-in-cosmos of which they themselves are components.

1 By "natural world" with man "natural" within it, the reader should understand that background of inquiry which since Darwin's time has become standard for perhaps all fields of serious scientific enterprise with the single exception of inquiry into knowings and knowns. We shall not employ the words "naturalism" or "naturalistic." We avoid them primarily because our concern is with free research, where the word "nature" specifies nothing beyond what men can learn about it; and, secondarily, because various current metaphysical or "substantial" implications of what

is called "naturalism" are so alien to us that any entanglement with them would produce serious distortion of our intentions.

² The word "all" is, of course, one more vague word. Heretofore we have avoided it altogether — or hope we have. An adequate technical language for our purposes would have one word for the "all" of scientific specification, and another for the "all" of symbolic definition. As we have previously said, our discussions limit themselves strictly to the former use.

³ Compare the three conditions of a search for names set down at the start of Chapter II, Section I, and accompanied by the three negations: that no purely private report, no "foundations" beyond the range of hypothesis, and no final declaration secure from the need of further inquiry can safely be accepted or employed.

⁴ Max Wertheimer, *Productive Thinking* (New York, 1945), p. 179 reports a conversation with Einstein concerning the latter's early approaches to relativity. In answer to a direct question Einstein said: "There is no . . . difference . . . between reasonable and arbitrary axioms. The only virtue of axioms is to furnish fundamental propositions from which one can derive conclusions that fit the facts."

⁵ Dewey: *Logic, the Theory of Inquiry* (New York, 1938), pp. 16-19.

⁶ Bentley: *Behavior, Knowledge, Fact* (Bloomington, Indiana, 1935), Chap. XXX. It is in the behavioral field particularly that this characteristic must never for a moment be neglected.

⁷ One further comment on the word "postulation" is needed. We are not here attempting to determine its final terminological status, but merely specifying the use we are now making of it. In the end it may well be that it should be assigned to the region of Symbol (Chapter II, Section IV, #8) and a different word employed in such territory as we are now exploring. We are choosing "postulation" instead of "hypothesis" for the immediate task because of its greater breadth of coverage in ordinary use. Freedom, as always, is reserved (Chapter II, Section III, and Chapter XI) to make improvements in our provisional terminology when the proper time comes.

⁸ Chapter II, Section IV and Chapter I, Section I.

⁹ Chapter II, Section III.

¹⁰ Chapter II, Section IV and Chapters IV and V.

¹¹ One of the authors of this volume (J. D.) wishes to make specific correction of certain statements in his *Logic; the Theory of Inquiry* about *observation*. As far as those statements limit the word to cases of what are called "sense-perception" — or, in less dubious language, to cases of observation under conditions approaching those of laboratory control — they should be altered. For the distinction made in that text between "observation" and "ideation" he would now substitute a distinction between two phases of observation, depending on comparative temporal-spatial range

or scope of subjectmatter. What is called observation in that text is only such observations as are limited to the narrower ranges of subjectmatter; which, however, hold a distinctive and critical place in the testing of observations of the more extensive type.

12 For the word "behavior," see Chapter II, n. 15.

13 Chapter II, Section IV, #2.

14 With variations of "more or less" (though still "irreconcilable"), and with special limiting cases on one side or the other in which winner takes all.

15 "Magic" (dictionary definition): "Any supposed supernatural art."

16 Though always with the risk of other thirds "to bite 'em; And so proceed *ad infinitum*."

17 Watson's early "behaviorism" (far remote, of course, from the factual behavior of our inquiry) included an identification of linguistic procedure as physiological process of vocal organs — an identification that lacked not merely the transactional view we employ, but even an interactional consideration of the environment. An excellent recent illustration of much more refined treatment is that of Roy Woods Sellars, *The Journal of Philosophy*, XLI (1944) who writes (p. 688): "I think we can locate the psychical as a *natural isolate* in the functioning organism and study its context and conditions." The issue could hardly be more neatly drawn between the "process" we are to investigate and the purported "things" the X, Y, and Z postulates offer for examination.

18 Cf. postulations B5 and B6, below. For "objects," see Chapter II, Section IV.

19 Chapter I, Section X.

20 One of our earlier experimental formulations may be mentioned: (*a*) existing epistemologies are trivial or worse; (*b*) the source of the trouble lies in primitive speech conventions; (*c*) in particular, the presentation of a "mind" as an individual "isolate," whether in "psychical" or in "physiological" manifestation, is destructive.

21 The system is named Fact (Chapter II, Section IV, #1).

22 For legitimate procedures in provisional detachments, see postulations D8 and G3.

23 Chapter II, Sections II and III.

24 Chapter II, Section IV, #1. For the distinction provisionally employed between the word "naming" and "designation," see Chapter II, Section IV, #8.

25 No priority is assumed for A over B or *vice versa*. Postulations A enter first into our immediate treatment as the needed offset to the current fracturings and pseudo-realistic strivings of X, Y, and Z.

26 Not to be overlooked is the express statement in the text that these postulations *B* are for research through namings, and are *not* set up for all types of search and formulation whatsoever. We cultivate our present gardens, leaving plenty of room for other gardens for future workers.

27 "Varies . . . in accordance with" might be profitably replaced by "is in function with," if we could be sure that the word "function" would be understood as indicating a *kind* of problem, and not as having some positive explanatory value for the particular case. Unfortunately too many of the uses of "function" in psychological and sociological inquiry are of the pontifical type. The problem is to indicate the aspectual status, despite the poverty of available language (Introduction, and Chapter II, n. 1). For discussion of the content of postulation *B2*, see Chapter II, Section IV, #4, and compare also the postulation of continuity, *Logic, the Theory of Inquiry*, p. 19, *et al.*

28 Postulations *A* have this characteristic in contrast with postulations *Z*. The free development of subjectmatters in *B2* and *B3* coincides in effect with the express rejection of "reals" in *B9*, *C7*, and *H1*. It also removes the incentive to the romantic types of "emergence" which often enter when "substantive reals" depart.

29 Bentley, "The Factual Space and Time of Behavior," *The Journal of Philosophy*, XXXVIII (1941), pp. 477-485. No interference is intended with the practical pre-scientific attitudes towards space and time so far as their everyday practical expression is concerned. Although long since deprived of dominance in the physical sciences, these attitudes remain dominant in psychological and sociological inquiry, and it is this dominance in this region that is rejected under our present postulation. See also the footnote to *D3*, postulation *H4*, and comment in the text following postulations *D*.

30 Chapter II, Section IV, #7. Bentley: "The Human Skin: Philosophy's Last Line of Defense," *Philosophy of Science*, VIII (1941), 1-19.

31 Chapter II, Section IV, #6. Compare postulation *A4*.

32 *B9* restates what results if *B2* is accepted and put to work thoroughly — "the addition of the adjective 'real' to the substantive 'facts' being only for rhetorical emphasis" (Dewey, "Context and Thought," *University of California Publications in Philosophy*, XII, [1931], 203-224). Compare also the statement by Stephen C. Pepper, *The Journal of Philosophy*, XLII (1945), 102: "There is no criterion for the reliability of evidence . . . but evidence of that reliability — that is corroboration." Professor Pepper's discussion of what happens "under the attitude of expecting an unquestionable criterion of truth and factuality to be at hand" runs strongly along our present line.

33 Both "focus" and "aspect" are double-barrelled words, in William James's sense. One cannot focus without something to focus with (such as a lens in or out of his eye) or without something to focus on. As for the

word "aspect" (see also Chapter II, n. 11), this word originally stressed the viewing; an archaic meaning was a gaze, glance, or look, and a transitive verb still is usable, "to aspect." In more recent English "aspect" has been transferred in large measure to "object," but there are many mixed uses, even some that introduce locations and directions of action as between observer and observed. In any case the word applies to the "object," not absolutely but with reference to an observer, present or remote.

34 Chapter II, Section IV, #8.

35 Two of our earlier experimental formulations may be helpful in their variation of phrasing. Thus: (a) knowings are natural events; (b) they are known by standard methods; (c) enough is known about knowings and knowns to make the use of such methods practicable. Again: (a) knowers are in the cosmos along with what is known and to be known; (b) knowings are there too, and are to be studied (observed) in the same way as are other subjectmatters.

36 Dewey: "How is Mind to be Known?" *The Journal of Philosophy,* XXXIX (1942), pp. 29-35.

37 Chapter II, Section I.

38 Chapter II, Section I: "We proceed upon the postulate that *knowings* are always and everywhere inseparable from *the knowns* — that the two are twin aspects of common fact."

39 The word "social" is not used, primarily because of its confused status. It is sometimes opposed to "individual," sometimes built up out of "individuals," and, as it stands, it fails to hint at the transactional approach we express. "Culture" is comparatively non-committal, and can be understood much more closely as "behavioral," in the sense we have specified for that word.

40 In contrast to the usual program of concentrating the impermanence (or the fear of it) in the knowing, and assigning the permanence, in measure exceeding that of its being known, to the knowns.

41 An earlier formulation, combining something of both the present postulations *D* and *E,* and perhaps of interest for that reason, ran as follows: (a) knowledge is a sign system; (b) names are a kind of naturally developed sign; (c) naming and "specifying existence" are one process. These statements, however, must all be taken transactionally, if they are to represent our approach properly.

42 Chapter II, Section III. In other words, under our postulation names do not enter as physical objects, nor as tools or instruments used by a psychical being or object, nor as being constructively separate from behavior in some such form as "products," nor as any other manner of externalization dependent on some supersubtle internalization. Under our postulation all such dismemberments are rejected as superfluous. The procedure, therefore, includes no such nostalgic plaint as that of the legendary egg to the hen: "Now that you have laid me, do you still love me?"

[43] Full duration and extension is not represented adequately and exclusively by such specialized devices as clock-ticks and foot-rules (see *B*7). Though these have developed into magnificent approximations for physics, they lack necessary pasts and futures across continents such as are involved in histories, purposes, and plans. They are therefore inadequate for inquiry into knowings, namings, and other behaviors.

[44] Compare the requirements set up in our appraisal of the logics (Chapter I, Sections I and X) that talkings be treated as "the men themselves in action."

[45] Cf. Chapter I, Section X; Chapter II, Section IV. A full behavioral spacetime form must be employed, comprising (but not limited by) physical and physiological spaces and times. The application of physical and physiological techniques is of course highly desirable, so far as they reach. Objectionable only are claims to dominate beyond the regions where they apply.

[46] Our own experience in the present inquiry is evidence of this, although the postulation ought to be acceptable at sight throughout its whole range of application. Starting out to find careful namings for phases of the subjectmatter discussed in the literature, we were quickly drawn into much closer attention to the named; this phase of the inquiry in turn depended for success on improvement in the namings. The two phases of the inquiry must proceed together. Rigidity of fixation for the one leads to wreckage for the other.

[47] An illustration that casts light on the status of naming and named with respect to each other may be taken from the earlier economics, which tried to hold consumption and production apart but failed miserably. Again, one may study the schemes of debtors and the protective devices of creditors, but unless this is done in a full transactional presentation of credit-activity one gains little more than melodrama or moralizing — equally worthless for understanding.

[48] This procedure was followed, so far as was practicable, in our examination of the logics, where the intention was never criticism of individuals, but always exhibition of the characteristics of the logical-linguistic mechanisms at work at present in America. As a technique of inquiry this is in sharp contrast with the ordinary practice. Through it we secured various exhibits of subjectmatters admitted — indeed even boasted — by their investigators to be neither fish, nor flesh, nor good red herring — neither physical, nor mental, nor linguistic; aliens in the land of science, denizens of never-never land; and likewise of various procedures in the name of consistency, tolerating the abandonment of the simplest standards of accuracy in naming at every other step. Unfortunately, specimens being few, we cannot carry on discussion under the anonymity which an entomologist can grant his bugs when he handles them by the tens and hundreds of thousands. To refer to a writer by name is much the same *sort* of thing as to mention a date, or as to name a periodical with its volume and page numbers. So far as inquiry into "knowledge" is con-

cerned, the "you" and the "I" have their ethical and juridical valuations
but offer little definiteness as to the activity under way; and this is
certainly as true of the epistemologist's variety of "subject," as it is of
any other. Recall the famous observation of William James, which has
thus far been everywhere neglected actually in psychological and sociological research, that "the word 'I' . . . is primarily a noun of position
like 'this' and 'here.' " (*A Pluralistic Universe*, New York, 1909, p. 380:
Essays in Radical Empiricism, New York, 1912, p. 170.)

49 The classical illustration of the sanctification of the reduplicative non-
observable as an explanation of the observable is, of course, to be found in
the third interlude Molière provided for *Le malade imaginaire*, in which
the candidate for a medical degree explains the effect of opium as due to
its *virtus dormitiva*. Its words should be graven on the breastbone of every
investigator into knowledge. The candidate's answer was:

Mihi a docto Doctore
Domandatur causam et rationem quare
Opium facit dormire.
A quoi respondeo,
Quia est in eo
Virtus dormitiva,
Cujus est natura
Sensus assoupire.

Peirce, in quoting this (5.534), remarks that at least the learned doctor
noticed that there was *some* peculiarity about the opium which, he implies, is better than not noticing anything at all.

50 As one stage in dealing with environments physiologists found it necessary to take account of "internal" environments, as in Claude Bernard's
"milieu." Since then they have passed to direct consideration of transdermal processes, which is to say: their adequate complete statements could
not be held *within* the skin but required descriptions and interpretations
running *across* it in physiological analogue of what behaviorally we style
"transactional."

51 Chapter II, Sections IV and V.

52 The word "manipulation" is used in its standard widened application
and not in limitation to the "manual."

53 Theorists such as Russell and other logicists are found who in their
prideful panoply demand (at least when occasion seems ripe) that no
science be recognized as such until it has been dubbed Sir Science and thus
legitimatized by Logic.

54 For introductory considerations, see Bentley, *Linguistic Analysis of
Mathematics*, (Bloomington, Indiana, 1932).

55 Chapter II, Section I.

56 The old plan of dumping "knowledge" into a "mind" as its peculiar
variety of "nature" and thus evading the labor of research, has long since
ceased to be attractive to us.

⁵⁷ This particular orientation does not preclude recognition of differences between namings that designate subjectmatters across indefinitely extended durations and expanses and those designating subjectmatters definitely limited in these respects. It is suggested, though not here postulated, that such differences may present the grounds for the rigid separations alleged in various traditional theories of knowledge to exist between theoretical and practical, and between rational and empirical, components; likewise for those alleged as between subjectmatters of sense-perception and of scientific knowlege, in ways that constitute radical obstacles to interpretation.

⁵⁸ Impressionistically one could say that duration is of the "very nature" of the event, of its "essence," of its "body and texture," though these are types of phrasing to avoid in formal statement, no matter how helpful they may seem for the moment. To illustrate: consider the "texture" of the "situations" in Dewey's *Logic, the Theory of Inquiry* as compared with the usual discussions of his viewpoint. These "situations," both "indeterminate" and "determinate," are cultural. Any report, discussion, or criticism that does not recognize this is waste effort, so far as the issues involved are concerned.

⁵⁹ Non-durational applications of such words as "sensation" and "faculty" in psychology have resulted in making these words useless to advanced systematic inquiry. Current words requiring continual watchfulness in this respect are such as "concept," "relation," "abstract," "percept," "individual," "social." In contrast our use of Fact, Event, and Designation is designed for full durational form, however faulty some of the phrasings in provisional report may remain.

CHAPTER FOUR

INTERACTION AND TRANSACTION

I

O UR preliminary sketch of the requirements for a firm terminology for knowings and knowns placed special stress on two procedures of knowledge [1] called Transaction and Specification. Specification was distinguished from Definition and the immediate development of Transaction was connected with Specification rather than with Definition.

We propose in succeeding chapters to discuss Transaction and Specification at some length, each on its own account, and to show how important it is for any theory of knowledge that their characteristics as natural processes of knowing-men and things-known should be fully understood. Before undertaking this, however, it will be well to display in the present chapter, the extent to which the transactional presentation of objects, and the determination of objects as themselves transactional, has been entering recent physical research. In so doing, the transactional presentation will be brought into contrast with the antique view of self-actions and with the presentation of classical mechanics in terms of interactions. The discussion will not be widened, however, beyond what is needed for the immediate report.

The reader will recall that in our general procedure of inquiry no radical separation is made between that which is observed and the observer in the way which is common in the epistemologies and in standard psychologies and

103

psychological constructions. Instead, observer and observed are held in close organization. Nor is there any radical separation between that which is named and the naming. Comparably knowings and knowns, as inclusive of namings and observings, and of much else as well, are themselves taken in a common system of inquiry, and not as if they were the precarious products of a struggle between severed realms of "being." It is this common system of the knowing and the known which we call "natural," without either preference or prejudice with respect to "nature," such as now often attends the use of that word. Our position is simply that since man as an organism has evolved among other organisms in an evolution called "natural," we are willing under hypothesis to treat all of his behavings, including his most advanced knowings, as activities not of himself alone, nor even as primarily his, but as processes of the full situation of organism-environment; and to take this full situation as one which is before us within the knowings, as well as being the situation in which the knowings themselves arise.[2]

What we call "transaction," and what we wish to show as appearing more and more prominently in the recent growth of physics, is, therefore, in technical expression, neither to be understood as if it "existed" apart from any observation, nor as if it were a manner of observing "existing in a man's head" in presumed independence of what is observed. The "transaction," as an object among and along with other objects, is to be understood as unfractured observation — just as it stands, at this era of the world's history, with respect to the observer, the observing, and the observed — and as it is affected by whatever merits or defects it may prove to have when it is judged, as it surely will be in later times, by later manners.

II

When Comte cast a sweeping eye over the growth of knowledge as far as he could appraise it, he suggested three stages or levels which he called the theological, the meta-physical, and the positive. One would not want to accept these stages today, any more than one would want to adopt Comte's premature scheme for the organization of the sciences. Nevertheless, his general sketch has entered substantially into everyone's comprehension. Roughly speaking, the animistic personifications and personalizations of the world and its phenomena were prevalent in the early days; hypostatizations such as physical "forces" and "substances" followed them; only in recent centuries have we been gaining slowly and often painfully, that manner of statement called positive,[3] objective, or scientific. How the future may view even our best present opinions is still far from clear.

Let us consider a set of opposed tendencies which, for the moment, in everyday English we may call the narrowing and widening of the scope of scientific observation with respect to whatever problem is on hand. By way of introduction, we may trace such an alternation of viewpoints for the most general problems of physics from Newton to Maxwell.

For many generations, beginning with Galileo after his break with the Aristotelian tradition, and continuing until past the days of Comte, the stress in physical inquiry lay upon locating units or elements of action, and determining their interactions. Newton firmly established the system under which particles could be chosen and arrayed for inquiry with respect to motion, and so brought under definite report. But not all discovery resulted in the establishment or use of new particles. In the case of heat, for example, it did not come to pass that heat-particles were identified. "The progress of science," say Einstein and Infeld, "has destroyed the older concept of heat as a substance."[4] Particles of a definitely Newtonian type were, it is true, retained in the work of Rumford and Joule, and later of Gibbs; and energy was advocated for a long time as a new substance with heat as one of its forms. But the particle fell upon statistical days (evil, indeed, from the point of view of its older assuredness), and what heat became in the end was a configuration in molecular ranges rather than a particulate presence. Faraday's brilliant observation found that all which happened electrically could not be held within the condenser box nor confined to the conducting wire. Clerk Maxwell took Faraday's observations and produced the mathematical formulation through which they could be expressed.[5] Maxwell's work furnished the structure for the developments of Roentgen, Lorentz, Planck, and Einstein, and their compeers, and for the more recent intra-atomic exploration. His posthumous book, *Matter and Motion*, has a lucidity which makes it a treasure to preserve and a model that all inquirers, especially those in newly opening fields, can well afford to study. The following is from the Preface to this book, dated 1877, and included in the British edition of 1920, edited by Sir Joseph Larmor:

Physical science, which up to the end of the eighteenth century had been fully occupied in forming a conception of natural phenomena as the result of forces acting between one body and another, has now fairly entered on the next stage of progress — that in which the energy of a material system is conceived as determined by the configuration and motion of that system, and in which the ideas of configuration, motion, and force are generalized to the utmost extent warranted by their physical definitions.

Although Maxwell himself appreciated what was taking place, almost two generations were needed before physicists generally began to admit it: *teste*, their long hunting for that greatest of all victims of the Snark that was Boojum, the ether: the process of re-envisionment is far from completed in physics even yet. The very word "transaction," which we are to stress, was, indeed, used by Maxwell himself in describing physical events; he even speaks of "aspects" of physical transactions in much the sense that we shall employ that word.[6] Thus:

If we confine our attention to one of the portions of matter, we see, as it were, only one side of the *transaction* — namely, that which affects the portion of matter under our consideration — and we call this aspect of the phenomenon, with reference to its effect, an External Force acting on that portion of matter, and with reference to its cause we call it the Action of the other portion of matter. The opposite aspect of the stress is called the Reaction on the other portion of matter.

Here we see the envisionment that Maxwell had gained in the electromagnetic field actually remodeling his manner of statement for mechanical systems generally. Maxwell was opening up new vistas from a footing in the firmest organization of inquiry the world had ever possessed — that of the Newtonian mechanics. Though our own position is one in which the best we can hope for is to be able to introduce a small degree of order into an existing chaos, we can use his work, and the results that came from it, in our support, believing as we do that, as progress is made, the full system of human inquiry may be studied as if substantially one.

III

With this much of introductory display let us now set down in broad outlines three levels of the organization and presentation of inquiry in the order of their historical appearance, understanding, however, as is the way with evolutions generally, that something of the old, and often much of it, survives within or alongside the new. We name these three levels, those of Self-Action, Interaction, and Transaction. These levels are all human behaviors in and with respect to the world, and they are all presentations of the world itself as men report it. We shall permit ourselves as a temporary convenience the irregular use of hyphenization in these names as a means of emphasizing the issues involved in their various applications. This is comparable to a free use of capitalization or of quotation marks, and to the ordinary use of italics for stress. It has the particular value that it enables us to stress the inner confusions in the names as currently used.[7]

Self-action: where things are viewed as acting under their own powers.

Inter-action: where thing is balanced against thing in causal interconnection.

Trans-action: [8] where systems of description and naming are employed to deal with aspects and phases of action, without final attribution to "elements" or other presumptively detachable or independent "entities," "essences," or "realities," and without isolation of presumptively detachable "relations" [9] from such detachable "elements."

These provisional characterizations will be followed in a later chapter by alternatives showing the variety of points of view from which the issues that are involved must be approached. The reader will note that, while names are given as if for the events observed, the characterizations are in terms of selective observation, under the use of phrasings such as "are viewed," "is balanced against," and "are employed." These are the two aspects of the naming-named transaction, for which a running exhibit is thus given, pending clarification as the discussion advances.

The character of the primitive stage of Self-action can be established easily and clearly by a thousand illustrations, past and present — all confident in themselves as factual report in their times, without suspicion of the way in which later generations would reduce them to the status of naïve and simple-minded guesswork.

For Trans-action at the latest end of the development we can show a clean status, not as assertion of its existence, but as a growing manner of observation of high efficiency at the proper time and place, now rapidly advancing to prominence in the growth of knowledge.

As for Inter-action, it furnished the dominant pattern of scientific procedure up to the beginning of the last generation. However, as a natural result of its successes, there grew up alongside it a large crop of imitations and debasements — weeds now ripe for the hoe. To avoid very possible misunderstandings, it is desirable to give a sub-classification of the main types of procedure that may from time to time present themselves as, or be appraised as, interactions. We find:

(a) Independently formulated systems working effi-ciently, such as Newtonian mechanics.

(b) Provisionally separated segments of inquiry given an inter-actional form for convenience of study, though with underlying recognition that their results are subject to reinterpretation in wider systems of description; such, for example, as the investigation of certain inter-actions of tissues and organs within the skin of an organism, while remembering, nevertheless, that the "organism-as-a- whole" transactionally viewed (with perhaps also along with it a still wider transactional observation of the "organism-in-environment-as-a-whole") must come into account before final reports are reached.

(c) Abuses of (a) such as often occurred when, before the Einstein development, efforts were made to force all knowledge under the mechanistic control of the Newton-ian system.[10]

(d) Grosser abuses much too common today, in which mixtures of self-actional "entities" and inter-actional "par-ticles" are used to produce inter-actional explanations and interpretations *ad lib.*: as when selves are said to inter-act with each other or with environmental objects; when small portions of organisms are said to inter-act with environ-mental objects as in the traditional theories of sensation; when minds and portions of matter in separate realms are brought by the epistemologies into pseudo-interactional forms; or, probably worst of all, when a word's meaning is severed from the word's actual presence in man's be-havior, like a sort of word-soul from a word-body.

IV

Returning now to physics for a further examination of its increasing use of transaction, we may preface discussion with a few general words on self-action. We need not go far back into cultural history to find the era of its dominance. It took Jupiter Pluvius to produce a rainstorm for the early Romans, whereas modern science takes its *pluvius* free from Jupiter. The *Lares* and *Penates* which "did" all that happened in the household multiplied so excessively in Rome that in time they became jokes to their own alleged beneficiaries. The Druid had, no doubt, much tree lore useful for his times, but to handle it he wanted a spirit in his tree. Most magic has this type of background. It took Robin Goodfellow, or one of his kind, a Brownie perhaps, to make cream turn sour. In modern times we have flocks of words of respectable appearance that spring from this source: such words as "substance," "entity," "essence," "reality," "actor," "creator," or "cause," and thus, indeed, the major part of the vocabulary of metaphysics.[11]

Aristotle's physics was a great achievement in its time, but it was built around "substances." Down to Galileo men of learning almost universally held, following Aristotle, that there exist things which completely, inherently, and hence necessarily, possess Being; that these continue eternally in action (movement) under their own power — continue, indeed, in some particular action essential to them in which they are engaged. The fixed stars, under this view, with their eternal circular movements, were instances. What did not, under the older pattern, thus act through its inherent power, was looked upon as defective Being, and the gradations ran down to "matter" on its lowest level, passive and inert.

Galileo's work is generally recognized as marking the overthrow of Self-action in physical doctrine, and it was just this feature which aroused so much hatred among the men of the ancient tradition. An excellent account — probably the best yet given — will be found in Max Wertheimer's book *Productive Thinking*.[12] Departing from the Aristotelian view that eternal force had to be applied to any inert body to put it in motion and to keep it in motion, Galileo made use of an inclined plane in substitution for a falling weight, as a direct aid to observation. Here he identified acceleration as the most significant feature for his purposes. He then considered the opposed case of a weight tossed upwards, using similarly an ascending inclined plane for his guide, and identified negative acceleration. Together, these yielded him the limiting case of the horizontal plane constructively lying between the descending and the ascending planes. He thus identified the fact (more pretentiously spoken of as a "principle" or "law") of inertia in its modern form: a mass once in motion continues in motion in a straight line, if not interfered with by other moving masses. Its motion, in other words, is no longer supposed to be dependent on the continued push applied to it by an "actor." This discovery was the needed foundation for the interactional development to come. Moreover, the new view itself was transactional with respect to the situation of its appearance: what, namely, had been an incident or result of something else was now taken up into direct report as event.[13] Hobbes quickly anticipated what Newton was later to establish, and Descartes made it his prime law of nature. For Newton it became the first law of motion, leading, through a second law concerning direction and proportionality of force, to the third law, namely, that action and reaction are equal and opposed — in other words, to the establishment of the full inter-actional system of mechanics.

The Newtonian construction — unexcelled for its efficiency within its sphere — viewed the world as a process of "simple forces between unalterable particles."[14] Given a closed system of this kind the inter-actional presentation had now been perfected. This, however, had been achieved at the cost of certain great omissions. Space and time were treated as the absolute, fixed, or formal framework within which the mechanics proceeded — in other words, they were omitted from the process itself. The failure to inquire into the unalterability of the particle was similarly an "omission," though one could freely select whatever "unalterables" one wished for experimental introduction as different problems arose. One immediate effect of Newton's success *within* his accepted restrictions was to hold him to the corpuscular theory of light and make him hostile to the competing wave theory of Huygens.

Einstein's treatment, arising from new observations and new problems, brought space and time into the investigation as among the events investigated. It did more than that: it prepared the scene for the particle itself to go the way of space and time.[15] These steps were all definitely in the line of the transactional approach: the seeing together, when research requires it, of what before had been seen in separations and held severally apart. They provide what is necessary at times and places to break down the old rigidities: what is necessary when the time has come for new systems.

The new foundation that has been given physics on a transactional basis, replacing the old inter-actional extremism, has not yet been made complete. Rival treatments and interpretations have their special places, and what the outcome will be is not wholly clear. Einstein himself devotes his efforts to securing a general field theory, but singularities remain in the field, with which he has not as yet been able successfully to deal. Whether "field" *in physics* is to represent the full situation, or whether it is to be used for an environment to other components is not *our* problem, and is not essential to a general consideration of the transactional phase of inquiry. Our assertion is the right to see in union what it becomes important to see in union; together with the right to see in separation what it is important to see in separation — each in its own time and place; and it is this right, when we judge that we require it for our own needs, for which we find strong support in the recent history of physics. The physicist can readily find illustrations of the two-fold need in his daily work. The changes in stress across the generations, from force as a center to the *vis viva* of Leibnitz, and then on to energy as a special kind of thing in addition to material things, and to the development of the de Broglie equation connecting mass and energy, are in point. Energy now enters more and more in the guise of a described situation rather than in that of an asserted "thing." Long ago some significance, apart from mere puzzlement, was found in the facts that an electric current was not present without a circuit and that all that happened was not "inside" the wire. Twenty years ago physicists began to ask whether light could "start" from a light source, near or distant, if it did not have its place of arrival waiting for it. Today, as indicative of the status of physics, we get discussions strewn with sentences such as the following: " 'The path of a light ray,' without including the environment of the light ray in the description, is an incomplete expression and has no operational meaning"; "The term 'path of a particle' has no more operational meaning than 'path of a photon' in ordinary optics"; "Speaking exactly, a particle by itself without the description of the whole experimental set-up is not a physical reality"; "We can not describe the state of a photon on its way from the sun"; "The law [of causality] in its whole generality cannot be stated exactly if the state variables by which the world is described are not mentioned specifically." [16]

Our aim in this examination of the transformation of viewpoints in physics has been solely to make clear how largely the manner of approach we propose to employ for our own inquiry into knowings and knowns has been already developed by the most potent of all existing sciences. We may supplement what has been said, for the benefit of any still reluctant philosophical, epistemological, or logical reader, by a few citations from the Einstein and Infeld work previously quoted. "The earth and the sun, though so far apart," were, under Newton's laws, "both actors in the play of forces. . . . In Maxwell's theory there are no material actors" (p. 152); "We remember the [mechanical] picture of the particle changing its position with time. . . . But we can picture the same motion in a different way. . . . Now the motion is represented as something which *is*, which exists . . . and not as something which changes . . ." (pp. 216-217); "Science did not succeed in carrying out the mechanical program convincingly, and today no physicist believes in the possibility of its fulfillment" (p. 125); "The concepts of substances, so essential to the mechanical point of view, were more and more suppressed" (p. 148); "The properties of the field alone appear to be essential for the description of phenomena; the differences in source do not matter" (p. 138); "The electromagnetic field is, in Maxwell's theory, something real" (p. 151).

So far as the question of what is called "physical reality" arises in this connection, a reference to a well-known discussion between Einstein and Niels Bohr about ten years ago is pertinent. In contrast with his transactional (i.e., free and open) treatment of *physical* phenomena, Einstein has remained strongly self-actional (i.e., traditionally constrained) in his attitude towards man's activity in scientific enterprise. His position is that "physical concepts are free creations of the human mind" (*op. cit.*, p. 33), and that "the concepts of the pure numbers . . . are creations of the thinking mind which describe the reality of our world" (*ibid.*, p. 311).[17] Bohr, in contrast, appears to have a much freer view of a world that has man as an active component within it, rather than one with man by fixed dogma set over against it. In the discussion in question, which involved the issues of momentum in wave theory, Einstein and his associates, Podolsky and Rosen, chose a criterion of reality based upon prediction to the effect that "if" (without disturbance) "one can predict with certainty the value of a physical quantity," then "there exists an element of physical reality corresponding to this physical quantity." In order to have a complete theory (and not merely a "correct" one), they held that "every element of the physical reality must have a counterpart in the physical theory"; and further they offered their proof that either "the quantum-mechanical description of reality given by the wave function is not complete," or "when the operators corresponding to two physical quantities do not commute, the two quantities cannot have simultaneous reality." In reply Bohr, employing his "notion of complementarity," held that the Einstein-Podolsky-Rosen "criteria of physical reality" contained "an essential ambiguity" when applied to quantum phenomena. He asserted further that while relativity had brought about "a modification of all ideas regarding the absolute character of physical phenomena," the still newer features of physics will require "a radical revision of our attitude as regards physical reality." [18] What is involved here is an underlying, though not explicitly developed, conflict as to the manner in which mathematics (as symbolic) applies to physics (as fact-seeking). This in turn involves the organization of symbol with respect to name among the linguistic behaviors of men.

1 The word "knowledge" has the value here of a rough preliminary description, loosely indicating the field to be examined, and little more.

2 For formal recognition and adoption of the "circularity" involved in the statement in the text, see Chapter II, Section IV, #2.

3 Comte's "positive" retained something from his "metaphysics," just as his "metaphysics" retained something from his "theological." He substitutes "laws" for "forces," but gives them no extensive factual construction. "Logical positivism" has anachronistically accepted this Comtean type of law, emptied it of what factuality it had, and further formalized it. Such a "positive" does not get beyond short-span, relatively isolated, temporal sequences and spatial coexistences. Its background of expression, combined with a confused notion of the part mathematics plays in inquiry, is what often leads scientists to regard "laws" as the essential constituents of science, instead of stressing directly the factual constructions of science in space-time.

4 Albert Einstein and Leopold Infeld, *The Evolution of Physics*, (New York, 1938), p. 51. We shall use the Einstein-Infeld book for repeated

citation, not at all for confirmation of our views or for support of our development, but in order to have before the reader's eyes in the plainest English, authoritative statements of certain features of physics which everyone ought to know, but which in the fields of knowledge-theory are put to use by few. Since we shall have a good deal to do (although little expressly to say) with the way in which rigidly established views block needed progress — a point to which Max Wertheimer, whom we shall later quote, has recently given vivid illustration — a further comment by Einstein and Infeld is significant: "It is a strange coincidence that nearly all the fundamental work concerned with the nature of heat was done by non-professional physicists who regarded physics merely as their great hobby" (Ibid., p. 51).

5 "The most important event in physics since Newton's time," say Einstein and Infeld of Maxwell's equations, "not only because of their wealth of content, but also because they form a pattern for a new type of law" (Ibid., p. 148).

6 Matter and Motion, Article XXXVIII. The italics for the word "transaction" are supplied by us.

7 Our problem here is to systematize the three manners of naming and knowing, named and known. Self-action can hardly be written, as writing and reading proceed today, without its hyphen. Transaction, we shall in the end argue, should be established in such a way that hyphenization would be intolerable for it except, perhaps, in purely grammatical or etymological examination. Inter-action, in contrast, within the range of our present specialized field of study, will appear to be the verbal thief-of-the-world in its commoner uses, stealing away "men's minds," mutilating their judgments, and corrupting the very operation of their eyesight. The word "thing" as used in the characterizations in the text is deliberately chosen because it retains its idiomatic uses, and is almost wholly free from the more serious of the philosophers' distortions which commonly go with the whole flock of words of the tribe of "entity." For our future use, where a definite outcome of inquiry in its full behavioral setting is involved, the word "object" will be employed.

8 "Transaction," in ordinary description, is used for the consideration as detached of a "deal" that has been "put across" by two or more actors. Such a verbal shortcut is rarely objectionable from the practical point of view, but that is about all that can be said for it. For use in research adequate report of the full event is necessary, and for this again adequate behavioral description must be secured. Dewey's early employment of the word "transaction" was to stress system more emphatically than could be done by "interaction." (See his paper "Conduct and Experience" in Psychologies of 1930. [Worcester, Mass.] Compare also his use of "integration" in Logic, the Theory of Inquiry.) The beginnings of this attitude may be found in his paper "The Reflex Arc Concept in Psychology" (1896). Bentley's treatment of political events was of the transactional type in his The Process of Government (Chicago, 1908), though, of course, with-

out the use of that name. John R. Commons has used the word comparably in his *Legal Foundations of Capitalism* (New York, 1924) to describe that type of economic inquiry in which attention centers on the
working rules of association rather than on material goods or human
feelings. George H. Mead's "situational" is often set forth in transactional
form, though his development is more frequently interactional rather
than transactional.

9 It should be fairly well evident that when "things" are too sharply
crystallized as "elements," then certain leftovers, namely, the "relations,"
present themselves as additional "things," and from that pass on to becoming a variety of "elements" themselves, as in many current logics. This
phase of the general problem we do not intend here to discuss, but we
may stop long enough to quote the very instructive comment Max Wertheimer recently made on this sort of thing. He had made a careful study
of the way in which a girl who was secretary to the manager of an office
described to him the character of her office setup, and he devoted a
chapter to her in his book *Productive Thinking* (New York, 1945). His
analysis of her account showed it defective in that it "was blind to the
structure of the situation" (p. 137), and he was led to the further comment that her procedure was "quite similar to the way a logistician would
write a list of relations in a relational network" (p. 138). Compare also
Wertheimer's paper "On Truth," *Social Research* (1934), 135-146.

10 The positions we shall take are in several important respects close to
those taken by Richard C. Tolman in his address prepared for the symposium in commemoration of the 300th anniversary of Newton's birth
("Physical Science and Philosophy," *The Scientific Monthly*, LVII (1943),
166-174). Professor Tolman uses a vocabulary of a different type from
that which we employ — one relying on such words as "subjective," "objective," "abstraction," "conceptual" etc. — but these wordings are not
the significant matter we have in mind. The essential points are that he
treats distinctions between the sciences as resting in the techniques of
inquiry that are available (pp. 171-172), and that he strongly opposes as
a "fallacious assumption" the view that "phenomena at one level of abstraction can necessarily be completely treated at a lower level of abstraction" (p. 174). (Compare our procedure, in Chapter II, Section IV, #4).
We insert this note not to involve Professor Tolman in our construction,
but to provide an alternative form of expression for views comparable in
these respects to our own that may better suit the needs of persons who
find our own manner unfamiliar or undesirable.

11 The distinction between ancient rigidities of naming and scientific
names of the firm (but not rigid) type, such as we desire to attain in our
own inquiry, stands out clearly here. The ancient substances needed
rigidity, fixation of names to things in final one-to-one correspondence.
Pre-Darwinian classification of living forms showed the rigid trend as opposed to modern freedom of development. We have surviving today in
obscure corners numerologies and other superstitions under which things
are controlled by the use of the right names. We even find remnants of

the ancient view in many of our modern logics which seek domination by verbal development. Bertrand Russell's logical atomism with its never-ceasing striving after minutely named "realities" may be mentioned in this connection.

12 Quotations of pertinent phrases from both Aristotle and Galileo are given by Einstein and Infeld in the opening chapter of their book previously cited. Wertheimer concentrates attention on the "structure" or "Gestalt" which governed Galileo's search. Seen as a stage of development in understanding and presentation in the cultural setting in which it was produced, this is in the line of our treatment. Seen, however, as Wertheimer has continued to see it, as a mental activity of self-actional parentage applied to an outer world of objects, it falls far short of the manner of statement which we believe to be necessary. The "mind" Wertheimer relies on is far too reminiscent of the older days in which the "physical" opposed to it was an all-too-solid fixture. Wertheimer, in his last book, has nevertheless dropped much of the traditional mentalistic phraseology; and this with no loss to his presentation.

13 In his early study of perception Max Wertheimer made the comparable demonstration that motion could be *directly* perceived. "Experimentelle Studien über das Sehen von Bewegung," *Zeitschrift für Psychologie*, LXI (1912), 161-265.

14 Einstein and Infeld, *op. cit.*, pp. 58, 255.

15 "In so far as wave mechanics has recognized two words that used to be associated with electrons — *position* and *momentum* — and has provided mathematical expressions as sort of tombstones to correspond to these words, it has done so with the least invocation of trouble to itself," W. F. G. Swann, "The Relation of Theory to Experiment in Physics," *Reviews of Modern Physics*, XIII (1941), 193.

16 These phrasings are all from Philipp Frank's excellent monograph, *Foundations of Physics*, the most recent publication of the *International Encyclopedia of Unified Science* (I, No. 7, [1946], 39, 45, 48, 53).

17 Various significant comments on Einstein's attitude in this respect, which Wertheimer largely shares, will be found scattered through the latter's book, *Productive Thinking*, previously cited.

18 "Can Quantum-Mechanical Description of Physical Reality be Considered Complete?" A. Einstein, B. Podolsky, and N. Rosen, *Physical Review*, XLVII (1935); Niels Bohr, *ibid.*, XLVIII (1935).

CHAPTER FIVE

TRANSACTIONS AS KNOWN AND NAMED

I

FOLLOWING an exhibit in the preceding chapter of the extent to which the manner of observing we call "transactional" is being employed in recent physics, we wish now to show something of its entry into physiology. On this basis we shall discuss its importance for behavioral inquiry and we shall especially stress the outstanding need for its employment in inquiries into knowings and knowns as human behaviors, if such inquiries are to achieve success.

A brief reminder of the terminology provisionally employed is desirable. In a natural factual cosmos in course of knowing by men who are themselves among its constituents, naming processes are examined as the most readily observable and the most easily and practicably studied of all processes of knowing.[1] The name "Fact" is applied to such a cosmos with respect both to its naming-knowing and its named-known aspects. The naming aspect of Fact is styled Designation; the named aspect is styled Event. The problem as to whether knowings-knowns of other forms [2] than namings-nameds should be brought into such inquiry prior to its development is postponed on about the same basis that a biologist proceeds with inquiry into either plant or animal life prior to securing a sharp differentiation between the two or a sharp separation of both of them together from physical event. In general, it is to be observed that the range of the known which we have thus far been developing under the name "event" is, later

119

in this book, to be presented as the full range which the word "existence" can cover in coherent application.

The name "Object" is applied to Event well established as the outcome of inquiry. The name "Specification" is applied to that most efficient form of Designation which has developed in the growth of modern science.[3] Transaction is, then, that form of object-presentation in improved Specification, which is becoming more and more importantly employed in the most advanced scientific inquiry, though still grossly disregarded in backward enterprises, and which is wholly neglected in present-day inquiries into knowledge as the knowing-known procedures of men. Transaction will be discussed in the present chapter and Specification in the next.

To reduce the occasion for some of the ordinary forms of misunderstanding, and to avoid frequent reminder of them in the text, attention is now called to certain positions common in whole or in large degree to current epistemologies, psychologies, and sociologies. These are positions which are *not* shared by us, and which may *in no case* be read into our work whether pro or con by persons who wish properly to appraise it.

1. We employ no basic differentiation of subject *vs.* object, any more than of soul *vs.* body, of mind *vs.* matter, or of self *vs.* not-self.

2. We introduce no knower to confront what is known as if in a different, or superior, realm of being or action; nor any known or knowable as of a different realm to stand over against the knower.

3. We tolerate no "entities" or "realities" of any kind, intruding as if from behind or beyond the knowing-known events, with power to interfere, whether to distort or to correct.

4. We introduce no "faculties" or other operators (however disguised) of an organism's behaviors, but require for all investigation direct observation and usable reports of events, without which, or without the effort to obtain

which, all proposed procedure is to be rejected as profitless for the type of enterprise we here undertake.

5. In especial we recognize no names that pretend to be expressions of "inner" thoughts, any more than we recognize names that pretend to be compulsions exercised upon us by "outer" objects.

6. We reject the "no man's land" of words imagined to lie between the organism and its environmental objects in the fashion of most current logics, and require, instead, definite locations for all naming behaviors as organic-environmental transactions under observation.

7. We tolerate no finalities of meaning parading as "ultimate" truth or "absolute" knowledge, and give such purported finalities no recognition whatever under our postulation of natural system for man in the world.

8. To sum up: Since we are concerned with what is inquired into and is in process of knowing as cosmic event, we have no interest in any form of hypostatized underpinning. Any statement that is or can be made about a knower, self, mind, or subject — or about a known thing, an object, or a cosmos — must, so far as we are concerned, be made on the basis, and in terms, of aspects of event which inquiry, as itself a cosmic event, finds taking place.

II

It was said of Transaction in Chapter IV that it represents that late level in inquiry in which observation and presentation could be carried on without attribution of the aspects and phases of action to independent self-actors, or to independently inter-acting elements or relations. We may now offer several additional characterizations [4] correlated with the preliminary one and indicating the wide range of considerations involved. We may take the ancient, indeed, largely archaic, stages of self-action for granted on the basis of what has already been said of them and subject to the illustrations that will be given hereafter, and we may economize space by confining immediate attention to a comparison of transaction with interaction.

Consider the distinction between the two as drawn in terms of description. If inter-action is inquiry of a type into which events enter under the presumption that they have been adequately described prior to the formulation of inquiry into their connections, then —

Transaction is inquiry of a type in which existing descriptions of events are accepted only as tentative and preliminary, so that new descriptions of the aspects and phases of events, whether in widened or narrowed form, may freely be made at any and all stages of the inquiry.

Or consider the distinction in terms of names and naming. If inter-action is found where the various objects inquired into enter as if adequately named and known prior to the start of inquiry, so that further procedure concerns what results from the action and reaction of the given objects upon one another, rather than from the reorganization of the status of the presumptive objects themselves, then —

Transaction is inquiry which ranges under primary observation across all subjectmatters that present themselves, and proceeds with freedom toward the re-determination and re-naming of the objects comprised in the system.

Or in terms of Fact. If inter-action is procedure such that its inter-acting constituents are set up in inquiry as separate "facts," each in independence of the presence of the others, then —

Transaction is Fact such that no one of its constituents can be *adequately* specified as fact apart from the specification of other constituents of the full subjectmatter.

Or with respect to Elements. If inter-action develops the particularizing phase of modern knowledge, then —

Transaction develops the widening phases of knowledge, the broadening of system within the limits of observation and report.

Or in terms of Activity. If inter-action views things as

primarily static, and studies the phenomena under their attribution to such static "things" taken as bases underlying them, then —

Transaction regards extension in time to be as indispensable as is extension in space (if observation is to be properly made), so that "thing" is in action, and "action" is observable as thing, while all the distinctions between things and actions are taken as marking provisional stages of subjectmatter to be established through further inquiry.

Or with special attention to the case of organism and environment. If inter-action assumes the organism and its environmental objects to be present as substantially separate existences or forms of existence, prior to their entry into joint investigation, then —

Transaction assumes no pre-knowledge of either organism or environment alone as adequate, not even as respects the basic nature of the current conventional distinctions between them, but requires their primary acceptance in common system, with full freedom reserved for their developing examination.[5]

Or more particularly with specialized attention to knowings and knowns. If, in replacement of the older self-action by a knower in person, inter-action assumes little "reals" interacting with or upon portions of the flesh of an organism to produce all knowings up to and including both the most mechanistic and the most unmechanistic theories of knowledge,[6] then —

Transaction is the procedure which observes men talking and writing, with their word-behaviors and other representational activities connected with their thing-perceivings and manipulations, and which permits a full treatment, descriptive and functional, of the whole process, inclusive of all its "contents," whether called "inners" or "outers," in whatever way the advancing techniques of inquiry require.

And finally, with respect to inquiry in general. Wherever inter-actional presentation, on the basis of its special

successes in special fields, asserts itself dogmatically, or
insists on establishing its procedure as authoritative to the
overthrow of all rivals, then —

Transactional Observation is the fruit of an insistence
upon the right to proceed in freedom to select and view all
subjectmatters in whatever way seems desirable under
reasonable hypothesis, and regardless of ancient claims on
behalf of either minds or material mechanisms, or any of
the surrogates of either.[7]

Thoroughly legitimate interactional procedures, it will
be recalled from our previous discussion,[8] are all those
which, like classical mechanics, are held adequately within
their frameworks of hypothesis; and also those others which
represent provisional partial selections of subjectmatters
with recognition of the need for later statement in wider
system. Abuses of interactional procedure are found, on
the other hand, in the endeavors now happily fast disap-
pearing, to force classical mechanistic control upon other
enterprises of inquiry; and in the many quasi-interactional
mixtures of diluted self-actors and pseudo-particles which
remain largely in control of inquiry in the psychologies,
sociologies, and epistemologies.

III

If we turn now to consideration of the biological fields of
inquiry we find that much, but not all, of the old-fashioned
self-actional has been discarded. The "vital principle" is
an outstanding illustration. Employed until recent decades
to mark the distinction of "life" from "mechanism," it
proved in the end to amount to nothing more than a sort
of honorific naming. What is left of it, when it is not a
mere appendage to some irrelevant creed, is mostly found
lurking in obscure corners, or entering by way of incidental implication. Today the marvelous descriptions we
possess of living processes provide adequate differentiation
from the very different, even if themselves equally marvel-

ous, descriptions of physical processes. The orthogenesis of Henry Fairfield Osborn sought to read "direction" into evolutionary lines with the implication of "control," but more and more today, despite his elaborate exhibits, biologists hold that developed description by itself is a far more useful "interpretation" than any appeal to "directives."[9]

Today we find transactional as well as interactional procedures used in the *details* of physiological and biological inquiry; but for *general* formulations we find little more than preliminary approaches to the transactional. This is seen on the large scale in the heavily theoretical separation that is maintained between the organism and the environment and the attribution of many activities to the former as if in independence.[10] As over against the vitalisms the "cell theory" in its radical form stands as a representative of interactional treatment. Views of the type called "organismic," "organismal," etc., except where they contain reminiscences of the old *self*-actional forms, stand for the transactional approach intra-dermally. Such special names as "organismic" were felt to be needed largely because the word "organic," which could serve as an adjective either for "organism" or for "organ," had been too strongly stressed in the latter usage. Transactional treatment, if dominant, would certainly desire to allot the leading adjective rather to the full living procedure of the organism than to minor specialized processes within it; and if ancillary adjectives were needed as practical conveniences, then it would adapt them to the ancillary inquiries in interactional form.[11] The anticipated future development of transdermally transactional treatment has, of course, been forecast by the descriptive spade-work of the ecologies, which have already gone far enough to speak freely of the evolution of the habitat of an organism as well as of the evolution of the organism itself.

The history of the cell in physiology is of great significance for our purposes. For almost a hundred years after Schleiden and Schwann had systematized the earlier scattered discoveries,[12] the cell was hailed as the basic life unit. Today there are only limited regions of physiological report in which the cell retains any such status. What the physiologist sees in it is not what it is, or is supposed to be " in itself," but what it is within its actual environment of tissues. Some types of inquiry are readily carried on in the form of interactions between one cell and other cells. So far as this type of treatment proves adequate for the work that is in hand, well and good. But other types of inquiry require attention in which the interactional presentation is not adequate, and in which broader statements must be obtained in full transactional form in order to secure that wider conveyance of information which is required. One can, in other words, work with cells independently, or with cells as components of tissues and organs; one can put organs into interaction, or one can study the organs as phases of organisms. Biographical treatment of the "organism as a whole" may or may not be profitable. If it is not, this is usually not so much because it fails to go deeply enough into cellular and organic details, as because it fails to broaden sufficiently the organic-environmental setting and system of report. Its defect is precisely that it centers much too crudely in the "individual" so that whether from the more minute or from the more extended viewpoint, the "individual" is precariously placed in knowledge, except as some reminiscence of an ancient self-actional status is slipped in to fortify it for those who accept that kind of fortification.

The gene, when it was first identified by name and given experimental study "on suspicion," seemed almost as if it held the "secret of life" packed into its recesses. Laboratory routine in genetics has become stylized, and is today easy to carry on in standard forms. The routine experimenter who emerges from its interesting specialties and lifts his voice as a radio pundit is apt to tell us all in a single breath, unabashed, that many a gene lives a thousand generations unchanged, and that each new-born organism has precisely two genes of each and every kind in each and every cell, one from each parent. One wonders and hunts his textbooks on grammar and arithmetic. But under wider observation and broader viewpoints we find little of that sort of thing. With gene-position and gene-complex steadily gaining increased importance for interpretative statement, the gene, like many a predecessor that has been a claimant for the rank of element or particle in the universe, recedes from its claims to independence *per se*, and becomes configurational within its setting. The genetic facts develop, but the status of self-actor attributed to the gene at the start proves to be a "fifth-wheel" characteristic: the physiological wagon runs just as well without the little genetic selves — indeed, all the better for being freed from their needless encumbrance.[13] In much the way that in the preceding chapter we employed a recent interpretive book in the physical range, for the significance of its wordings rather than for fixation of authority, we may here cite from Julian Huxley's *Evolution, the Modern Synthesis* (New York, 1942). We are told: "Genes, all or many of them, have somewhat different actions according to what neighbors they possess" (p. 48); "The effect produced by any gene depends on other genes with which it happens to be co-operating". . . . "The environment of the gene must include many, perhaps all other genes, in all the chromosomes" (p. 65); "The discreteness of the genes may prove to be nothing more than the presence of predetermined zones of breakage at small and more or less regular distances along the chromosomes" (p. 48) ; "Dominance and recessiveness must be regarded as modifiable characters, not as unalterable inherent properties of genes" (p. 83); "To say that rose comb is inherited as a dominant, even if we know that we mean the genetic factor for rose comb, is likely to lead to what I may call the one-to-one or billiard-ball view of genetics". . . . "This crude particulate view . . . of unanalyzed but inevitable correspondence . . . is a mere restatement of the preformation theory of development" (p. 19). We have here a clear illustration of the newer feeling and newer expression for physiology comparable to that of other advanced sciences.[14]

Organisms do not live without air and water, nor without food ingestion and radiation. They live, that is, as much in processes across and "through" skins as in processes "within" skins. One might as well study an organism in complete detachment from its environment as try to study an electric clock on the wall in disregard of the wire leading to it. Reproduction, in the course of human history, has been viewed in large measure self-actionally (as fiction still views it) and then interactionally. Knowledge of asexual reproduction was an influence leading to re-interpretation on a fully racial basis, and recent dairy practices for insemination make the transdermally transactional appearance almost the simple, natural one.

Ecology is full of illustrations of the interactional (where the observer views the organism and the environmental objects as if in struggle with each other); and it is still fuller of illustrations of the transactional (where the observer lessens the stress on separated participants, and sees more sympathetically the full system of growth or change). The issue is not baldly that of one *or* the other approach. It is not even an issue as to which shall be the basic underlying construction — since foundations in general in such questions are much less secure than the structures built upon them.[15] It is, in view of the past dominance of the interactional procedure in most scientific enterprise, rather an issue of securing freedom for wider envisionment.

The development of taxonomy since Linnaeus throws much light on the lines of change. He brought system and order among presumed separates. The schematism of taxonomy has at times sought rigidity, and even today still shows such tendencies among certain diminishing types of specialists. The very wording of Darwin's title, *The Origin of Species*, was a challenge, however, to the entire procedure of inquiry as it had been carried on for untold years.

Its acceptance produced a radical change in taxonomic understanding — a method which rendered imperative observation across extended spatio-temporal ranges of events previously ignored. Taxonomy now tends to flexibility on the basis of the widened and enriched descriptions of advancing knowledge.[16]

The distinction of transactional treatment from interactional — the latter often with surviving traces of the self-actional — may be seen in the way the word "emergence" is often used. At a stage at which an inquirer wants to keep "life," let us say, within "nature," at the same time not "degrading" it to what he fears some other workers may think of "nature" — or perhaps similarly, if he wants to treat "mind" within organic life — he may say that life or mind "emerges," calling it thereby "natural" in origin, yet still holding that it is all that it was held to be in its earlier "non-natural" envisionment. The transactional view of emergence, in contrast, will not expect merely to report the advent out of the womb of nature of something that still retains an old non-natural independence and isolation. It will be positively interested in fresh direct study in the new form. It will seek enriched descriptions of primary life processes in their environments and of the more complex behavioral processes in theirs. It is, indeed, already on the way to gain them. The advances in the transactional direction that we can note in biological inquiries, while, of course, not as yet so striking as those in physical sciences, are nevertheless already extensive and important.[17]

IV

We have considered physiological inquiry in transactional forms and we have mentioned, in passing, other biological inquiries such as those concerning trends of evolution, adaptations, and ecologies. We turn now to the wide ranges of adaptive living called behaviors, including thereunder everything psychological and everything sociological in human beings, and embracing particularly all of their knowings and all of their knowns. If physiology cannot successfully limit itself to the interactions between one component of living process within the skin and other components within it, but must first take a transactional view within the skin, following this with further allowance for transdermal process, then very much more strongly may behavioral inquiries be expected to show themselves as transdermally transactional.[18] Manifestly [19] the subject-matter of behavioral inquiries involves organism and environmental objects jointly at every instant of their occurrence, and in every portion of space they occupy. The physiological setting of these subjectmatters, though itself always transactionally organic-environmental, submits itself to frequent specialized investigations which, for the time being, lay aside the transactional statement. The behavioral inquiries, in contrast, fall into difficulties the very moment they depart from the transactional, except for the most limited minor purposes; their traditional unsolved puzzles are indeed the outcome of their rejecting the transactional view whenever it has suggested itself, and of their almost complete failure to allow for it in any of their wider constructions. The ancient custom, of course, was to regard all behaviors as initiated within the organism, and at that not by the organism itself, but rather by an actor or resident of some sort — some "mind," or "psyche," or "person" attached to it — or more recently at times by some "neural center" imitative of the older residents in character. The one-sided inadequacy of this view is what, so often, has called out an equally one-sided opposed view, according to which the organism is wholly passive, and is gradually moulded into shapes adapted to living by independent environmental conditions, mechanistically treated. Both of these views, one as much as the other, are alien to us.

Summing up positions previously taken, we regard behaviors as biological in the broad sense of that word just as much as are any other events which biologists more immediately study. We nevertheless make a technical, — indeed almost a technological — distinction between physiological and behavioral inquiries comparable to the technological distinction between physical and physiological. This is simply to stress the difference in the procedures one must use in the respective inquiries, and to note that the technical physiological statement, no matter how far it is developed, does not directly achieve a technical behavioral statement. One may, in other words, take into account all known physical procedures about the moon, and likewise all known physiological procedures of the human body, and yet not arrive, through any combination or manipulation whatsoever, at the formulation, "rustic, all agape, sees man in moon." This last needs another type of research, still "natural," but very different in its immediate procedures. The distinction is never one of "inherent materials," nor one of "intellectual powers," but always one of subjectmatter at the given stage of inquiry.[20]

As for the self-actional treatment of behaviors (much of which still remains as a heritage of the past in the laboratories) it is probably safe to say that after physicists knocked the animism out of physical reports, the effect was not to produce a comparable trend in organic and behavioral fields, but just the reverse. All the spooks, fairies, essences, and entities that once had inhabited portions of matter now took flight to new homes, mostly in or at the human body, and particularly the human brain. It has always been a bit of a mystery as to just how the commonplace "soul" of the Middle Ages, which possessed many of the Aristotelian virtues as well as defects, came to blossom out into the overstrained, tense, and morbid "psyche" of the last century or two. To Descartes, whether rightly or wrongly, has fallen much of the blame. The "mind" as "actor," still in use in present-day psychologies and sociologies, is the old self-acting "soul" with its immortality stripped off, grown dessicated and crotchety. "Mind" or "mental," as a preliminary word in casual phrasing, is a sound word to indicate a region or at least a general locality in need of investigation; as such it is unobjectionable. "Mind," "faculty," "I. Q.," or what not as an actor in charge of behavior is a charlatan, and "brain" as a substitute for such a "mind" is worse. Such words insert a name in place of a problem, and let it go at that; they pull out no plums, and only say, "What a big boy am I!" The old "immortal soul" in its time and in its cultural background roused dispute as to its "immortality" not as to its status as "soul." [21] Its modern derivative, the "mind," is wholly redundant. The living, behaving, knowing organism is present. To add a "mind" to him is to try to double him up. It is double-talk; and double-talk doubles no facts.

Interactional replacements for self-actional views have had minor successes, but have produced no generally usable constructions. This is true regardless of whether they have presented the organic inter-actors, which they set over against physical objects, in the form of minds, brains, ideas, impressions, glands, or images themselves created in the image of Newtonian particles. Despite all the fine physiological work that has been done, behavioral discussions of vision in terms of images of one kind or another are in about as primitive a state as they were a hundred years ago. [22] The interactional treatment, as everyone is aware, entered psychological inquiry just about the time it was being removed from basic position by the physical sciences from which it was copied. [23]

The transactional point of view for behaviors, difficult as it may be to acquire at the start, gains freedom from the old duplicities and confusions as soon as it is put to firm use. Consider ordinary everyday behaviors, and consider them without subjection to either private mentalities or particulate mechanisms. Consider closely and carefully the reports we make upon them when we get rid of the conversational and other conventional by-passes and short-cuts of expression.

If we watch a hunter with his gun go into a field where he sees a small animal already known to him by name as a rabbit, then, within the framework of half an hour and an acre of land, it is easy — and for immediate purposes satisfactory enough — to report the shooting that follows in an interactional form in which rabbit and hunter and gun enter as separates and come together by way of cause and effect. If, however, we take enough of the earth and enough thousands of years, and watch the identification of rabbit gradually taking place, arising first in the sub-naming processes of gesture, cry, and attentive movement, wherein both rabbit and hunter participate, and continuing on various levels of description and naming, we shall soon see the transactional account as the one that best covers the ground. This will hold not only for the naming of hunter, but also for accounts of his history back into the pre-human and for his appliances and techniques. No one would be able successfully to speak of the hunt*er* and the hunt*ed* as isolated with respect to hunt*ing*. Yet it is just as absurd to set up hunt*ing* as an event in isolation from the spatio-temporal connection of all the components.

A somewhat different type of illustration will be found in the comparison of a billiard game with a loan of money, both taken as events. If we confine ourselves to the problem of the balls on the billiard table, they can be profitably presented and studied interactionally. But a cultural account of the game in its full spread of social growth and human adaptations is already transactional. And if one player loses money to another we cannot even find words in which to organize a fully interactional account by assembling together primarily separate items. Borrower can not borrow without lender to lend, nor lender lend without borrower to borrow, the loan being a transaction that is identifiable only in the wider transaction of the full legal-commercial system in which it is present as occurrence.

In ordinary everyday behavior, in what sense can we examine a talking unless we bring a hearing along with it into account? Or a writing without a reading? Or a buying without a selling? Or a supply without a demand? How can we have a principal without an agent or an agent without a principal? We can, of course, detach any portion of a transaction that we wish, and secure provisional descriptions and partial reports. But all this must be subject to the wider observation of the full process. Even if sounds on the moon, assuming the necessary physical and physiological waves, match Yankee Doodle in intensity, pitch, and timbre, they are not Yankee Doodle by "intrinsic nature," in the twentieth century, whatever they might have been thought to be in the Dark Ages, or may perhaps be thought to be today by echoistic survivals of those days;[24] they need action if they are to yankeedoodle at all.

When communicative processes are involved, we find in them something very different from physiological process; the transactional inspection must be made to display what takes place, and neither the particles of physics nor those of physiology will serve. Many a flint chip fools the amateur archaeologist into thinking it is a flint tool; but even the tool in the museum is not a tool in fact except through users of such tools, or with such tool-users brought into the reckoning. It is so also with the writing, the buying, the supplying. What one can investigate a thing *as*, that is what it *is*, in Knowledge and in Fact.

V

When we come to the consideration of the knowings-knowns as behaviors, we find Self-action as the stage of inquiry which establishes a knower "in person," residing in, at, or near the organism to do (i.e., to perform, or have, or be — it is all very vague) the knowing. Given such a "knower," he must have something to know; but *he* is cut off from it by being made to appear as a superior power, and *it* is cut off from *him* by being made to appear just as "real" as he is, but of another "realm."

Interaction, in the interpretation of knowings, is a somewhat later stage which assumes actual "real" things like marbles which impinge on certain organic regions such as nerve endings or perhaps even brain segments. Here we still have two kinds of "reals" even though superficially they are brought somewhat closer together in physical-physiological organization. The type of connection is superficial in this case because it still requires a mysticism similar to that used for self-actions to bridge across from the little real "thing" to the little "real" sensation as organic, psychic, or psychologic — where by the word "mysticism" is meant nothing "mystic" itself, but merely some treatment that does not yield to description, and quite often does not want to.

The transactional presentation is that, we believe, which appears when actual description of the knowledge process is undertaken on a modern basis. At any rate it is the kind of presentation which has resulted from our own attempts at direct observation, description, and naming; it is for aid in appraising our results that we have, in this present chapter and the one immediately preceding it, examined comparable procedures in other scientific fields and upon other scientific subjectmatters. The steps we have taken, it will be recalled, are to say that we can not efficiently name and describe except through observation; that the word "knowledge" is too broadly and vaguely used to provide a single subjectmatter for introductory inquiry; that we can select as a compact subjectmatter within "knowledges" generally the region of knowings-through-namings; that here observation at once reports that we find no naming apart from a named, and no named apart from a naming in such separation that it can be used as direct subject of *behavioral* inquiry — whatever physical or physiological observations we can incidentally make on the namings and the named in provisional separations; that such observations in fused systems *must* be steadily maintained if we are to attain complete behavioral report; and that, if this procedure requires an envisionment for be-

havioral purposes of space and time that is more extensive
and comprehensive than the earlier physical and physiological reports required, such envisionment is then what
we must achieve and learn to employ.

The outcome of self-actional and interactional procedures, so far as any competent theory of knowledge is
concerned, has been and still is chaos, and nothing more.
One can easily "think of" a world without a knower, or
perhaps even of a knower without a world to belong to,
and to know. But all that "think of" means in such a
statement is "to mention in crude language," or "to speak
crudely." The hypostatizing fringes of language are what
make this "easy." While "easy," it is nevertheless not "possible," if "possible" covers carrying through to a finish,
and if "think" means sustained consideration that faces
all difficulties, holds to coherent expression, and discards
manifestly faulty experimental formulations wherever and
whenever it finds them — in short, if the "thinking" strives
to be "scientifically" careful. A "real world" that has no
knower to know it, has, so far as human inquiry is concerned (and this is all that concerns us), just about the
same "reality" that has the palace that in Xanadu Kubla
Kahn decreed. (That, indeed, has had its reality, but it
was not a reality beyond poetry, but in and of it.) A
knower without anything to know has perhaps even less
claim to reality than that. This does not deny the geologic
and cosmic world prior to the evolution of man within it.
It accepts such a world as known to us, as within knowledge, and as with all the conditionings of knowledge; but
it does not accept it as something superior to all the knowledge there is of it. The attribute of superiority is one that
is, no doubt, "natural" enough in its proper time and
place, but it too is "of and in" knowledge, not "out of" or
"beyond." [25] In other words, even these knowings are
transactions of knowing and known jointly; they themselves as knowings occupy stretches of time and space as
much as do the knowns of their report; and they include

the knower as himself developed and known within the known cosmos of his knowledge.

How does it come to pass, one may ask, if the naming-named transaction as a single total event is basic as we say it is, that historically our language has not long since developed adequate special naming for just this basic process itself? The answer lies partially in the fact that, so far as ordinary conversational customs are concerned, it frequently happens that the most matter-of-fact and commonplace things are taken for granted and not expressly written down. For the rest of the answer, the part that concerns the professional terminology of knowledge and of epistemology, the sad truth is that it has long been the habit of the professionals to take words of the common vocabulary, stiffen them up somewhat by purported definition, and then hypostatize "entities" to fit. Once given the "entities" and their "proper names," all factual contact, including carefully managed observation, defaults. The names ride the range (in the west) and rule the roost (in the east). All too often the bad names get crowned while the good names get thumbs down. The regions in which this happens are largely those in which procedure is governed by the grammatical split between the subject and the object of the sentence rather than by observation of living men in living linguistic action. In such theoretical interpretations an unobservable somewhat has been shoved beneath behavioral naming, so that "naming as such" is personified into a ready-made faculty-at-large simply waiting for entities to come along for it to name; though most regrettably without that supernatural prescience in attaching the right name to the right animal which Adam showed in the Garden of Eden. The absurdity is thus standardized; after which not merely epistemology but linguistics, psychology, sociology, and philosophy proceed to walk on artificial legs, and wobbly-creaky legs at that. Turn the subject and object of the sentence into disconnected and unobservable kinds of entities, and this is what happens.

The organism, of course, seems in everyday life and language to stand out strongly apart from the transactions in which it is engaged. This is superficial observation. One reason for it is that the organism is engaged in so many transactions. The higher the organism is in the evolutionary scale, the more complicated are the transactions in which it is involved. Man especially is complex. Suppose a man engaged in but one transaction and that with but one other man, and this all his life long. Would he be viewed in distinction from that transaction or from that other man? Hardly. Much analysis, if an analyzer existed, would at least be necessary to separate him out as a constituent of what went on. A "business man" would not be called a business man at all if he never did any business; yet the very variety of his other transactions is what makes it easy to detach him and specialize him as a "business man." Consider the great variety of his other transactions, and it becomes still easier to make "a man" out of him in the sense of an "essence" or "substance," or "soul" or "mind," after the pattern demanded by the general noun. He comes thus, in the end, to be considered as if he could still be a man without being in *any* transaction. It is precisely modern science which reverses this process by driving through its examinations more thoroughly. When actions were regarded as separate from the actor, with the actor regarded as separate from his actions, the outcome, individually and collectively, was to bring "essence" into authority. The procedures of Galileo, Newton, and Darwin, steadily, bit by bit, have destroyed this manner of observation; and the procedures which must follow hereafter will complete it for the most complex human behavioral activities. They will reverse the old processes and bring the transactions into more complete descriptive organization without the use of either self-actional powers, or interactional "unalterable particles" behind them.[26]

---

[1] See Chapter II, Section III. Chapter III, Sections I and III.

2 These other forms include not only the full range of the perceptive-manipulative (Signal), but also those of non-naming linguistic processes such as mathematics (Symbol). For the words "event" and "existence" see Chapter II, Note 22, and the characterizations given the words in Chapter XI.

3 The word "science" in our use stands for free experimental observation and naming, with the understanding that the advanced branches of scientific inquiry are necessary aids to the backward branches, but never their dictators.

4 The reader will recall that in the present treatment we do not hope to get beyond characterization, but must leave the greater accuracy of specification for future development, when additional phases of the issue have been examined. The use of hyphenization as a device for emphasizing interior confusions in words continues now and then in the text. The following from the British weekly *Notes and Queries* a hundred years ago may be profitably examined by the muddled victims of unhyphenized "interaction" today: "A neglect of mental hyphenization often leads to mistake as to an author's meaning, particularly in this age of morbid implication."

5 How much need there is for precision in these respects is well indicated by a paragraph in a recent book on the general characteristics of evolution by one of America's most distinguished biologists. His phrasings were first that "the organism develops . . . structures and functions," next that "the organism becomes adapted to . . . conditions," and finally that "evolution produces . . . etc." First the organism is actor, next the environment is actor, and lastly "evolution" is hypostatized to do the work. And all in a single paragraph. Such phrasings indicate, of course, inattention to the main issues involved.

6 Descartes, in his discussion of vision in the first five or six chapters of his *Dioptrique,* gives a fascinating account of sensation as mechanistically produced. It should be specially valuable to modern laboratory workers in the field since it lacks the ordinary protective jargon of professional life, and gets down to the verbal bone of the matter. Descartes was far from liking it in its full application, but in the case of vision, he did not see how he could avoid its apparatus of tubes, rods, and animal spirits.

7 The reader of philosophical specialization may be interested in comparing Kant's substance, causation, and reciprocity. Cassirer's substance and function has interest so far as he develops it. The words "analysis" and "synthesis" suggest themselves, but a cursory survey of discussions in that form has shown little of interest. More suggestive, perhaps, for the philosophical specialist, is the now almost wholly discarded "objective idealism" of men like Green, Bradley, and Caird. The basic terminology of this group of men, using "absolute mind" as a starting point, may be stripped off so as to open the way to see more clearly what they were practically seeking. They show us a full system of activity, a dislike for crude

dualisms, and a desire to get rid of such breakages as those the epistemologies capitalize. Along with this went a tolerance for, and even an interest in, the growth, and in that sense the "life," of the system itself. Our own development, of course, in contrast, is of the earth earthy, representing strictly an interest in improved methods of research, for whatever they are worth here and now.

8 Chapter IV, Section II.

9 Osborn's use of the word "interaction" is characteristically in contrast with ours. In developing his "energy" theory in his book *The Origin and Evolution of Life* (London, 1917) he considered action and reaction as usually taking place simultaneously between the parts of the organism, and then added interaction as an additional something connecting non-simultaneous actions and reactions. Interactions therefore appeared as a new product controlling the others, illustrated by such forms as instincts, functions of co-ordination, balance, compensation, co-operation, retardations, accelerations, etc. The "directing power of heredity" was thus set forth as "an elaboration of the principle of interaction" (pp. 4-6, 15-16).

10 A prevailing type of logical reflection of this older attitude towards the organism will be found in Carnap's assertion that "It is obvious that the distinction between these two branches [physics and biology] has to be based on the distinction between *two kinds of things* which we find in nature: organisms and nonorganisms. Let us take this latter distinction as granted" (*Logical Foundations of the Unity of Science, International Encyclopedia of Unified Science*, I, No. 1, 45; italics not in the original). As against this rigidified manner of approach, compare the discussion of the organism and behavior in John Dewey's *Logic, the Theory of Inquiry*, (New York, 1938), pp. 31-34.

11 For the intra-organic transactional observation, with occasional still wider envisionments, see the works of J. v. Uexkull, W. E. Ritter, and Kurt Goldstein. Lawrence J. Henderson's book *The Fitness of the Environment*, (New York, 1913) should also be examined. Ritter lists among the most forceful of the earlier American advocates of the "organismal theory" as against the extreme forms of the "cell theory" C. O. Whitman, E. B. Wilson, and F. R. Lillie. Goldstein refers in biology to Child, Coghill, Herrick, and Lashley; in psychiatry to Adolf Meyer and Trigant Burrow; in psychology to the *Gestalt* school; and adds references in philosophy to Dilthey, Bergson, Whitehead, and Dewey. Henderson, with reference to Darwin's "fitness," says that it is a "mutual or reciprocal relationship between the organism and the environment," and again that "the fitness of the environment is both real and unique" (*op. cit.*, p. xi, pp. 267-271). To rate as more fundamental than any of these is the discussion by J. H. Woodger in his *Biological Principles* (London, 1929), a book which is far from having received the attention it deserves. Especially to examine are Chapters V on the theory of biological explanation, VII on structure-function, and VIII on the antithesis between organism and environment.

12 For the slow process of identifying the cell as distinctive structure, see the discussion by E. B. Wilson in *The Cell in Development and Heredity*, 3d ed. (New York, 1937), pp. 2-4.

13 Such an entitative superfluity exemplifies the position we are taking throughout our entire discussion: Why retain for the purpose of general interpretation "entities" (i.e., supposititious things-named) that no longer figure in actual inquiry, nor in adequate formulation of its results? Why not get rid of such items when worn out and dying, instead of retaining their sepulchral odor till the passing generations cause even the latter to die away? The split of "nature" into two "realms" — two superfluities — is the instance of such entitative survival to which we elsewhere find it necessary to give ever-renewed consideration.

14 The results secured by R. Goldschmidt and Sewall Wright should also be compared. For the former, see his *Physiological Genetics* (New York, 1938). For the latter see "The Physiology of the Gene," *Physiological Review*, XXI (1941). T. Dobzhansky and M. F. Ashley Montagu write (*Science*, CV, June 6, 1947, p. 588): "It is well known that heredity determines in its possessor not the presence or absence of certain traits, but, rather, the responses of the organism to its environments."

15 Georg Simmel, *Soziologie: Untersuchungen über die Formen der Vergesellschaftung*, Zweite Auflage. (Leipzig, 1922), p. 13.

16 E. Mayr, *Systematics and the Origin of Species*, (New York, 1942). The author (pp. 113-122) offers a highly informative account of the learning and naming issues in biological nomenclature, ranging from the "practical devices" of the systematist to the "dynamic concepts" of the evolutionist, and compares a variety of treatments including the morphological, the genetic, the biological-species, and the criterion of sterility. His discussion moves back and forth between the natural processes of naming and the facts-in-nature to be named. When we come later to discuss characterization, description, and specification, it will be evident (1) that the account can be given from the point of view of either aspect, and (2) that the recognition of this very complementarity is basic to our whole procedure. The twenty-two essays in the volume *The New Systematics* (Oxford, 1940) edited by Julian Huxley also furnish much material for profitable examination in this connection.

17 For a discussion of the entry of the fundamental field theory of physics into biology, see "A Biophysics Symposium," (papers by R. E. Zirkle, H. S. Burr and Henry Margenau) *The Scientific Monthly*, LXIV (1947), 213-231. In contrast, for typical instances of the abuse of field and other mathematical terminology in psychology, *see* Ivan D. London, "Psychologists's Misuse of the Auxiliary Concepts of Physics and Mathematics" *The Psychological Review*, LI, (1944), pp. 226-291.

18 See Bentley, "The Human Skin: Philosophy's Last Line of Defense," *Philosophy of Science*, VIII (1941), 1-19. Compare J. R. Firth, *The Tongues of Men* (London, 1937), pp. 19-20. "The air we talk and hear

by, the air we breathe, is not to be regarded as simply outside air. It is inside air as well. We do not just live within a bag of skin, but in a certain amount of space which may be called living space which we continue to disturb with some success. And the living space of man is pretty wide nowadays. Moreover we never live in the present." "In dealing with the voice of man we must not fall into the prevalent habit of separating it from the whole bodily behaviour of man and regarding it merely as a sort of outer symbol of inward private thoughts."

19 This is "manifest," of course, only where observation has begun to be free. It is far from manifest where ancient categories and other standardized forms of naming control both the observation and the report.

20 Chapter II, Section #4 to #8. We do not undertake to make a comparable distinction between psychological and sociological inquiries. This latter distinction is standard among "self-actional" treatments, where the "individual" enters in the traditional exaggeration customary in most interactional treatments. Transactionally viewed, a widening or narrowing of attention is about all that remains indicated by such words as "social" and "individual." As we have elsewhere said, if one insists on considering individual and social as different in character, then a derivation of the former from the latter would, in our judgment, be much simpler and more natural than an attempt to produce a social by joining or otherwise organizing presumptive individuals. In fact most of the talk about the "individual" is the very finest kind of an illustration of isolation from every form of connection carried to an extreme of absurdity that renders inquiry and intelligent statement impossible.

21 The historical differentiations between spirit, soul, and body throw interesting light on the subject. Any large dictionary will furnish the material.

22 For example, Edwin G. Boring in *A History of Experimental Psychology* (New York, 1929), p. 100, speaking of the work of Johannes Mueller, writes: "In general, Mueller remains good doctrine today, although we know that perceived size is neither entirely relative nor entirely proportional to visual angle." This despite the fact that he had ascribed to Mueller the view that "It is the retina that the sensorium perceives directly," and added that "it is plain that, for Mueller, the theory of vision is merely the theory of the excitation of the retina by the optical image." This is perhaps mainly carelessness in statement, but what a carelessness!

23 The recent work of Egon Brunswik goes as far, perhaps, on the transactional line as any. He recently ("Organismic Achievement and Environmental Probability," *Psychological Review*, L (1943), 259n) suggested coupling "psychological ecology" with "ecological psychology" in what seemed a functional manner from both sides. In contrast Kurt Lewin, speaking at the same meeting, suggested the name "ecological psychology" but rather for the purpose of getting rid of factors undesirable in his

mentalistically fashioned "life-space" than for improvement of system. Clark Hull, also on the same program, holds that organic need and organic environment must be "somehow jointly and simultaneously brought to bear" upon organic movement (the phrasing from his book *Principles of Behavior*, [New York, 1943], p. 18, where he italicizes it) and he bridges across the gap by a series of intervening variables of a fictional, pseudological character.

24 Echolatry might be a good name to apply to the attitudes of our most solemn and persevering remembrancers of things past—and done with. "Echoist," by the way, is a good word in the dictionaries, and should not be wholly lost from sight.

25 Many a man is confident in saying that he knows for certain (and often with a very peculiar certainty) what is behind and beyond his personal knowings. We are well aware of this. Nevertheless, we do not regard it as good practice in inquiry when dependable results are sought.

26 A discussion of "The Aim and Progress of Psychology" by Professor J. R. Kantor (*American Scientist*, XXXIV, [1946], 251-263) published after the present paper was written, may be examined with profit. It stresses the modern "integrated-field stage" of science, with special reference to psychology, in contrast with the earlier "substance-property" and "statistical-correlation" stages.

CHAPTER SIX

SPECIFICATION

I

HAVING discussed at length the status of those events of the known and named world which we have styled "transactions," we proceed now to examine that linguistic activity through which Transaction is established: namely, Specification.[1]

Specification, in our provisional terminology, is the most efficient form of Designation, and Designation is that behavioral procedure of naming which comprises the great bulk of linguistic activities, and which, in the line of evolution, lies intermediate between the earlier perceptional activities of Signaling and the later and more intricately specialized activities of Symboling.

It will be recalled that we have inspected Fact most generally as involving and covering at once and together the naming process and the "that" which the naming is about. The choice of the word "fact" to name the most general transaction of "knowledge," was made because in practically all of its many varied uses this word conveys implications of the *being known* along with those of the *what* that is known; moreover, Fact applies to that particular region of the many regions covered by the vague word "knowledge" in which namings are the prominent feature. It is in this region that "knowledge" is most generally considered to be "knowledge of existence" in perhaps the only sense of the word "existence" having practical utility — that, namely, in which the existence is being affirmed with a considerable measure of security as to its details.[2]

Taking Fact as inclusive of both the naming and the named in common process, we adopted Designation for the naming phase of the transaction, and Event for the phase of the named. Events (or "existences," if one is prepared to use the latter word very generally and without specialized partisan stress) were distinguished as Situations, Occurrences, and Objects; and Objects were then examined in their presentations as Self-actions, Inter-actions, and Trans-actions — all of this, of course, not as formal classification, but as preliminary descriptive assemblage of varieties. The "self," "inter," and "trans" characteristics appear in Situations and Occurrences as well as in Objects, but it is in the more determinate form of Objects that the examination can most closely be made.

When we now turn to the examination of the processes of Designation we must on the one hand place designation definitely within the evolutionary range of behaviors; on the other hand we must examine the stages of its own development, leading up to Specification as its most efficient and advanced stage. The first of these tasks is necessary because a disjunction without a conjunction is usually more of a deception than of a contribution; but the pages we give to it furnish no more than a sketch of background, the further and more detailed treatment being reserved for a different connection.[3] In the second of these tasks we shall differentiate Cue, Characterization, and Specification as the three stages of Designation, and shall give an account of Specification freed from the hampering limitations of the symbolic procedures of Definition.[4]

II

Designation, as we have said, covers naming. "Naming" would itself be an adequate name for the processes to be considered under Designation — and it would be our preferred name — if the name "name" itself were not so tangled and confused in ordinary usage that different

groups of readers would understand it differently, with
the result that our own report would be largely *mis*-under-
stood. For that reason, before going further, we shall insert here a few paragraphs about the common understand-
ings as to "name," and as to their difference from the
specialized treatment we introduce as Designation. Some
of these positions have been discussed before, and others
will be enlarged upon later.

Naming we take as behavior, where behavior is process
of organism-in-environment. The naming type of behavior, by general understanding so far as present information goes, is one which is characteristic of *genus homo* in
which almost alone it is found. Except as behavior — as
living behavioral action — we recognize no name or naming whatever. Commonly, however, in current discussions,
name is treated as a third type of "thing" separate both
from organism and from environment, and intermediate
between them. In colloquial use this makes little difference. But in the logics and epistemologies, a severed realm
of phenomena, whether explicit or implicitly introduced,
matters a great deal. Such an intervening status for
"name," we, by hypothesis, reject.

Name, as a "thing," is commonly spoken of as a tool
which man or his "mind" uses for his aid. This split of a
"thing" from its function is rejected. Naming is before
us not as a tool (however it may be so described from
limited viewpoints), but as behavioral process itself in
action, with the understanding, nevertheless, that many
forms of behavior, and perhaps all, operate as instrumental
to other behavioral processes which, in turn, are instrumental to them.

Treatments of name as thing or tool accompany (or are
accompanied by; the point is not here important) the
splitting of "word" from "meaning" — "word," whether
crudely or obscurely, being taken as "physical," with
"meaning" as "mental." The split of a sign-vehicle from
a sign, stressed as one of maximum theoretical importance

in certain recent efforts at construction in this general field, is merely the old rejected split in a new guise. Under the present approach such a treatment of name, or of any other word, is regarded as deficient and inefficient, and is therefore banished.[5]

Under the above approach naming is seen as itself directly a form of knowing, where knowing is itself directly a form of behavior; it is the naming type of knowing behavior (if one wishes to widen the scope of the word "knowledge"), or it is the distinctive central process of knowledge (if one prefers to narrow the scope of the word "knowledge" thus far). Our hypothesis is that by treating naming as itself directly knowing, we can make better progress than in the older manners.

Naming does things. It states. To state, it must both conjoin and disjoin, identify as distinct and identify as connected. If the animal drinks, there must be liquid to drink. To name the drinking without providing for the drinker and the liquid drunk is unprofitable except as a tentative preliminary stage in search. Naming selects, discriminates, identifies, locates, orders, arranges, systematizes. Such activities as these are attributed to "thought" by older forms of expression, but they are much more properly attributed to language when language is seen as the living behavior of men.[6] The talking, the naming, is here oriented to the full organic (currently "organismic" or "organismal") process rather than to some specialized wording for self, mind, or thinker, at or near, or perhaps even *as*, a brain.

All namings are positive. "Not-cow" is as much positive naming as is "cow" — whatever the cow itself might think about that. The cow's local point of view does not govern all theoretical construction. If the negatives and the positives alike stand for something, this something is as thoroughly "existential" in the one case as in the other.

Written names are behavioral process as much as spoken names are. Man's diminishment of the time-period, say, to the span of his day or of his life, does not govern decision as to what is behavioral or what is not.

The "what" that is named is no fiction. "Hercules" was a name in its time for something existently cosmic or cultural — not as "reality at large," but always as "specified existence." "Sea-serpents" and "ghosts" have played their parts, however inactive they may be as existential namings today. Trilobites are inactive, but they nevertheless made animal history.

These viewpoints that we have set down are not separates fortuitously brought together. They are transactional. They form, for this particular region of inquiry, the substance of what is meant by "transaction" in our use. That they will not "make sense" from the inter-actional point of view, or from the self-actional point of view, is only what is to be expected. They make sufficient sense as fact to be usable by us in hypothesis, and the test of their value will be in the outcome of such use.

III

If we are to examine Designations as behaviors, we must first establish the characteristics of behavior as we see it. That the name "behavior," however elsewhere used, can, in biological studies, be applied without misunderstanding to certain adjustmental types of animal activities, will hardly be disputed. That a behavioral statement in this sense is not itself directly a physiological statement, nor a physiological statement itself directly a behavioral one, will likewise hardly be disputed, as matters stand today, however much one may hope or expect the two forms of statement to coalesce some time in the future, or however valuable and indeed indispensable the primary understanding of the physiological may be for any understanding of the behavioral. Extend either form of statement as far as you wish, holding it closely within its own vocabulary; it will, nevertheless, not directly convert itself into the other.

Moreover attempts to limit the application of the word "behavior" to the overt muscular and glandular activities of an organism in the manner of a generation ago have not proved satisfactory. Too much development in terms of the participation of the "whole organism" — or, better said, of "the rest of the organism" has of late been made; and recent attempts to revive the older narrow construction for the interpretation of knowledge have had misfortunes enough to serve as ample warnings against such programs.

We shall take the word "behavior" to cover all of the adjustmental activities of organism-environment, without limiting the word, as is sometimes done, to overt outcomes of physical or physiological processes. This latter treatment involves too crude a disregard of those factual processes which in older days were hypostatized as "mental," and which still fall far short of acquiring "natural" description and reports. In the older psychologies (and in many still with us), whether under "mental" or "physiological" forms of statement, the distinction of the typically human behaviors from non-human and also of behaviors generally from the non-behavioral, was made largely in terms of "faculties" or "capacities" assumed to be inherent in the organism or its running mate, the "mind" or "soul." Thus we find "purposiveness" stressed as the typically "animal" characteristic; or accumulations of complexly-interrelated habits, or certain emotional, or even moral, capacities. In our case, proceeding transactionally, nothing, so far as we know, of this "capacitative" manner of statement remains in stressed use at critical points of research. Regarding behaviors as events of organism-environment in action, we shall find the differentiation of behavioral processes (including the purposive) from physical or physiological to rest upon types of action that are observable directly and easily in the full organic-environmental locus.

Sign: Developing behaviors show indirections of action of types that are not found in physical or physiological processes. This is their characteristic. The word "indirection" may, no doubt, be applicable to many physiological processes as compared with physical, but it is not the word by itself that is important, The particular type of indirection that is to be found in behaviors we shall call *Sign*, and we shall so use the word "sign" that where sign is found we have behavior, and where behavior occurs sign-process is involved. This is an extremely broad usage, but we believe that, if we can make a sound report on the factual case, we are justified in applying the word as we do.[7]

At a point far down in the life-scale Jennings identified sign as a characteristic behavioral process forty years ago. He was studying the sea-urchin, and remarked that while it tends to remain in dark places and light is apparently injurious to it, "yet it responds to a sudden shadow falling upon it by pointing its spines in the direction from which the shadow comes." "This action," Jennings continues, "is defensive, serving to protect it from enemies that in approaching may have cast the shadow. The reaction is produced by the shadow, but it *refers,* in its biological value, to something behind the shadow." [8]

This characteristic of Sign is such that when we have followed it back in protozoan life as far as we can find traces of it, we have reached a level at which we can pass over to the physiological statement proper and find it reasonably adequate for what we observe as happening. This makes the entry of the "indirection" which we call "sign" a fair border-line marker between the physiological and the behavioral. The sign-process characterizes perceptions all the way up the path of behavioral evolution; it serves directly for the expanded discussion of differentiated linguistic representation; it deals competently with the "properties" and the "qualities" that have for so long a time at once fascinated and annoyed philosophers and epistemologists; it can offer interpretation across all varieties of expressive utterance up to even their most subtle forms. All these phases of behavior it can hold together simply and directly.

Having adopted an interchangeability of application for sign and behavior, our position will be as follows: If we fall away from it, that fact will be evidence of defect in our development; if we fall seriously away that will be indication of an insecurity in our basic hypotheses themselves; if we can maintain it throughout — not as *tour de force* but as reasonably adequate factual statement — this will furnish a considerable measure of evidence that the manner of construction is itself sound.

We have indicated that behavior is envisaged transactionally and that sign itself is a transaction. This means that in no event is sign in our development to be regarded as consisting of an "outer" or detached "physical" thing or property; and that in no event is it to be regarded as the kind of an ear-mark that has no ear belonging to it, namely, as a detached "mental thing." Sign, as we see it, will not fit into a self-actional interpretation at all; nor will it fit into an interactional interpretation.

If this is the case an important question — perhaps the most important we have to face — is the exact location of sign. Precisely *where* is the event that is named when the name "sign" is applied? Sign is process that takes place only when organism and environment are in behavioral transaction. Its locus is the organism and the environment, inclusive of connecting air, electrical and light-wave processes, taken all together. It is these in the duration that is required for the event, and not in any fictive isolation apart from space, or from time, or from both. A physiologist studying breathing requires air in lungs. He can, however, temporarily take for granted the presence of air, and so concentrate his own attention on the "lungs" — on what *they* do — and then make his statement in that form. He can, that is, for the time being, profitably treat the transaction as interactional when the occasion makes this advantageous. The student of the processes of knowings and knowns lacks this convenience. He can not *successfully* make such a separation at any time. Epistemologies that isolate two components, that set them up separately and then endeavor to put them together again, fail; at least such is our report on the status of inquiry, and such our reason for proceeding transactionally as we do.

It is evident that time in the form of clock-ticks and space in the form of foot-rules yield but a poor description of such events as we report signs to be. Treat the events as split into fragments answering to such tests as clocks and rules may give, and you have a surface account, it is true, but one that is poor and inaedequate for the full transaction. Even physics has not been able to make the advances it needs on any such basis. The spatial habits of the electrons are bizarre enough, but they are only the prologue. When physicists find it practicable to look upon 92 protons and 142 neutrons as packed into a single nucleus in such a way that the position of each is "spread out" over the entire nuclear region, certainly it should be permissible for an inquirer into man's behavioral sign-processes to employ such pertinent space-forms with pasts and futures functioning in presents, as research plainly shows to be necessary if observation is to be competent at all. At any rate any one who objects to freedom of inquiry in this respect may properly return to his own muttons, for subsequent proceedings will not interest him at all.

Taking Sign, now, as the observable mark of all behavioral process, and maintaining steadily transactional observation in replacement of the antique fixations and rigidities, we shall treat Signal, Designation, and Symbol as genera of signs, and so of behaviors. Similarly within the genus Designation, we may consider Cue, Characterization, and Specification as species. In this we shall use "genus" and "species" not metaphorically, but definitely as natural aids to identification.

Signal: All the earlier stages of sign up to the entry of language we group together under the name "signal." Signal thus covers the full sensori-manipulative-perceptive

ranges of behavior, so far as these are unmodified by linguistic behaviors. (Complex problems of linguistic influencings will surely have to be faced at later stages of inquiry, but these need not affect our terminology in its
preliminary presentation.) Signals like all signs are transactional. If a dog catches sight of the ear of a rabbit and
starts the chase, signal behavior is involved. The signal
is not the rabbit's ear for itself, nor is it the identification
mechanism in the dog; it is the particular "fitness" of environment and organism — to use Henderson's word; it is
the actual fitting in the performance. Pavlov's conditioned
reflex, as distinguished from simple reflexes that can tell
their stories directly in terms of physical-physiological excitations and reactions, is typical signaling, and Pavlov's
own use of the word "signal" in this connection is the main
reason for our adoption of it here.[9] The Pavlov process
must, however, be understood, not as an impact from without nor as a production from within, but as a behavioral
event in a sense much closer to his own descriptions than
to those of many comparable American laboratory inquiries. It must be a feature of the full stimulus-response situation of dog and environmental objects together. If we
take bird and berry in place of dog and rabbit, berry is as
much a phase of signal as bird is. Divorce the two components — disregard their common system — and there *is*
no signal. Described in divorcement the whole picture is
distorted. Signaling is always action; it is event; it occurs;
and only as occurrence does it enter inquiry as subjectmatter. It is not only transactional as between dog and
rabbit and between bird and berry, but each instance of it
is involved in the far wider connections of the animal's
behaviors. No such fact is ever to be taken as an isolate
any more than one animal body is to be taken as an isolate
from its genus, species, race, and family. If one takes either
the sensory, the motor, or the perceptional as an isolate,
one again distorts the picture. Each case of signal, like
every other case of sign, is a specific instance of the con-

tinued durational sign-activity of life in the organic-environmental locus. The motor phase has its perceptive-habitual aspect, and the perceptive phase has its motor aspect, with training and habit involved.

IV

Designation: Designation develops from a basis in Signaling. Signaling is organic-environmental process that is transactional. Designation in its turn is transactional organic-environmental process, but with further differentiation both with respect to the organism and with respect to the environment. With respect to the organism the "naming" differentiates; with respect to the environment the "named" differentiates. On neither side do we consider detachment as factual. The organism is not taken as a "capacity" apart from its environmental situation. The environment is not taken as "existing" in detachment from the organism. What is "the named" is, in other words, not detached or detachable environmental existence, but environment-as-presented-in-signaling-behavior. In other words, signalings are the "named," even though the namer in naming develops a language-form presumptively presenting an "outer" as detachable. Neither "naming" nor "named" under our procedure is taken as either "inner" or "outer," whether in connections or separations. The process of designation becomes enormously more complex as it proceeds; in it environmental determinations and namings unfold together. We make our approach, however, not in terms of the late complex specializations, but instead in terms of the growth in its early stages. The *what* that is assumed in the earliest instances is, then, not a *thing* in detachment from men (as most logicians would have us believe); much less is it some "ultimate reality," "provisional reality," "subsistence," or metaphysical "existence" (whatever such "things" may be taken to be). What is "cued" in the earliest forms of naming is some action-requirement within the sign-process, that is, within behavior. When one of a pair of birds gives a warning cry to his mate, or when a man says "woof" to another man as sign of bear-trail or bear-presence, it is behavior that is brought in as named; it is transactionally brought in, and is transaction itself as it comes. One can go so far back along the evolutionary line that the bird-call or the "woof" or some more primitive predecessor of these has, under such observation and report as we can make, not yet reached so much as the simplest differentiating stage with respect to "naming and named." But when the differentiating stage *is* reached, then the "named" that differentiates within the behavior is an impending behavioral event — an event in process — the environing situation included, of course, along with the organism in it. Both bird-call and woof indicate something doing, and something to be done about it.

The transactional locus of a designation in one of its earliest forms is very narrow — just the range of the creatures in communication, and of the sensori-manipulative-perceptive events directly presented in the communication. When and as the designation-event develops more complexity, the locus widens. Intermediate stages of namings intervene. Some of them push themselves temporarily into the foreground of attention, but even so are in fact members of a total inclusive transaction, and are given isolation and independence only in theories that depart from or distort observation. One may name a law, say the price-control act, without ever putting one's "finger" on it. In fact our experts in jurisprudence talk indefinitely about a statutory or other law without being able to specify what any law *is,* in a way equivalent to a direct "fingering." And while, in this talking and writing about the law, limiting intervening namings become temporarily the focus of direct attention, the *what* that is named is the law in its entire reach.

It is in this transition to more and more complex designations that the descriptive accounts are most likely to go astray. The cry "Wolf" is quickly brought to rest through actions that yield a "yes" or "no." The cry "Atomic Bomb" is evidently on a different level. It is in the cases of highly developed designations that it is most necessary to take our clue from the simpler cases so as to be firmly and solidly aware that name can not be identified as a process in an organism's head or "mind," and that the named can not be identified with an object taken as "an entity on its own account"; that the naming-transaction has locus across and through the organisms-environments concerned in all their phases; and that it is subject to continued development of indefinite scope so that it is always in transit, never a fixture.

We shall give attention to the two less complex stages of designation, namely, Cue and Characterization, merely far enough to lead up to the presentation of Specification as the perfected (and ever-perfecting) stage of naming, and so as to provide the ground for its differentiation from symbol and definition. So far as the terminology used is concerned, it may seem strange to group the thing-name, Cue, with the action-names, Characterization and Specification, as we are doing. But since all designations are designations in and of behavioral activities, the preliminary noun-form used does not greatly matter. We might, perhaps, set up Cue, Common Noun, Term [10] as one series of names to range the field; or, as an alternative, we might use Ejaculation, Characterization, and Specification. Provided the behavioral transactions are taken as names with respect to developing action, the selection of terminology may well be left open for the present.

Cue: By Cue is to be understood the most primitive language-behavior. Wherever transactional sign on the signal level begins to show differentiation such that out of it will grow a verbal representation of any signal process, we have the beginnings of Cue. It is not of prime importance whether we assert this as first arising on the sub-human animal level, and say that language comes into being there, or whether we place the first appearance of true language among men. The general view is that the regions of cue, in contrast with those of signal, are characteristically communicative, but this issue, again, is not one of prime importance. Such questions lie in the marginal regions which modern science (in distinction from older manners of inquiry) does not feel it necessary to keep in the forefront of attention. Life is life, whether we can put a finger on the line that marks the boundary between it and the non-living, or whether a distinction here is far beyond our immediate powers; and much energy will be saved if we postpone such questions till we have the facts. Biology learned about its marginal problems from the viruses and could have got along just as well or better without the oceans of opinionative disputation over the "vital principle" in older days.

The illustrations of designation above were mainly from the lower levels and will serve for cue. Cue, as primitive naming, is so close to the situation of its origin that at times it enters almost as if a signal itself. Face-to-face perceptive situations are characteristic of its type of locus. It may include cry, expletive, or other single-word sentences, or any onomatopoeic utterance; and in fully developed language it may appear as an interjection, exclamation, abbreviated utterance, or other casually practical communicative convenience. Though primarily name grown out of signal, it may at times have the guise of more complex name reverted to more primitive uses. We may perhaps say that cue is signal with focal localization shifted from organism-object to organism-organism, but with object still plain in reach.

The transition from signal to cue may be indicated in a highly artificial and wholly unromantic way through a scheme which, fortunately, is devoid of all pretense to authority as natural history. On the branches of a tree live three snakes protectively colored to the bark, and enjoying vocal chords producing squeaks. Transients at the tree are squeaking birds: among them, A-birds with A-squeaks that are edible by snakes, and B-birds with B-squeaks that pester snakes. Bird-squeaks heard by snakes enter as signals, not as bird-squeaks alone, nor as snake-heard sounds alone, but strictly as events in and of the full situation of snake-bird-tree activity. Snake-squeaks, ono-matopoeically patterned, are cues between snakes — primitive verbalisms we may call them, or pre-verbalisms. The evolutionary transition from bird-squeaks warning snakes, to snake-squeaks warning snakes is not one from external signs to internal signs, nor from the automatic to the mental, but just *a slight shift in the stresses of the situation.* When cue appears, we have a changed manner of action. When cue is studied transactionally, we change our stress on these subjectmatters of inquiry. Our change is slight, and one of growth in understanding, elastic to the full development of inquiry. It is not a breakage such as a self-actional account produces, nor even a set of minor breakages such as interactional treatment involves. The change to transactional treatment permits descriptions such as those on which perfected namings are built up.

The cue-stage of designation was not mentioned in our sketch of terminology in Chapter II, our arrangement there being designed to give preliminary stress to the distinction of definition from specification. Signal was chosen as a name for the perceptive-manipulative stage of sign process largely on the basis of Pavlov's use of it. Cue was chosen for its place because all "dictionary definitions" (except one or two that lack the sign character altogether) make it verbal in nature. It may be, however, especially in view of Egon Brunswik's recent studies,[11] that the words "cue" and "signal" could better be made to shift places. Our purpose here is solely to establish at once the manners of disjunction and of conjunction of cue and signal, and an interchange of names would not be objectionable.

Characterization: Out of cue there develops through

clustering of cues — i.e., through the growth of language — that type of naming which makes up almost all of our daily conversation. It is the region of evolving description, which answers well enough for current practical needs, but is limited by them in scope. The wider the claims it makes, the less value it has. It is the region where whale in general is a fish because it lives in the water like any "proper" fish. Words cease to be of the type of "this," or "that," or "look," or "jump quick," and come to offer a considerable degree of connection among and across environmental situations, occurrences, and objects. The cues overlap and a central cue develops into a representative of a variety of cues. The interconnections are practical in the colloquial sense of everyday life. Horse is named with respect to the way one does things with and about horses, and with respect to the way horse does things with and about us. The noun enters as an extension of the pronoun, which is a radically different treatment from that of ordinary grammar. The characterizations move forward beyond the "immediately present" of the cues as they widen their connections, but for the most part they are satisfied with those modes of linguistic solvency which meet the requirements set by an immediately present "practical" communicative situation.

The first great attempt to straighten out the characterizations and bring them under control was perhaps made by the Greek sophists, and this led the way to Aristotle's logic. The logics that have followed Aristotle, even those of today that take pride in calling themselves non-Aristotelian, are still attempting to bring characterizations under the control of rules and definitions — to get logical control of common namings. All theories of linguistics, at least with a rare exception or two, make their developments along these lines. In the region of characterization the view arises that if naming occurs there must exist a "some one" to do the naming; that such a "some one" must be a distinctive kind of creature, far superior to the observed world — a creature such as a "mind" or personified "actor"; and

that for such a "some one" to give a name to "anything,"
a "real" thing or "essence" [12] must exist somewhere apart
and separate from the naming procedure so as to get itself
named. (The word "must" in the preceding sentences
merely reports that where such practical characterizations
are established they think so well of themselves that they
allege that every form of knowledge "must" adapt itself
to them.) Alien as this is from modern scientific practice,
it is, nevertheless, the present basis of most linguistic and
logical theory and of what is called "the philosophy of
science." [13] It is in this stage that namings and the named
get detachable existences assigned to them by reflecting or
theorizing agents, their immediate users being, as a rule,
protected against this abuse by the controls exercised in
conversational exchange by the operative situation directly present to those who participate in the oral transaction. Indeed, one may go so far as to doubt whether
the distorted theory would have arisen if it had not been
for the development of written documents with their increasing remoteness from determination by a directly observed situation. Given the influence of written, as distinct
from spoken, language, it is dubious whether theoretical
or philosophical formulations could have taken any form
other than the one they now have, until a high degree of
the development of the methods of inquiry now in use in
advanced subjects had provided the pattern for statement
in the form we term specification as complementary with
transaction.

Description: Before passing to specification it will be
well to attend to the status of names and naming with
respect to descriptions. Phrasings develop around namings,
and namings arise within phrasings. A name is in effect
a truncated description. Somewhat similarly, if we look
statically at a stable situation after a name has become well
established, a description may be called an expanding
naming. The name, in a sense which is useful if one is
careful to hold the phrasing under control, may be said

to name the description, and this even more properly at times than it is said to name the object. For naming the object does not legitimately, under our approach, name an object unknown to the naming system; what it names is the object-named (with due allowance for the other forms of knowing on the sensori-manipulative-perceptive level of signal); and the object-named is far more fully set forth in description than by the abbreviated single word that stands for the description. Beebe[14] mentions a case in which a single word, Orthoptera, in the Linnaean scheme precisely covered 112 words which Moufet had required for his description a hundred years earlier. The process of description begins early and is continuous while naming proceeds in its own line of growth, whatever arbitrary substitutes for it may at times be sought. Take two yellow cats and one black cat. Some little while afterwards, culturally speaking (a few tens of thousands of years, perhaps) primitive man will mark the color distinction, not as color for itself, but as color in contrast with other color. Put his color-naming in system with cat-naming, and you have the beginnings of description. "Cat" begins now to stand not merely for anti-scratch reaction, or for cat-stew, but for an organization of words into description. Bertrand Russell and several of his contemporaries have had a great deal of trouble with what they call "descriptions" as compared with what Russell, for instance, calls "logical proper names." Fundamentally Russell's "proper names" are analogues of the cue — reminiscent of primeval yelps and of the essences and entities that descend from them, to which it is that Russell wishes to reduce all knowledge. At the far extreme from his form of statement stands specification as developed out of characterization by expanding descriptions which in the end have attained scientific caliber. It is to Specification rather than to survivals of primitive catch-words that our own procedure directs itself in connection with progress in knowledge. Our most advanced contemporary cases of scientific identification should certainly not be compelled to comply with a demand that they handcuff themselves "logically" to a primitive type of observation and naming, now scientifically discarded.

V

Specification: Specification is the type of naming that develops when inquiry gets down to close hard work, concentrates experimentally on its own subjectmatters, and acquires the combination of firmness and flexibility in naming that consolidates the advances of the past and opens the way to the advances of the future. It is the passage from conversational and other "practical" namings to namings that are likewise practical — indeed, very much more practical — for research. The whale ceases to be a fish on the old ground that it lives in water and swims, and becomes established instead as a mammal because of characterizations which are pertinent to inquiries covering wide ranges of other animals along with the whale, bringing earlier "knowns" into better system, and giving direction to new inquiries. "Fish," as a name, is displaced for whale, not because it fails to conform to "reality," but because in this particular application it had been limited to local knowings which proved in time to be obstructive to the further advance of inquiry in wider ranges. Scientific classificatory naming, as it escapes from the bonds of rigidity, illustrates the point in biology. In physics it is illustrated by the atom which ceases to be a little hard, round, or cubical "object" that no one can make any smaller, harder, or rounder, and has become instead a descriptive name as a kind of expert's shorthand for a region of carefully analyzed events. Incidentally this procedure of specification is marked by notable inattention to the authority so often claimed for ancient syllogistic reasoning carried on in patterns fixed in advance.[15] The surmounting of the formal or absolute space and time of Newton, and the bringing of space and time together under direct physical description, is the outstanding illustration of the work of specification in recent physics, and our account in a preceding chapter[16] of the advance of transactional presentation of physical phenomena might in large part have been developed as a report upon specification. The developmental process in "science" is still far from complete. In biological work, organism and object still often present themselves in the rough as characterizations without specification, even though much specification has occurred in the case of physiological inquiry. In psychological and societal subjectmatters procedures are even more backward. It is astonishing how many workers in these latter fields relegate all such issues to "metaphysics" and even boast that they are "scientific" when they close their eyes to the directly present (though unfortunately most difficult) phases of their inquiry.

In our preliminary account of naming we have said that it states and connects. Cue states and characterization connects. Specification goes much further. It opens and ranges. By the use of widened descriptions it breaks down old barriers, and it is prepared to break down whatever shows itself as barrier, no matter how strongly the old characterizations insist on retention. What it opens up it retains for permanent range from the furthest past to the best anticipated futures. Also it retains it as open. It looks back on the ancient namings as at least having been designational procedure, no matter how poor that procedure was from man's twentieth-century point of view. It looks upon further specifications as opening a richer and wider world of knowledge. In short it sees the world of knowledge as in growth from its most primitive forms to its most perfected forms. It does not insert any kind of a "still more real" world behind or beneath its world of knowledge and fact.[17] It suspects that any such "real" world it could pretend to insert behind the known world would be a very foolish sort of a guessed-at world; and it is quite content to let full knowledge come in the future under growth instead of being leaped at in this particular instant. It welcomes hypotheses provided they are taken for what they are. Theories which sum up and organize facts in ways which both retain the conclusions of past inquiries and give direction to future research are themselves indispensable specifications of fact.

The word "specification" will be found making occasional appearances in the logics though not, so far as we have observed, with definitely sustained use. A typical showing of contrasted use appears in Quine's *Mathematical Logic,* where a "principle of application or specification" is embodied in Metatheorem *231. The name "specification" itself hardly appears again in his book, but the principle so named — or, rather, its symbolic embodiment — once it has entered, is steadily active thereafter. Nonsymbolically expressed, this principle "leads from a general law, a universal quantification, to each special case falling under the general law." In other words, whereas we have chosen the name "specification" to designate the most complete and accurate description that the sustained inquiry of an age has been able to achieve based on all the inquiries of earlier ages, this alternative use by Quine employs it for the downward swoop of a symbolically general law to fixate a substitute for the name of the thing-named. This is manifestly one more illustration of the extremes between which uses of words in logical discussion may oscillate.

Specification, as we thus present it, *is* science, so far as the word "science" is used for the reporting of the known. This does not mean that out of the word "science" we draw "meanings" for the word "specification," but quite the contrary. Out of a full analysis of the process of specification we give a closer meaning to the word "science" as we find it used in the present era. Scientists when confronting an indeterminacy alien to classical mechanics, may seem as agitated as if on a hot griddle for a month or a year or so; but they adapt themselves quickly and proceed

about their business. The old characterizations did not
permit this; the new specifications do; this is what is typical
of them. There is a sense in which specification yields the
veritable object itself that is present to science; specification, that is to say, as one aspect of the process in which the
object appears in knowledge, while, at the same time, the
object, as event, yields the specification. It is not "we"
who are putting them together in this form; this is the way
we find them coming. The only object we get is the object
that is the result of inquiry, whether that inquiry is of the
most primitive animal-hesitation type, or of the most advanced research type. John Dewey has examined this
process of inquiry at length on its upper levels — those
known as "logic" — and has exhibited the object in the
form of that for which warranted assertion is secured.[18]

The scientific object, in this broad sense, is that which
exists. It reaches as far into existence as the men of today
with their most powerful techniques can reach. In our
preliminary suggestions for terminology we placed event
in contrast with designation as the existential aspect of
fact. We should greatly prefer to place the word "existence" where we now provisionally place event, and shall
probably do so when we are ready to write down the determinations at which we aim. Exist, the word, is derivative of the Latin *sto* in its emphatic form, *sisto,* and names
that which stands forth. What stands forth requires temporal and also spatial spread. Down through the ages the
word "existence" has become corrupted from its behavioral
uses, and under speculative philosophy has been made to
stand for something which is present as "reality" and on
the basis of which that which is "known" is rendered as
"phenomenon" or otherwise to the knower. Common
usage, so far as the dictionaries inform us, leans heavily
towards the etymological and common-sense side, though,
of course, the philosophical conventions get their mention.
The common man, not in his practical use, but if asked
to speculate about what he means, would probably offer

his dogmatic assurance that the very "real" is what exists. *Solvitur ambulando* is a very good practical solution of a practical question, but *solvitur* in the form of a dogmatic assertion of reality is something very different. Dr. Johnson (if it was Dr. Johnson) may kick the rock (if it was a rock), but what he demonstrates is kicked-rock, not rock-reality, and this only within the linguistic form then open to him. We believe we have ample justification for placing existence where we now place event in our terminological scheme — only delaying until we can employ the word without too much risk of misinterpretation by hearer or reader. If, however, we do this, then specification and existence are coupled in one process, and with them science; though again it must be added, not science in a purely "physical" or other narrow rendering of the word, but science as it may hope to be when the best techniques of observation and research advance into the waiting fields.

VI

The passage from characterization to specification is not marked by any critical boundary. Nor is the passage from everyday knowledge to scientific knowledge, nor that from everyday language to scientific language. Our attention is focused on lines of development and growth, not on the so-called "nature" of the subject-matter of inquiry. If we are wrong about observing events in growth, then the very inquiry that we undertake in that form should demonstrate that we are wrong. Such a demonstration will be more valuable than mere say-so in advance that one should, or should not, make such an attempt. The regions of vagueness remain in specification, but they decrease. They are Bridgman's "hazes." Their main implication is, however, transformed. The earlier vagueness appeared as defect of human capacity, since this latter did not seem to succeed in reaching the infinite or the absolute as it thought it ought to. The newer vagueness, under the operation of specification, is a source of pride. It shows that work to date is well done, and carries with it the assurance of betterment in the future.

It is common for those who favor what is called "naturalism" to accept, with qualifications, many phases of the development above. We are wholly uninterested in the phases of the "ism," and solely concerned with techniques of inquiry. For inquiry into the theory of knowledge, to avoid wastage and make substantial progress, we believe the attitude indicated must be put to work one hundred per cent, and without qualification either as to fields of application or ranges of use. We have, however, not yet discussed the manner in which symbol and definition, which we do not permit to interfere with designation, may be put to work in the service of the latter. Nor have we shown the intimate connection between the techniques of specification and the establishment of transaction as permissible immediate subject-matter and report. These problems are among those remaining for a further inquiry which, we trust, will be continued along the lines we have thus far followed.

---

[1] We shall continue, as heretofore, to capitalize some of our main terms where stress on them seems needed, and particularly where what is in view is neither the "word" by itself nor the "object" by itself, but the general presentation of the named-as-in-naming. We shall continue also the occasional use of hyphenization as a device for emphasis.

[2] For naming and knowing see Chapter II, Section III. For comment on "existence" see Chapter XI.

[3] Of psychology today one can sharply say (1) if its field is behavior, and (2) if human behavior includes language, then (3) this behavioral language is factor in all psychology's presentations of assured or suspected fact, and (4) psychological construction today shows little or no sign of taking this linguistic factor into account in its double capacity of being itself psychologic fact and at the same time presenter of psychologic fact. The problem here is, then, the terminological readjustment of psychological presentation to provide for this joint coverage of the naming and the named in one inquiry.

[4] The word "definition" is used throughout the present chapter, as in-

preceding chapters, to stand for procedures of symboling as distinct from those of designating. This choice was made mainly because recent developments of technique, such as those of Tarski, Carnap, and symbolic logicians generally, have either adopted or stressed the word in this sense. After the present chapter, however, we shall abandon this use. In preparing our succeeding chapter, to appear under the title "Definition," we have found such complex confusions that misunderstanding and misinterpretations seem to be inevitable, no matter how definition is itself "defined." The effect of this change will be to reduce the word "definition" from the status of a "specification" to that of a "characterization" as this distinction is now to be developed. Progress towards specification in the use of the word "definition" is, of course, what is sought, no matter how unattainable it may seem in the existing logical literature.

5 The issue here is not one of personal "belief," whether pro or con. It is one of attitude, selection, decision, and broader theoretical formulation. Its test is coherence of achievement. *Practical* differentiations of specialized investigation upon half a dozen lines with respect to word, or along half a dozen other lines with respect to word-meaning, are always legitimate, and often of great practical importance. For some account of the abuses of sign and sign-vehicle see Chapter XI.

6 However, if language is not regarded as life-process by the reader, or if thought is regarded as something other and higher than life-process, then the comparison in the text will not be acceptable to him.

7 The *Oxford Dictionary* has twelve main dictionary definitions of sign, and a number of subdivisions. The *Century* has eleven. In modern discussion the uses are rapidly increasing, but no one usage is yet fixed for the field we are at work in. Usages range from saying that sign is a form of energy acting as a stimulus, followed by the application of the word for almost any purpose that turns up, to presenting it as a product of mind-proper. No one use can claim the field till it has been tried out against others; and certainly no candidate should even enter itself until it has been tried out in its own backyard and found capable of reasonably coherent usage.

8 H. S. Jennings, *Behavior of the Lower Organisms* (New York, 1906), p. 297. Jennings has himself never made a development in terms of sign, despite the highly definite description he so early gave it. Karl Bühler, who was one of the first men to attempt a broad use of a sign-process for construction, quoted this passage from Jennings in his *Die Krise der Psychologie*, (Jena, 1927), p. 80, at about the time it began to attract attention among psychologists in the United States.

9 Allowing for a difference in the forms of expression shown by the use of such a word as "relation," Bartley and Chute in *Fatigue and Impairment in Man* (New York, 1947) plan to differentiate the word "signal" along very much the lines of our text. They write (p. 343): "Neither items in the physical world nor perceived items are themselves signals. A signal merely expresses the relation between the two, as determined by

the functional outcome." They, however, still retain the word "stimulus" separately for the "physical items from which the signals arise."

[10] Decision as to the use of the word "terms" is one of the most difficult to make for the purposes of a safe terminology. Mathematics uses the word definitely, but not importantly. Logics, as a rule, use it very loosely, and with much concealed implication.

[11] Egon Brunswik, "Organismic Achievement and Environmental Probability," *Psychological Review*, L (1943), 255. See also Tolman and Brunswik, "The Organism and the Causal Texture of the Environment," *Psychological Review*, XLII (1935), 43. Both cue and signal overlap in ordinary conversational use, a fact of interest here. George H. Mead occasionally used "signal" in much the region where we use "cue." Mead's treatment of the animal-man border regions will be of interest (*Mind, Self, and Society*, [Chicago, 1934], pp. 61-68, 81, *et al.*).

[12] The recent revival of the word "essence" in epistemological discussion, as in Santayana's writings, is of itself convincing evidence of this statement.

[13] The difficulties in which the logics find themselves are examined in Chapters I and VIII.

[14] William Beebe, Editor, *The Book of Naturalists*, (New York, 1944), p. 9.

[15] The issues, of course, are of the type so long debated under the various forms of contrast between what is called empiricism and what is called rationalism, these names merely marking the condition surrounding their entry into specialized modern prominence. Such issues are, however, held down by us to what we believe we are able to report under direct observation of the connections between language and event in current scientific enterprise in active operation.

[16] Chapter IV. For a complete account, of course, a full appraisal of the participation of mathematics would be necessary; that is, of the system of organization of symbol with name.

[17] Philipp Frank, *Between Physics and Philosophy* (Cambridge, 1941), using a terminology and a psychological base very different from ours, writes: "Our modern theoretical physics, which admits progress in all parts of the symbol system, is skeptical only when viewed from the standpoint of school philosophy" (p. 102) ; "There are no boundaries between science and philosophy" (p. 103) ; "Even in questions such as those concerning space, time and causality, there is scientific progress, along with the progress in our observations" (p. 102) ; "The uniqueness of the symbol system can be established within the group of experiences itself without having recourse to an objective reality situated outside, just as the convergence of a sequence can be established without the need of discussing the limit itself" (p. 84).

[18] John Dewey, *Logic, the Theory of Inquiry*, (New York, 1938), p. 119.

CHAPTER SEVEN

THE CASE OF DEFINITION

I

IT is now time to give close attention to the status of the word "definition" in present-day discussions of knowings and knowns, and especially in the regions called "logic." We began by accepting the word as having soundly determinable specialized application for mathematics and formal logic, but by rejecting it for use with the procedures of naming.[1] Naming procedures were styled "designations," and their most advanced forms, notable especially in modern science, were styled "specifications." Thereby definition and specification were held in terminological contrast for the uses of future inquiry.

Throughout our inquiry we have reserved the privilege of altering our terminological recommendations whenever advancing examination made it seem advisable. This privilege we now exercise in the case of the word "definition." For the purposes of the present discussion we shall return the word to its ordinary loose usage, and permit it to range the wide fields of logic in its current great variety of ways. This step was forced upon us by the extreme difficulty we found in undertaking to examine all that has to be examined under "definition," while we ourselves stood committed to the employment of a specialized use of the word. It is much better to abandon our suggested preference than to let it stand where there is any chance that it may distort the wider inquiry.

Our present treatment in effect deprives the word "defi-

nition" of the status we had planned to allot it as a "specification" for procedures in the mathematical and formal
logical fields. Since we had previously rejected it as a
specification for namings, it will now as a name, for the
time being at least, be itself reduced to the status of a characterization.[2]

Regardless of any earlier comments,[3] we shall for the
present hold in abeyance any decision as to the best permanent employment of the word. The confusions that we
are to show and the difficulties of probing deep enough to
eliminate them would seem sufficient justification for rejecting the word permanently from any list of firm names.
On the other hand the development of its specialized use
in formal logic along the line from Frege and Hilbert down
to recent "syntactics" (as this last is taken in severance from
its associated "semantics") would perhaps indicate the possibility of a permanent place for it, such as we originally
felt should be allotted it.

If we begin by examining the ordinary English dictionaries, the Oxford, Century, Standard, and Webster's, for
the definitions they provide for definition itself, we shall
find them vague and often a bit shifty in setting forth the
nature of their own peculiar type of "definition," about
which they might readily be expected to be the most definite: namely, the traditional uses of words. Instead, they
are strongly inclined to take over some of the authority
of the philosophies and the logics, in an attempt to make
the wordings of these latter more intelligible to the general
reader. Two directions of attention are manifest, sharply
phrased in the earlier editions, and still present, though a
bit more vaguely, in the later. First, there is a distinction
between definition as an "act" (the presence of an "actor"
here being implied) and definition as the "product" of an
act (that is, as a statement in verbal form) ; and then there
is a distinction between the defining of a word and the
defining of a "thing," with the "thing," apparently, entering the definition just as it stands, as a component directly

of its own right, as a word would enter. What is striking here, moreover, is the strong effort to *separate* "act" and "product" as different *kinds* of "meanings" under differently numbered entries, while at the same time *consolidating* "word" and "thing" in close *phrasal union,* not only inside the definition of "act" but also inside that of "product." In the Oxford Dictionary (1897) [4] entry No. 3 is for the "act" and entry No. 4 is for the statement *produced* by the act. The "act," we are told, concerns "what a thing is, or what a word means," while the "product" provides in a single breath both for "the essential nature of a thing," and for the "form of words by which anything is defined." Act and product are thus severed from each other although their own "definitions" are so similar they can hardly be told apart. So also with the Century (1897), in which act and product are presented separately in definitions that cover for each not only "word or phrase," but also what is "essential" of or to a "thing." The Standard has offered continuously for fifty years as conjoined illustrations of definition: "a *definition* of the word 'war'; a *definition* of an apple." The latest edition of Webster (revision 1947) makes "essential nature" now "archaic"; runs acts and processes of explaining and distinguishing together, with formulations of meaning such as "dictionary definitions" added to them for good measure; and then secures a snapshot organization for Logic by a scheme under which "traditional logic" deals with the "kinds of thing" in terms of species, genera, and specific differences, while "later schools of logic" deal with statements "either of equivalences of connotation, or intension, or of the reciprocal implications of terms."

Now, a distinction between words and things other than words along conventional lines is easy to make. So is one between an "act" and the products of acts, especially when an "actor," traditionally hypostatized for the purpose, is at hand ready for use. In the present case of the dictionaries, what apparently happens is that if an actor is once

obtained and set to work as a "definer," then all his "defin-
ings" are taken to be one *kind* of act, whether concerned
with words or with things: whereupon their products are
taken as equally of one *kind,* although *as* products they
belong to a realm of "being" different from that to which
actors as actors belong. In the present inquiry we shall
have a continuous eye on the dealings logical definition has
with words and things, and on the manner in which these
dealings rest on its separation of product from acts. We
shall not, however, concern ourselves directly with the
underlying issues as to the status of acts and products with
respect to each other.[5] As to this it is here only to be remarked that in general any such distinction of product
from act is bad form in modern research of the better sort.
Fire, as an "actor," expired with phlogiston, and the presence of individually and personally existing "heat" is no
longer needed to make things hot.

These remarks on what the ordinary dictionaries accomplish should keep our eyes close to the ground — close to
the primary facts of observation — as we advance in our
further examinations. Whether a dictionary attempts pat-
ternings after technical logical expressions, whether it tries
simplified wordings, or whether it turns towards evasive-
ness, its troubles, under direct attention, are in fairly plain
view. Elsewhere the thick undergrowth of verbiage often
subserves a concealment.

II

This inclusion of *what a thing is* with *what a word says*
goes back to Aristotle. Aristotle was an observer and
searcher in the era of the birth of science. With him, as
with his contemporaries, all knowledge, to be sound, or,
as we should say today, to be "scientific," had to win
through to the completely fixed, permanent, and unchangeable: to the "essence" of things, to "Being." Knowledge was present in definition, and *as* definition.[6] Word
and thing, in this way, came before him conjoined. The

search for essences came to be known classically as "clarification." [7] Clarification required search in two directions
at once. Definition must express the essences; it must also
be the process of finding them. Species were delimited
through the "forms" that make them *what* they are. It
was in the form of Speech (*Logos*) that logic and ontology
must come into perfect agreement.

Aristotle thus held together the subjectmatters which
came together. He did not first split apart, only to find
himself later forced to try to fit together again what had
thus been split. The further history is well known to all
workers in this field. The Middle Ages retained the demand for permanence, but developed in the end a sharp
split between the name and thing, with an outcome in
"isms." On one side were the nominalists (word-dizzy, the
irreverent might say), and on the other side the realists
(comparably speaking, thing-dizzy). Between them came
to stand the conceptualists, who, through an artificial device which even today still seems plausible to most logicians, inserted a fictitious locus — the "concept" — in which
to assemble the various issues of word and thing. The age
of Galileo broke down the requirements of immutability,
and substituted uniformities or "laws" for the old "essences" in the field of inquiry. Looking back upon that
age, one might think that the effect of this change on logic
would have been immediate and profound. Not so. Even
today the transformation is incomplete in many respects,
and even the need for it is often not yet brought into the
clear. John Stuart Mill made a voyage of discovery, and
developed much practical procedure, as in the cases of naming and induction, but his logic held to dealings with
"laws" as separate space-time connections presented to
knowledge, and was essentially pre-Darwinian in its scientific setting, so that many of the procedures it stresses
are now antiquated. [8]

The Aristotelian approaches were, however, sufficiently
jarred to permit the introduction in recent times of "non-

Aristotelian" devices. These were forecast by a new logic of relations. These "relations," though not at all "things" of the ancient types, nevertheless struggled from the start (and still struggle) to appear as new variations of the old, instead of as disruptive departures from it. Logical symbols were introduced profusely after the pattern of the older mathematical symbols, but more as usable notations than as the recognition of a new outlook for logic.

In addition to the greatly changed appearance since Greek days of the "objects" presented as "known," as the so-called "contents" of knowledge,[9] there are certain marked differentiations in techniques of presentation (in the organization of "words" and "sentences" to "facts") which are of high significance for the logic of the future. For one thing, there is the difference between what "naming" has come to be in science since Darwin, and what it was before his time; for another, there is the difference between what a mathematical symbol is in mathematics today and what it was when it was still regarded as a type of naming.[10] Neither of these changes has yet been taken up into logical understanding to any great extent, however widely discussion in the ancient forms of expression has been carried on. The common attempt is to reduce logical, mathematical, and scientific procedures to a joint organization (usually in terms of some sort of single mental activity presumed at work behind them) in such a way as to secure a corresponding forced organization of the presumptive "things," logical, mathematical, and scientific, they are supposed to deal with.

One may illustrate by such a procedure as that of Bertrand Russell's "logical atomism," in which neither Russell nor any of his readers can at any time — so far as the "text" goes — be quite sure whether the "atoms" he proposes are minimal "terms" or minimal "reals." Comparably, in those logical systems which use "syntactics" and "semantics," as soon as these distinctions have been made, an attempt follows to bring them together again by "interpre-

tations." But the best of these "interpretations" are little
more than impressionistic manifestations of wishfulness,
gathering within themselves all the confusions and uncertainties which professedly have been expelled from the
primary components. Although the "definitions" in such
treatments are established primarily with reference to "syntactics" they spawn various sub-varieties or queer imitations on the side of "semantics." We seem to have here
exhibits of the conventional isolations of form from content, along with a companionate isolation of things from
minds, of a type that "transactional" [11] observation and
report overcome.

In summary we find word and thing in Aristotle surveyed together but focused on permanence. In the later
Middle Ages they came to be split apart, still with an eye
on permanence, but with nothing by way of working organization except the tricky device of the "concept" as a
third and separate item. Today logic presents, in this historical setting, many varieties of conflicting accounts of
definition, side-slipping across one another, compromising
and apologizing, with little coherence, and few signs of so
much as a beginning of firm treatment. We shall proceed
to show this as of the present. What we may hope for in the
future is to have the gap between name and object done
away with by the aid of a modern behavioral construction
which is Aristotelian in the sense that it is freed from the
post-Aristotelian dismemberment of man's naming activities from his named world, but which at the same time
frees itself from Aristotle's classical demand for permanence in knowledge, and adapts itself to the modern view
of science as in continuing growth.[12] Act and product
belong broadly together, with product, as proceeds, always
in action, and with action always process. Word and thing
belong broadly together, with their provisional severance
of high practical importance in its properly limited range,
but never as full description nor as adequate theoretical
presentation, and always *in* action.

III

Since, as we have said, we are attempting to deal with this situation on the ground level, and in the simplest wordings we can find, it may be well to preface it with a brief account of an inquiry into definition carried on throughout in highly sophisticated professional terminology, which exhibits the confusions in fact, though without denouncing them at their roots. Walter Dubislav's *Die Definition* [13] is the outstanding work in this field. In discussing Kant and Fries he remarks that they do not seem to observe that the names they employ bring together into close relations things that by rights should be most carefully held apart; and in another connection he suggests that one of the important things the logician can do is to warn against confounding definitions with verbal explications of the meaning of words. His analysis yields five types (*Arten*) of definitions, the third of which, he is inclined to think, is merely a special case of the first. These are: (1) Special rules of substitution within a calculus; (2) Rules for the application of the formulas of a calculus to appropriate situations of factual inquiry; (3) Concept-constructions; (4) Historical and juristic clarifications of words in use; (5) Fact-clarifications, in the sense of the determination of the essentials (*Inbegriff*) of things (*Gebilde*), these to be arrived at under strictly logical-mathematical procedure out of basic presuppositions and perceptual determinations, within a frame of theory; and from which in a similar way and under similar conditions all further assertions can be deduced, but with the understanding (so far as Dubislav himself is concerned) that things-in-themselves are excluded as chimerical.[14] A comparison of the complexly terminological composition of No. 5 with the simple statements of Nos. 1, 2, and 4, or even with the specialized appearance of simplicity in No. 3, gives a fair idea of the difficulties of even talking about definition from the older viewpoints.

IV

Definition may be — and often is — talked about as an incidental, or even a minor, phase of logical inquiry. This is the case both when logic is seen as a process of "mind" and when the logician's interest in it is primarily technological. In contrast with this view, the processes of definition may be seen as the throbbing heart — both as pump and as circulation — of the whole knowledge system. We shall take this latter view at least to the extent that when we exhibit the confusions in the current treatments of definition, we believe that we are not exhibiting a minor defect but a vital disease. We believe, further, that here lies the very region where inquiry into naming and the named is the primary need, if dependable organization is to be attained. The field for terminological reform in logic generally is much wider, it is true, than the range of the word "definition" alone, and a brief reminder of these wider needs may be in order. In logic a definition may enter as a proposition, or as a linguistic or mental procedure different from a proposition; while, alternatively, perhaps all propositions may be viewed as definitions. A proposition itself may be almost anything;[15] it consists commonly of "terms," but terms, even while being the "insides" of propositions, may be either words or nonverbal "things." The words, if words enter, may either be meanings, or have meanings. The meanings may be the things "themselves" or other words. Concepts may appear either as "entities" inserted between words and things, or as themselves words, or as themselves things. Properties and qualities are perhaps the worst performers of all. They may be anything or everything, providing it is not too definite.

The following exhibits, some of confusion, others of efforts at clarification, are offered much as they have happened to turn up in current reading, though supplemented by a few earlier memoranda and recollections. We shall display the confusions directly on the body of the texts, but intend thereby nothing invidious to the particular writers. These writers themselves are simply "the facts of the case," and the case itself is one, at this stage, for observation, not for argumentation or debate.

For philosophers' views we may consult the philosophical dictionaries of Baldwin (1901), Eisler (German, 1927), Lalande (French, 1928), and Runes (1942). If definition "clarifies," then the philosophical definitions of definition are far from being themselves definitions. Ancient terminologies are at work, sometimes with a slight modernization, but without much sign of attention to the actual life-processes of living men, as modern sciences tell us about them. Robert Adamson, in Baldwin, proceeds most firmly, but also most closely under the older pattern.[16] Both acts and resultant products are, for him, definitions, but the tops and bottoms of the process — the individual objects, and the *summa genera* — are "indefinables." [17] Nominal definitions concern word-meanings, and real definitions concern the natures of things defined; analytic definitions start with notions as given, and synthetic definitions put the notions together; rational definitions are determined by thought, and empirical definitions by selective processes. This is all very fine in its way, but effectively it says little of present-day interest.

Lalande first identifies "definition" in a "general logic" dealing with the action of *l'esprit;* and then two types in "formal" logic, one assembling known terms to define the concept, the other enunciating equivalences. He also notes the frequent extension of the word "definition" to include all propositions whatsoever. Eisler adds to *Nominaldefinition* and *Realdefinition,* a *Verbaldefinition,* in which one word is merely replaced by others. Besides this main division he reports minor divisions into analytic, synthetic, and implicit, the last representing Hilbert's definition of fundamental geometrical terms.

Alonzo Church, in Runes's dictionary, stands closer to

contemporary practice, but shows still no interest in what
in ordinary modern inquiry would be considered "the facts
of the case," namely, actual uses. He mixes a partial report on contemporary practices with a condensed essay on
the proprieties to such an extent that it is difficult to know
what is happening.[18] For a first grouping of definitions, he
offers (a) (in logistic systems proper) nominal or syntactical
definitions which, as conventional abbreviations or substitutions, are merely a sort of minor convenience for the
logician, though nevertheless, it would seem, they furnish
him one hundred per cent of his assurance; and (b) (in
"interpreted logistic systems") semantical definitions which
introduce new symbols, assign "meanings" to them, and
can not appear in *formal* development, although they may
be "carried" implicitly by nominal definitions, and are
candidates for accomplishing almost anything that may be
wished, under a properly adapted type of "intent." As a
second grouping of definitions he offers the "so-called real"
definitions which are not conventions as are syntactical
and semantical definitions, but instead are "propositions of
equivalence" (material, formal, etc.) between "abstract entities"; which require that the "essential nature" of the
definiendum be "embodied in" the definiens; and which
sometimes, from other points of approach, are taken to
convey assertions of "existence," or at least of "possibility."
He notes an evident "vagueness" in "essential nature" as
this controls "real" definition, but apparently sees no
source of confusion or any other difficulty arising from the
use of the single word "definition" for all these various purposes within an inquiry, nor in the various shadings or mixtures of them, nor in the entry of definienda and definien-
tia, sometimes in "nominal" and sometimes in "real"
forms, nor in livening up the whole procedure, wherever
it seems desirable, with doses of "interpretative" intent.[19]

Here are other specimens, old and new, of what is said
about definition. Carnap expressly and without qualification declares that a definition "means" that a definiendum

THE CASE OF DEFINITION

"is to be an abbreviation for" a definiens, but in the same inquiry introduces definitions that are not explicit but recursive, and provides for definition rules as well as for definition sentences. Elsewhere he employs two "kinds" of definition, those defining respectively logical and empirical "concepts," and makes use of various reduction processes to such an extent that he is spoken of at times as using "conditioned" definitions.[20] Tarski makes definition a stipulation of meaning which "uniquely determines," differentiating it thus from "designation" and "satisfaction."[21] An often quoted definition of definition by W. L. Davidson is that "It is the object of Definition to determine the nature or meaning or signification of a thing: in other words definition is the formal attempt to answer the question 'What is it?'"[22] H. W. B. Joseph writes: "The definition of anything is the statement of its essence: what makes it that, and not something else."[23] J. H. Woodger limits the word for axiom-systems to "one quite definite sense," the "explicit" — understanding thereby substitutability; however differently the word might elsewhere be used.[24] Henry Margenau distinguishes between constitutive and operational.[25] A. J. Ayer has "explicit" or "synonymous" definition in contrast with philosophical "definition in use."[26] Morris Weitz employs the names "real" and "contextual."[27] A. W. Burks proposes to develop a theory of ostensive definition which describes "definition in terms of presented instances, rather than in terms of already defined concepts," and says that counter-instances as well as instances must be pointed at; such definition is thereupon declared to be classification.[28] W. E. Johnson decides that "every definition must end with the indefinable," where the indefinable is "that whose meaning is so directly and universally understood, that it would be mere intellectual dishonesty to ask for further definition"; he also thinks, interestingly enough, that it would "seem legitimate . . . to define a proper name as a name which *means* the same as what it *factually indi-*

cates." [29] G. E. Moore insists on a sharp separation between defining a word and defining a concept, but leaves the reader wholly uncertain as to what the distinction between word and concept itself might be in his system, or how it might be defined to others.[30] What current philosophizing can accomplish under the aegis of the loose and vagrant use of "definition" by the logics is illustrated by Charles Hartshorne in a definition of "reality" which ideal knowledge is said to "provide" or "give" us by the aid of a preliminary definition of "perfect knowledge." This "definition" of "reality" is: "The real is whatever is content of knowledge ideally clear and certain," [31] and in it, however innocent and simple the individual words may look separately, there is not a single word that, in its immediate context, is itself clear or certain.

The above specimens look a good deal like extracts from a literature of escape, and some might rate well in a literature of humor. No wonder that Professor Nagel says of Bertrand Russell (who may be regarded as one of the ablest and most active investigators of our day in such matters) that "it is often most puzzling to know just what he is doing when he says that he is 'defining' the various concepts of mathematics";[32] and that Professor Skinner, discussing the problems of operational definition with some of his psychological colleagues, tells them that while definition is used as a "key-term," it itself is not "rigorously defined," and that "modern logic . . . can scarcely be appealed to by the psychologist who recognizes his own responsibility." [33]

V

Turn next to recent reports of research into the question. A paper by H. H. Dubs, "Definition and its Problems," [34] gives an excellent view of the difficulties logicians face when they strive to hold these many processes together as one. Present theories of definition are recognized by him as confused, and the time is said to have arrived when it has become necessary to "think through" the whole subject afresh. Throwing dictionary definition [35] aside as irrelevant, "scientific definitions" are studied as alone of logical import, with logic and mathematics included among the sciences. Science itself is described as a linkage of concepts, and the general decision is reached for definition that it must tell us what the "concepts" are which are to be associated with a "term or word" so as to determine when, "in immediate experience or thought," there is present the "entity or event" denoted by that term or word.

Definitions, in Dubs' development, are classified as conceptual or non-conceptual. The former is, he says, what others often call "nominal" and occurs where term is linked only with term. The latter are inevitable and occur where the linkage runs back to "logical ultimates" or "indefinables." Cutting across this classification appears another into "essential" and "nominal" (sometimes styled "real" and "accidental") depending on whether we can or can not so define a term as to denote "all" the properties of the object or other characteristic defined. Practically, he reports, scientific definition consists almost entirely of the conceptual and the nominal, even though "scientific" has been adopted as the name of *all* definition pertinent to logic.

If we examine the non-conceptual indefinables in this presentation, we find that they consist of (*a*) causal operations (necessarily "wordless"), (*b*) direct pointings or denotings (that "cannot be placed in books"), and (*c*) intermediate hermaphroditic specimens, half pointings and half verbalizings. Dubs is not at all pleased to find his scheme of definition falling back upon the "indefinable," but his worry is mainly in the sense that he would prefer to reach "ultimates." He solaces himself slightly by hoping that it is just an affair of nomenclature. Nevertheless, since in certain cases, such as those of logic and mathematics, indefinables are seen entering which, he feels sure, are *not* ultimates, he feels compelled to keep the "indefinable" as an outstanding component of definition (or, shall we say, of the "definable"?) without permitting this peculiarity to detract from the hope that he has secured a new "practical and consistent" theory.

Especially to note is that while his leading statement about definition depends upon the use of such words as "concept," "term or word," "immediate experience," "thought," and "entity or event," no definition or explanation of any sort for these underlying words is given. They rate thus, perhaps, as the indefinables of the definition of definition itself, presumably being taken as so well known in their mental contexts that no question about them will be raised. We have already seen the indefinable mentioned by Adamson and Johnson (and the related "ostensive" by Burks), and we shall see more of the peculiar problem they raise as we go along.

Consider another type of examination such as that offered by John R. Reid under the title: "What are Definitions?" [36] Here the effort is to solve the problem of definition not by classifying, but by the building up, or "integration," of a "system of ideas" into an "articulated unity." Taking for consideration what he calls a "definitional situation," he distinguishes within it the following "factors" or "components": a "definitional relation," a "definitional operation," and a "definitional rule." While distinct, these factors are not to be taken as "isolated." The "rule" seemingly is given top status, being itself three-dimensional, and thus involving sets of symbols, sets of cognitive interpretants, and particular cases to which the rule can apply. He holds that we can not *think* at all without this definitional equipment, and stresses at the same time that the symbols, as part of the equipment, would not exist at all except in mental activity. This makes "mental activity" both cause and product, and apparently much the same is true for "symbol." The above points are elaborately developed, but all that is offered us in the way of information about definition itself is a recognition, in currently conventional form, that definitions may be either "syntactical" or "semantical," and that the word "definition" remains ambiguous unless it has an accompanying adjective thus to qualify it. This difference is assumed, but the differentiation is not studied; nor, apparently, is it considered to be of much significance in theory.

Not by pronouncement, but in their actual procedures, both Dubs and Reid bring definition under examination as a facultative activity in the man who does the defining and who is the "definer," and as having, despite its many varieties, a single "essential" type of output. Where Dubs undertakes through cross-classifications to make the flagrant conflicts in the output appear harmonious, Reid strives to establish unity through a multiplication of "entities," arriving thus only at a point at which the reader, according to his likings, will decide either that far too many entities are present, or nowhere near enough.[37]

VI

Let us turn next to the deliberation of a group of six scientists and logicians in a recent symposium from which we have already quoted one speaker's pungent comment.[38] On the list of questions offered by the American Psychological Association for especial examination was one (No. 10), which asked: "What is a Definition, operational or otherwise?" Two of the contributors, so far as they used the word "definition" at all, used it in conventional ways, and gave no direct attention to its problems, so we can pass them by. Two others, Feigl and Boring, used stylized phrasings, one in a slightly sophisticated, the other in a currently glib form, and have interest here merely to note the kind of tunes that can be played.

Feigl regards definition as useful in minor ways in helping to specify meanings for terms or symbols. Since it deals with terms or symbols it is always "nominal," and the "so-called real" definitions rate as mere descriptions or identifications. Nevertheless, although all definition is "nominal," it always terminates in something "not nominal," namely, observation. This might leave the reader uncertain whether a definition is still a definition after it has got beyond the nominal stage, but Feigl gets rid of this difficulty by calling it "a mere question of terminology." Boring defines definition as a "statement of equivalence," and says it can apply between a term and other terms or between a term and "events"—blandly inattentive to the question as to just in what sense a "term" can be *equivalent* to an "event." He further distinguishes definitions as either operational or non-operational, without, apparently, any curiosity as to the nature of the difference between the operational and the non-operational, nor as to what might happen to an assured equivalence on the operation table with or without benefit of anesthetic.

This leaves two contributors to the symposium, Bridgman, the physicist, and Skinner, the psychologist, to give useful practical attention to the business in hand, operational and definitional.[39] Bridgman, standing on the firm practical ground he has long held with respect to physical procedure, treats definitions as statements applying to terms. Such definitions, he says, presuppose checking or verifying operations, and are thus not only operational, but so completely so that to call them "operational" is a tautology. Skinner, making the same kind of hard, direct operational analysis of the psychological terms that Bridgman made twenty years ago for physical terms, tosses out by the handful the current evasive and slippery phrasings wherever he finds them, and lays the difficulties, both in the appraisals of operation and in the appraisals of definition, to the fact that underlying observation and report upon human behaviors are still far too incomplete to give dependable results. He rejects dualisms of word and meaning, and then settles down to the application of plain, practical, common sense to the terminology in use — to the problem, namely, of what words can properly stand for in observation and experimentation in progress, and to the tentative generalizations that can be made from the facts so established. Skinner agrees with Bridgman that operational analysis applies to all definitions. For him a good answer to the question "What is a definition?" would require, first of all, "a satisfactory formulation of the effective verbal behavior of the scientist." His own undertaking is to contribute to the answer "by example." The others in this symposium might well be asked to become definite as to the status of whatever it is they mean when they say "*non*-operational."

The examinations, both by Bridgman and by Skinner, are held to the regions we ourselves have styled "specification" in distinction from those of "symbolization." For us they lead the way from the antiquated manners of approach used by the other workers we have just examined to three papers, published in *The Journal of Philosophy* in 1945 and 1946, in which much definite progress has been made. They are by Abraham Kaplan, Ernest Nagel, and Stephen C. Pepper. We shall note the advances made and the openings they indicate for future work. We regret it if other equally advanced investigations have failed to attract our attention.

VII

Kaplan's paper is styled "Definition and Specification of Meaning." [40] In it he examines "specification of meaning" as a process for improving the applicability of terms, and as thus leading the way towards definition in the older logical sense of a "logical equivalence between the term defined and an expression whose meaning has already been specified." He sets up the connection between specification and equivalence of meaning as a goal, but does not undertake to deal with its problems, limiting himself here instead to an examination of some of the matters to take account of in such a theory. He acutely observes that much of the best work of science is done with "concepts" such as that

of species for which all the long efforts of the biologists
have failed to secure any "definition" whatever, and proceeds to ask how this can be possible if definition is so
potent and so essential as logicians make it out to be. Treating "specification of meaning" as "hypothetical throughout," he leads up to the question: How does such a development of meaning come to approximate, and in the
end to attain, the character of logical definition in which
the meanings are no longer held within the limits of hypothesis (though, nevertheless, under the reservation that
in the end, definition may possibly come to appear as "only
a special form of specification")?

A great field of inquiry is thus opened, but certain difficulties at once demand attention. Kaplan employs, as if
well understood, certain key-words in connection with
which he gives no hint of specification on their own account. These include such words as "concept," "term,"
and "meaning." In what sense, for example, in his own
development, does "specification of meaning" tell more
than "specification" alone? What additional "meaning"
is added by the word "meaning"? Is this "meaning" in any
way present apart from or in addition to its "specification"?
If "meaning" adds anything, should its particular contribution not be made clear at an early point in the treatment
— a point earlier, indeed, than Kaplan's present discussion?
What is the difference between "meaning" by itself and
"meaning of a term" — a phrase often alternatively used?
If "term" has to have a "meaning" and its "meaning" has
to be separately "specified," is the inquiry not being carried on at a stage twice removed — and unnecessarily removed at that — from direct observation? If three stages of
"fact" are thus employed, should not their differentiation
be clearly established, or their manner of entry at least
be indicated? These questions are asked, not to discourage,
but as encouragement for, the further examination which
Kaplan proposes, if the relations of equivalence and specification are to be understood.

VIII

Nagel, in his paper "Some Reflections on the Use of Language in the Natural Sciences," [41] understands by "definition" very much what Kaplan understands by specification. He does not, for the immediate purposes of his discussion of language, generalize the problem as Kaplan does, but he shows brilliantly the continuous revision and reconstruction of uses which an active process of definition involves. We have already cited, in passing, his valuable pages on the growing abandonment by mathematicians of their older expectations that their symbols should have efficient status as names. He provides an illuminating illustration of the underlying situation in the case of "constant instantial velocity" which by its very manner of phrasing makes it operationally the "name" of nothing at all, while nevertheless it steadily maintains its utility as a phrase.[42] He eliminates the claims of those types of expression which, applied in a variety of meanings through a variety of contexts, manage to fascinate or hypnotize the men who use them into believing that, as expressions, they possess "a generic meaning common to all" their varieties of applications. He could even have used his own word "definition" as an excellent example of such a form of expression. In the background of his vividly developed naturalistic appraisal of the processes of knowledge, all of these steps have high significance for further progress.

IX

Pepper's account of "The Descriptive Definition" [43] undertakes a form of construction in the very region which Kaplan indicates as locus of the great problem. His "descriptive definition" is so close to what we ourselves have described as "specification" that, so far as his introductory characterization goes, we could gladly accept his account of it, perhaps free from any reservation, as meeting our needs. It offers at the least a fair alternative report to that

which we seek. His framework of interpretation is, however, another matter, and his "descriptive definition," as
he sees it, is so intricately built into that framework that it
must be appraised as it there comes.

Like Kaplan, with his specification of meaning, Pepper
envisions the old logical definition as basic to the display
and justification of a descriptive definition. He notes that
"in empirical enquiry observers desire expressions which
ascribe meaning to symbols with the definite proviso that
these meanings shall be as nearly true to fact as the available evidence makes possible." To this end the reference
of description is "practically never" to be taken as "unalterable." He does not offer a fully positive statement,
but at least, as he puts it in one phrasing, the "reference"
of the symbol under the description is "intended" to be
altered whenever "the description can be made more nearly
true." The descriptive definition thus becomes "a convenient tool constantly responsible to the facts," rather
than "prescriptive in empirical enquiry." [44]

So far so good. Men are shown seeking knowledge of
fact, elaborating descriptions, and changing names to fit
improved descriptions. But Pepper finds himself facing
the query whether this is "definition" at all? Perhaps,
he reflects, the nominal and the real definitions of logical
theory, the equations, the substitutions, and the ostensive
definitions have exclusive rights to the field and will reject "descriptive" definitions as intruders? At any rate he
feels it necessary to organize descriptive definition with
respect to these others, and with a continuing eye on the
question whether he can get from or through them authority for what he wishes to accomplish. Though still com-
mitting himself to the wearing of a coat of many definitional colors, the organization he seeks is in a much more
modern spirit than the classifications of Dubs or the "articulated unity" of Reid.

He begins by making descriptive definition one of two
great branches of definition. Against it he sets nominal

definition. The former is known by its being "responsible to facts meant by the symbol." The latter is not thus responsible, but either assumes or ignores facts, or else is irrelevant to them. Nominal definition in turn has two species: the equational and the ostensive.

The equational species is said to be strictly and solely a matter of the substitution of symbols. Whether this is an adequate expression for all that goes on in the equational processes of mathematics and in the development of equivalences, and whether it is really adequate for his own needs, Pepper does not discuss. What he is doing is to adopt a manner of treatment that is conventional among logicians who deal with logical "products" displayed on logical shelves instead of with the logical activity of living men, even though his own procedure is, culturally speaking, much further advanced than is theirs. For our present purposes we need to note that in *his* program equational definition is substitution — it is *this, and nothing more.*

The ostensive species of definition is (or "involves" or "refers to") a non-symbolic meaning or source of meaning for a symbol. It is primarily and typically a "pointing at." Pepper here examines the "facts" before him with excellent results. He suggests the interpretation of such "pointing" as "indication," and then of "indication" as "operation." The indicative "operation" at which he arrives in place of ostensive definition along the older lines is, however, still allotted status as itself a "definition." In this, there is a survival of influences of the "word and thing" mixture, even at the very moment when important steps are being taken to get rid of such conventional congealment. Old-timers could talk readily of "ostensive *definition*" because they lived reasonably misty lives and avoided analysis in uncomfortable quarters. Pepper makes a pertinent analysis, and we are at once startled into asking: Why and how can such an ostensive or indicative operation be itself called a "definition" in any careful use of either of the words, "ostensive" or "definition"? Is there something

logically in common between finger-pointing without
name-using, and name-using without finger or other pointing action? If so, just *what* is it? And above all, just *where*
does it "existentially" have specific location?

Pepper's problem, now, is to organize the descriptive to
the ostensive and to the equational. The problem is of
such great importance, and every fresh exploration of it is
of such great interest, that we shall take the space to show
what is apt to happen when "substitution" in the guise of
"equation" is employed as organizer for a presumptively
less dependable "description." We are given three dia-
grams, and these with their accompanying texts should be
carefully studied. The diagram for equational definition
shows that the symbol, "*S*," is "equated with" and is "*equationally* defined by" other "symbols." The diagram for
ostensive definition shows that such an "*S*" "indicates"
and is "*ostensively* defined by" an "empirical fact," "*O*."
The diagram for descriptive definition expands to triadic
form. "*S*" is symbol as before. "*O*" is advanced from
"fact" to "field," while remaining empirical. "*D*" is added
to stand for description. Further distinctive of this diagram is the entry into its formulations of the words
"tentative," "hypothetical," and "verifies," along with "describes." The scheme of the diagram then develops in two
parallel manners of expression, or formulations:

	FORMULATION A	FORMULATION B
1.	$(D\text{-}O)$: D hypothetically describes	(or) is verified by .... O.
2.	$(S\text{-}D)$: S is tentatively equated with	(or) is descriptively defined by D.
3.	$(S\text{-}O)$: S tentatively indicates	(or) is ostensively defined by O.[45]

Under Formulation A, it would seem easy or "natural"
to condense the statements to read that, given a hypothetical description of "something," we can take a word to stand
tentatively for that description, and this word will then also
serve as a tentative indication of the "something." Under
Formulation B, we might similarly say (though various
other renderings are possible) that, given a verified description of something, that description descriptively defines a

word which in turn is (or is taken as) ostensively defined
by the something; or we might perhaps more readily think
of an ostensive hint leading through naming and description to verification or imagined verification followed by a
thumping return to "ostensive *definition.*" (In a discussion
in another place Pepper, to some extent, simplifies his report by saying of the descriptive definition that "strictly
speaking, it is an arbitrary determination of the meaning
of a symbol in terms of a symbol group, subject, however,
to the verifiability of the symbol group in terms of certain
indicated facts.")[46] But would it not be still more informative if one said that what substantially this all comes to
is a report that men possess language in which they describe events (facts, fields) — that they can substitute single
words for groups of words — that the groups of words may
be called descriptive definitions — and that the words so
substituted serve to indicate the facts described, and, when
regarded as "verified," are linked with "indicative operations" styled "ostensive"?

Thus simplified (if he will permit it) Pepper's development may be regarded as an excellent piece of work
towards the obliteration of ancient logical pretenses, and
it might well be made required reading in preliminary
academic study for every budding logician for years to
come. Our only question is as to the effectiveness of his
procedure, for he carries it on as if it were compelled to
subject itself to the antique tests supplied by the traditional
logical scheme. We may ask: if equation is substitution or
substitutability — precisely this, and nothing else — why
not call it substitution in place of equation? Would not
such an unequivocal naming rid us of a bit of verbal
trumpery, and greatly heighten definiteness of understanding? If equation runs pure and true from symbol to symbol, what possibly can "tentative" equating be as a type
of equating itself, and not merely as a preliminary stage in
learning? If one turns the phrase "is equated with" into
the active form "equals," how pleasing is it to find oneself

saying that "*S* tentatively equals *D*"? Or, if we are told, as in one passage, that the description is "not flatly equated" with the symbol, but only equated "to the best of our abilities," does this add clarity? Descriptions are meant to be altered, but equations not; again, the question arises, how is it that descriptive definitions can be equated? How can "verifies" become an alternative phrasing for "hypothetically describes"? Should not the alternative form in the diagram be perhaps, "hypothetically verifies," but then what difference would there be between it and "description" itself? In introducing the "ostensive," Pepper views it in the older manner as dealing with "facts of immediacy," despite his own later reduction of it to indicative operation, and his retention of it as definition.[47] But just what could a tentative immediacy be?

The main question, further, remains: Why employ one single name, even under the differentiations of genus and species, for such varied situations in human behavior? If we take "*e*" for equationally, "*o*" for ostensively, and "*d*" for descriptively, Pepper's varieties of definition may be set down as follows:

e-defined is where a word *S* is substitutable for other words.

o-defined is where a word is used operationally to indicate an object, *O*.

d-defined is where a word tentatively indicates an *O*, by being tentatively substitutable for a description, *D*, which latter hypothetically describes the *O;* or alternatively (and perhaps at some different phase of inquiry), *d*-defined is where a word is *o*-defined *via,* or in connection with, the verification" of the *D* by the *O.*

In preliminary, conventional forms of statement, the report would seem to be that the *e*-definition, *as he offers it* (though we do not mean to commit ourselves to such a view), seems to be primarily a matter of language-organization; the *o*-definition seems to lie in a region commonly, though very loosely, called "experience"; and the *d*-definition, so far as any one can yet see, does not seem to lie comfortably anywhere as a species of a common genus.

X

We have seen many conflicting renderings of the word "definition" offered us by acute investigators who are currently engaged in a common enterprise in a common field. Recalling these conflicts, may one not properly say that this display by itself, and just as it stands, provides sufficient reason for a thorough terminological overhaul; and that, without such an overhaul and reorganization, the normal practical needs for intercommunication in research will fail to be properly met? The one word "definition" is expected to cover acts and products, words and things, accurate descriptions and tentative descriptions, mathematical equivalences and exact formulations, ostensive definitions, sensations and perceptions in logical report, "ultimates," and finally even "indefinables." [48] No one word, anywhere in careful technical research, should be required to handle so many tasks. Where, outside of logic — except, perhaps, in ancient theology or modern stump-speaking — would such an assertion be tolerated as that of the logicians when, among the "definables" of definition, they push "indefinables" boldly to the front? Here seems to be a witches' dance, albeit of pachydermally clumsy logical will-o'-the-wisps. What more propriety is there in making definition cover such diversities than there would be in letting some schoolboy, poring perversely over the pages of a dictionary, report that the Bengal tiger, the tiger-lily, the tiger on the box, and the tiger that one on occasion bucks, are all species of one common genus: *Tiger?*

The types of definition we have inspected appear to fall roughly into three groups: namely, equivalence as in mathematics, specification as in science, and a traditionally derived mixed logical form which hopes and maneuvers to establish specifications ultimately under a perfected logical pattern of equivalences. The worst of the affair is that present-day logic not only accepts these different activities and all their varieties as evident phases of a common process, but actually sees the great goal of all its labors to lie in their fusion into a single process, or unit in the logical system. The outcome is just the chaos we have seen.

The problem here to be solved is not one for a debating society, nor is it one for a formal calculating machine. It requires to be faced in its full historical linguistic-cultural setting. The great phases of this setting to consider are: the *logos* and the Aristotelian essences; the late medieval fracture of namings from the named as separate "things" in the exaggerated forms of "nominals" and "reals"; the artifically devised "concept" inserted to organize them; the survival into modern times of this procedure by conceptual proxy under a common, though nowhere clarified, substitution of "word" (or "sentence") for "concept"; the resultant confusedly "independent" or "semi-independent" status of "words," "terms," and "propositions" as components of subjectmatter; and finally the unending logical discussion of the connections of science and mathematics carried on in the inherited terminology, or in slight modifications of it, with no adequate factual examination at any stage, of the modern developments of scientific designation and mathematical symbolization in their own rights.

In this setting, and in the illustrations we have given, one feature appears that has great significance for our present consideration as showing the excesses to which the existing terminological pretenses may lead. This is the entry, of which we have repeatedly taken note,[49] and which will now receive a little closer attention, of the "ultimates" and "indefinables" as components at once of "definition" and of "reality." What we have called "specifications" and "symbolizations" can surely rate as current coin of the logical fields, no matter who does the investigating, and

no matter how thorough or how precarious today's understanding of them is. The "indefinables" and the "ultimates," in contrast, are counterfeit. In them, as they enter
logical discussion, we have neither good working names,
nor intelligible equivalences, nor verifiable factual references, but instead pretenses of being, or of having more or
less the values of, all three at once. They enter through
"ostensive" definitions, or through some verbal alternative
for the ostensive, but in such a way that we are unable to
tell whether the "definition" itself is "about" something,
or "is" the something which it is "about," or how such
phrasings as "is" and "is about" are used, or just what
meanings they convey. John Stuart Mill remarked a hundred years ago that, however "unambiguously" one can
make known who the particular man is to whom a name
belongs "by pointing to him," such pointing "has not been
esteemed one of the modes of definition." [50] "Pointing" on
the basis of previous mutual understanding is one thing,
but the kind of understanding (or definition) that might
be developed from pointing alone in a communicational
vacuum, offers a very different sort of problem. Nevertheless, regardless of all such absurdities the ostensive definition, since Mill's time, has gained very considerable repute,
and is, indeed, a sort of benchmark for much modern logic,
to which, apparently, the possession of such a name as
"ostensive definition" is guarantee enough that somewhere
in the cosmos there must exist a good, hard fact to go with
the name. The ostensives, and their indefinables and ultimates, seem, indeed, to be a type of outcome that is un-
avoidable when logic is developed as a manipulation of old
terminologies using "definers," "realities," and "names"
as separate components, instead of being undertaken as an
inquiry into a highly specialized form of the behaviors of
men in the world around them. Ostensive behavior can be
found. Definitional behavior can be found. But the mere
use of the words "ostensive definition" is not enough to
solve the problem of their organization.

If we try, we may take these procedures of defining the indefinables apart so as to see, in a preliminary way at least, what they are made of and how they work. What are these indefinables and ultimates assumed to be (or, verbally, to stand for) as they enter definition? Are they regarded as either "physical" or "mental"? Usually not. Instead they are spoken of as "logical" entities or existences, a manner of phrasing as to which the less it is inquired into, the better for it. Certainly there are words involved, because, without its linguistic presentation as "ostensive," there is no way, apparently, in which such definition would be before our attention at all. Certainly, also, there are "things" involved — "things" in the sense of whatever it is which is beyond the finger in the direction the finger points. Certainly also there is a great background of habit and orientation, of behavior and environment, involved in every such pointing. More than this, in any community using language — and it is a bit difficult to see how definition in any form would be under close scrutiny except in a language-using community — a large part of the background of such pointing is linguistic. Suppose we consider as sample exhibits in the general region of pointings a masterless wild dog alert and tense with nose turned towards scent of game; a trained pointer in field with hunting master, the master pointing with hand for benefit of comrade towards sign of motion in brush; a savage hunter pointing or following with his eye another hunter's pointing; a tropic savage as guest in arctic watching Eskimo's finger pointed towards never-before-seen snow, and finally, the traditional Patagonian getting first sight of locomotive as Londoner points it out. Traditionally the Patagonian sees nothing of what a locomotive "is," and certainly it would be stretching matters to assume that the immediate case of "pointing" *defined* the locomotive to him.[52] Hardly anywhere would a theorist speak of the wild dog as engaged in definition. In the intervening cases there are various gradations of information established or imparted *via* sign.

THE CASE OF DEFINITION

Where does distinctive "definition" begin, and why?
Where does it cease, and why? These questions concern
varieties of events happening, and names needed in their
study.

It is our most emphatically expressed belief that such a
jumble of references as the word "definition" in the logics
has today to carry can not be brought into order until a
fair construction of human behaviors across the field is set
up, nor until within that construction a general theory of
language on a full behavioral basis has been secured.[51] We
have sketched tentatively in preceding chapters some of the
characteristics which we believe such construction will
have. Identifying behavior in general with organic-environmental sign-process, transactionally viewed, we have
noted the perceptive-manipulative activities at one end of
the range, and then three stages of the designatory use of
language, followed by another type of use in symbolization. Given such a map of the behavioral territory, the
various sorts of human procedure insistently lumped together under the name of "definition" could be allocated
their proper operating regions. Among them the "ostensive," now so absurdly present, should be able, under a
much needed transmutation, to find a proper home.

1 See especially Chapter II, Section IV, #5.

2 For this terminology, see Chapter VI, Section IV.

3 See Chapter II, Section IV, #5; Chapter VI, note 4; see also Chapter
XI.

4 We omit, of course, entries irrelevant to the problem of knowings and
knowns.

5 For some illustrations of the separation of "acts" and "products" in
the logics, under a variety of formulations, see Chapter I, particularly
Sections I and X. In Chapter IX product follows product and by-product
follows by-product; here Sections I and IV exhibit the range of wordings
employed. In Chapter VIII five of the six logicians examined make use
of separable products under one form or another as basic to their constructions.

6 "Opinion" was allowed for as dealing with uncertainties, but on a lower level. It was *not* science; it was *not* definition.

7 Felix Kaufmann is one of the comparatively few workers in this field who make deliberate and sustained — and in his case, powerful — efforts to develop "clarification" in the classical sense (*Methodology of the Social Sciences,* [New York, 1944]. He expressly affirms this approach (*Philosophy and Phenomenological Research*, Vol. V, 1945, p. 351) in the sense of *Meno*, 74 ff., and *Theaetetus*, 202 ff.

8 Mill managed to see adjectives as names (*Logic*, I, i, Chapter II, Section 2) but not adverbs. By way of illustration drawn from our immediate range of subjectmatters, consider how much sharper and clearer the adverb "definitely" is in its practical applications than is an adjectival assertion of definite*ness*, or a purported "nounal" determination of what "definition" substantively *is*.

9 Consider, for example, astronomy, with respect to which Greek science found itself inspecting a fixed solar system moving about the fixed earth, with sun and moon moving backward and forward, and the firmament of fixed stars rotating above. Its physics offered four fixed elements, different in essence with earth movements downward toward their proper "end"; fire movements upwards into the heavens; air and gas movements upwards as far as the clouds or moon; and water movements, and those of all liquids, back and forth. Its biology had fixed animal and plant species, which remained fixed until Darwin.

10 The problem in this respect began as far back as the first uses of zero or minus-one, and has only disappeared with the heavy present employment of the wave in mathematical formulation. Professor Nagel has lately given such fine illustrations of this status that, with his permission, we should like to recommend to the reader the examination of his pages as if directly incorporated at this point as a part of our text (*The Journal of Philosophy*, XLII, 1945, pp. 625-627).

11 See Chapter V.

12 Compare the development in John Dewey, *Logic, The Theory of Inquiry*, Chap. XXI, on "Scientific Method: Induction and Deduction," especially pages 419, 423, 424.

13 Third edition, (Leipzig, 1931), 160 pages (*Beihefte der "Erkenntnis"*, 1). Citations from pages 17, 131. Historically Dubislav finds four main "theories" of definition: the Aristotelian essence and its successors to date (*Wesensbestimmung*); the determination of concepts (*Begriffsbestimmung*); the fixation of meanings, historical and juristic (*Feststellung der Bedeutung . . . bzw., der Verwendung*); and the establishment of new signs (*Festsetzung über die Bedeutung . . . bzw., der Verwendung*).

14 The characterization of type No. 5 in the text above is assembled from two paragraphs of Dubislav's text (pp. 147, 148) which are apparently similar, but still not alike in content. Dubislav's own view as to

what should be regarded as definition makes use of type No. 1 along lines of development from Frege to Hilbert (with a backward glance at Pascal), and in the expectation that its "formal" can be made "useful" through definitions of type No. 2.

15 For illustrations and references as to propositions, see Chapter VIII, Section V.

16 Adamson, who was one of the most impartial observers and keenest appraisers of logical theory, himself remarked in *A Short History of Logic* (Edinburgh and London, 1911), pp. 19-20, that "looking to the chaotic state of logical textbooks . . . one would be inclined to say that there does not exist anywhere a recognized, currently received body of speculations to which the title logic can be unambiguously assigned."

17 The introduction of such an "indefinable," of which we shall later find various examples, is, in effect, to make proclamation of ultimate impotence precisely at the spot in logical inquiry where sound practical guidance is the outstanding need.

18 It is proper to recall that the contributors to Runes's dictionary had much fault to find with the way their copy was edited, and that, therefore, the dictionary text may not fully represent Professor Church's intention. The difficulty to be stressed is, however, not peculiar to his report. A similar confused mixture of what is "historical" with what is "factual" is general. The Runes classification, as we find it, is in this respect vague at almost every point of differentiation. More broadly for all four philosophical dictionaries, the manifestly unclarified phrasings seem to outnumber the attempted clarifications a dozen to one.

19 How curiously this sort of thing works out can be seen in the opening pages of Church's *Introduction to Mathematical Logic,* Part I (Princeton, 1944), in which he writes (p. 1): "In the formal development we eschew attributing any meanings to the symbols of the Propositional Calculus"; and (p. 2): "We shall be guided implicitly by the interpretation we eventually intend to give it." Repeated examinations which several interested inquirers have made into Church's words, "meanings," "natural," "necessary," "language," "implicit," and "interpretation," as he has used them in the context of the sentences just quoted, have given no aid towards reducing the fracture in his constructional bone. As pertinent to the issue it may be recalled that Kurt Gödel, in analyzing Russell's procedure, came to the conclusion that Russell's formalism could not "explain away" the view that "logic and mathematics (just as physics) are built up on axioms with a real content" (*The Philosophy of Bertrand Russell,* P. A. Schilpp, editor [Chicago, 1944] p. 142). Again, Hermann Weyl in the *American Mathematical Monthly,* (1946), p. 12, remarks of Hilbert that "he is guided by an at least vaguely preconceived plan for such a proof."

20 Carnap, R., *Introduction to Semantics* (Cambridge, 1942), pp. 17, 31, 158. "Testability and Meaning," *Philosophy of Science,* III, (1936), pp. 419-471, especially pp. 431, 439, 448; IV, (1937), pp. 1-40.

21 *Introduction to Logic* (New York, 1941), pp. 33-36, pp. 118 ff. "The Semantic Conception of Truth," *Philosophy and Phenomenological Research,* IV (1944), 345, and notes 20 and 35.

22 *The Logic of Definition* (London, 1885), p. 32.

23 *An Introduction to Logic* (Oxford, 1916), p. 72.

24 *The Axiomatic Method in Biology* (Cambridge, England, 1937), p. 4.

25 "On the Frequency Theory of Probability," *Philosophy and Phenomenological Research,* VI (1945), p. 17.

26 *Language, Truth and Logic* (New York, 1936), pp. 66-69. A comparison of the respective uses of the word "explicit" by Carnap, Woodger, and Ayer might be instructive.

27 "The Unity of Russell's Philosophy," in *The Philosophy of Bertrand Russell* (P. A. Schilpp, editor) (Chicago, 1944), pp. 120-121. The following pronouncement (p. 121) on the subject would seem worthy of profound pondering: "The value or purpose of real and contextual definitions is that they reduce the vaguenesses of certain complexes by calling attention to their various components."

28 "Empiricism and Vagueness," *The Journal of Philosophy,* XLIII (1946), p. 479.

29 *Logic* (Cambridge, England, 1921), Vol. I, pp. 105-106; p. 93.

30 "A Reply to My Critics," in *The Philosophy of G. E. Moore* (P. A. Schilpp, editor) (Chicago, 1942), pp. 663-666.

31 "Ideal Knowledge Defines Reality: What was True in 'Idealism,'" *The Journal of Philosophy,* XLIII (1946), p. 573.

32 In his contribution to *The Philosophy of Bertrand Russell,* edited by P. A. Schilpp, p. 326.

33 "Symposium on Operationism," *Psychological Review,* LII, (1945), pp. 270-271.

34 *Philosophical Review,* LII, (1943), pp. 566 ff.

35 It is interesting to note that one of his requirements for a dictionary definition is that it "must be capable of being written down." This is not demanded for the "scientific definition" for which there are "two and only two" specific requirements: it must be commensurate with what it defines, and it must define a term only in terms that have been previously defined.

36 *Philosophy of Science,* XIII, (1946), pp. 170-175.

37 Reid's asserted background for his inquiry into definition may be illustrated by the further citations: "A . . . relation is the symbolic product

of an . . . operation . . . according to . . . rule." "These distinctions are
. . . not only 'real' . . . but . . . fundamental for . . . understanding."
We must not deny "the irreducible complexity of the relevant facts."
"Definitions . . . are . . . not assertable statements." Reid is here frank
and plain about what ought to be in the open, but which in most discussions of definition is left tacit.

[38] "Symposium on Operationism," *Psychological Review,* LII, (1945),
pp. 241-294. Introduction by the editor, Herbert S. Langfeld. Contributions by Edwin G. Boring, P. W. Bridgman, Herbert Feigl, Harold E.
Israel, Carroll C. Pratt, and B. F. Skinner.

[39] Bridgman, however, is still deeply concerned with his old query as
to the "public" *vs.* the "private" in knowledge; and the other contributors
were so bemused by it that in the seventeen pages of "rejoinders and second thoughts" following the primary papers, one-third of all the paragraphs directly, and possibly another third indirectly, had to do with this
wholly fictitious, time-wasting issue.

[40] *The Journal of Philosophy,* XLIII (1946), pp. 281-288.

[41] *The Journal of Philosophy,* XLII (1945), pp. 617-630.

[42] His statement, of course, is not in terms of "naming." As he puts it,
such expressions "are *prima facie inapplicable* to anything on land or sea";
they "*apparently* have no pertinent use in connection with empirical subject-matter," as "no overtly identifiable motions of bodies can be characterized" by them. *Ibid.,* pp. 622-623.

[43] *The Journal of Philosophy,* XLIII, (1946), pp. 29-36.

[44] Merely as a curiosity, showing the way in which words used in logic
can shift back and forth, Peirce once undertook (2.330) to suggest much
the same thing as Pepper now develops. Pepper's language is that "a
nominal definition is by definition prescriptive." Peirce's wording was:
"this definition — or rather this precept that is more serviceable than a
definition." Precept and prescription are not the same etymologically, but
their uses are close. Peirce's "precepts" would be a close companion for
Pepper's descriptive definition; while Pepper's "prescription," in its none
too complimentary use, matches closely what Peirce felt compelled to
understand by definition.

[45] Certain features of the diagram should be mentioned in connection
with the above transcription. There is a bare possibility, so far as dia-
grammatic position goes, that the "tentatively indicates" and the "ostensively defined" on the *S-O* line should change places; our choice was made
to hold the "tentatives" and "hypothetical" together in one set. The *S-D*
and *S-O* statements under Formulation A (the latter transformed to read
"is . . . taken to indicate") are noted as "at the same time," which possibly indicates orders of succession elsewhere which we have overlooked.
(We are far from wishing to force any such successions into the treatment.)

The shiftings from active to passive verb forms may have some significance which we overlook, and the specific subject indicated for the passive verbs would be interesting to know. These difficulties are slight, and we trust none of them has interfered with a proper rendering by us of Professor Pepper's position.

46 *The Basis of Criticism in the Arts* (Cambridge, 1945), p. 31. The structural diagram in the book for the *D-O* of Formulation A uses the word "describes," and has not yet made the limitation "hypothetically describes."

47 *Ibid.*, pp. 27ff.

48 As we have already indicated, this confusion of a great variety of things under a single name is most probably maintained under some primitive form of reference of them all to a purportedly common source in a single human "capacity," "action," or "act," derivative of the medieval soul.

49 In the preceding reports we have had mention of indefinables by Adamson, Johnson, and Dubs. Ostensive definition has been variously treated by Pepper and Burks. Feigl also considers the ostensive definition, saying that it is "rather fashionable nowadays." He believes there should be no trouble with it, as it is either "a designation rule formulated in a semantical metalanguage" or "a piece of practical drill in the learning of the 'right use' of words." Dubs, for his part, finds it "not quite clear" enough to use.

50 *Op. cit.* Book I, Chapter VIII, Section 1. For a discussion in a wider background than the present of the whole problem of "demonstratives" including both the "pointings" and the "objects" pointed-at, see J. Dewey, *Logic, The Theory of Inquiry*, pages 53-54, 124, and 241-242.

51 We have already cited Skinner's view that without a developed behavioral base modern logic is undependable, and we repeat it because such a view so rarely reaches logicians' ears. Their common custom is to discard into the "pragmatic" all uncomfortable questions about logic as living process, forgetting that the "pragmatic" of Peirce and James, and of historical status, is quite the opposite, since it interprets meanings, concepts, and ideas in life. Skinner's conclusion is that eventually the verbal behavior of the scientists themselves must be interpreted, and that if it turns out that this "invalidates our scientific structure from the point of view of logic and truth-value, then so much the worse for logic, which will also have been embraced by our analysis."

52 Cf. the discussion of "demonstratives" in Dewey's *Logic, The Theory of Inquiry*, pp. 125-127.

CHAPTER EIGHT

LOGIC IN AN AGE OF SCIENCE[1]

I

AMONG the subjectmatters which logicians like at times to investigate are the forms of postulation that other branches of inquiry employ. Rarely, however, do they examine the postulates under which they themselves proceed.[2] They were long contented to offer something they called a "definition" for logic, and let it go at that. They might announce that logic dealt with the "laws of thought," or with "judgment," or that it was "the general science of order." More recently they are apt to connect it in one or another obscure way with linguistic ordering.

We may best characterize the situation by saying that while logicians have spent much time discussing how to apply their logic *to* the world, they have given almost no examination to their own position, as logicians, *within* the world which modern science has opened. We may take Darwin's great demonstration of the "natural" origin of organisms as marking the start of the new era in which man himself is treated as a natural member of a universe under discovery rather than as a superior being endowed with "faculties" from above and beyond, which enable him to "oversee" it. If we do this, we find that almost all logical enterprises are still carried on in pre-Darwinian patterns. The present writer is, indeed, aware of only two systems (and one of these a suggested project rather than a developed construction) which definitely undertake an approach in a modern manner. The rest are almost wholly operated under the blessing, if not formally in the name,

of "thinkers," "selves," or superior realms of "meanings."
The present memorandum will sketch the new form of approach and contrast it with typical specimens of the old.

Two great lines of distinction between pre-Darwinian
and post-Darwinian types of program and goals for logic
may readily be set down.

While the former are found to center their attention
basically upon *decisions* made by individual human beings
(as "minds," "deciders," or otherwise "actors"), the latter
describe broadly, and appraise directly, the presence and
growth of knowings in the world, with "decisions" entering as passing phases of process, but not as *the* critical acts.

While enterprises of pre-Darwinian types require certainties, and require these to be achieved with perfection,
absoluteness, or finality, the post-Darwinian logic is content to hold its results within present human reach, and
not strive to grasp too far beyond.

Examined under these tests the recent logics of the non-
Aristotelian, multivalued, and probability types all still
remain in the pre-Darwinian or "non-natural" group, however they may dilute their wordings with respect to the
certainties. A century ago Boole undertook to improve
logic by mathematical aid, and there was great promise in
that; but Russell, following the mind-steeped Frege, and
himself already thoroughly indoctrinated to understanding
and interpretation by way of "thought" or "judgment,"
reversed this, and has steadily led the fight to make logic
master and guardian [3] in the ancient manner, with never
a moment's attention to the underlying problem: *Quis
custodiet ipsos custodes?*

The lines of distinction we have mentioned above might,
perhaps, be made the basis for two contrasting sets of postulations. In some respects such postulations could be developed as sharply as those which geometers set up with
respect to parallels. But such a course would be practicable
only on the condition that the key words employed in them
could be held to sharply established meanings. However,

as logic and its surrounding disciplines now stand, this necessary linguistic precision cannot be attained. A single man might allege it, but his fellows would not agree, and at his first steps into the linguistic market-place he would find each logician he approached demanding the right to vary the word-meanings, and to shape them, here subtly, there crudely, out of all semblance to the proposed postulational use.[4]

Since such a course will not avail, we may try another. We may hunt down in several logics the most specific statements each of them has made in regard to the issues in question. We may then assemble these as best we can. We shall not in this way obtain postulations [5] in the sense in which more securely established inquiries can obtain them, but we may at times secure fair approximations. Where we can not get even this far forward, we can at least present skeletons of the construction of logical systems, such that they contain the materials out of which postulations may perhaps be derived if in the end the logicians involved will ever attend closely enough to what they are doing. If careful appraisals are to be secured, work of this kind is essential, even though it as yet falls far below the standards we could wish.

We shall consider six logical procedures, half of them in books published in 1944 and 1945, and all now under active discussion. We shall take them in three groups: first the "natural" [6] constructions of John Dewey and J. R. Kantor;[7] next, the sustained efforts of Morris R. Cohen and Felix Kaufmann to adapt old mentalistic-individualistic forms of control to modern uses; finally the desperate struggles of two outstanding logician-philosophers, Bertrand Russell and G. E. Moore, to secure victory with their ancient banners still waving. Our purpose is not so much to debate the rights and wrongs of these procedures, as it is to exhibit the differences in materials and workmanship, and to indicate the types of results thus far offered.

II

John Dewey's wide professional and public following derives more from his philosophical, educational, and social studies than from his logic. Nevertheless for over forty years he has made logic the backbone of his inquiry. His preliminary essays on the subject go back, indeed, to the early nineties. The *Studies of Logical Theory* appeared in 1903. The *Essays in Experimental Logic* in 1916, and *Logic, the Theory of Inquiry* in 1938, all in a single steadily maintained line of growth which stresses inquiry directly as the great subjectmatter of logic along a line of development foreseen and tentatively employed by Charles Sanders Peirce.[8] With Dewey the method and outcome of inquiry becomes warranted assertion. "Proof," which the older logics endeavored to establish under validities of its own for the control of knowledge, is here to be developed within, and as a phase of, inquiry; all certainty becomes subject to inquiry including the certainties of these very canons of logic which older logics had treated as the powerful possessors of certainty in their own right. Man is thus seen to advance in his logical action as well as in all his other affairs *within* his cosmos, so that the dicta and ultimacies of the older *super*-natural rationalities, presumptively possessed by men, fall forfeit. The basic attitudes adopted in Dewey's *Logic*, the makings of a postulation for it, will be found in his first chapter. We list six section headings from this chapter and supplement them with two other characteristic attitudes. These are numbered 1 to 8, and are followed by a dozen more specialized determinations, here numbered 9 to 20.

DEWEY [9]

1. "Logic is a progressive discipline" (p. 14);
2. "The subjectmatter of logic is determined operationally" (p. 14);
3. "Logical forms are postulational" (p. 16);
4. "Logic is a naturalistic theory; . . . rational operations *grow out of* organic activities" (pp. 18-19);

5. "Logic is a social discipline" (p. 19) ;
6. "Logic is autonomous; inquiry into inquiry . . . does not depend upon anything extraneous to inquiry" (p. 20) ;
7. "Every special case of knowledge is constituted as the outcome of some special inquiry" (p. 8) ;
8. "Logical theory is the systematic formulation of controlled inquiry" (p. 22) with "the word 'controlled' . . . standing for the methods of inquiry that are developed and perfected in the processes of continuous inquiry" (p. 11).
9. Inquiry, through linguistic development of terms and propositions, arrives in judgment at warranted assertions upon existence (Chapter VII) ;
10. Propositions and propositional reasonings are intermediate and instrumental in inquiry (pp. 113, 166, 181, 310, et al.) ; propositions are not found in independence or as isolates, but only as members of sets or series (p. 311) ;
11. Terms enter as constituents of propositions and as conditioned by them, never in independence or as isolates (p. 328) ;
12. Singular and generic propositions are conjugates, the former specifying "kinds," the latter organizations of "kinds" (pp. 358-9) ;
13. The development of propositions in "generic derivation or descent where differentiation into kinds is conjoined with differentiation of environing conditions" is an equivalent in logic to the biological advance which established the origin of species (pp. 295-6) ;
14. Singular propositions (and with them "particulars") appear as incomplete or imperfect, rather than as "simple," "atomic," or otherwise primordial (p. 336n, p. 342) ;[10]
15. The propositions called "universal" are intermediate stages of inquiry like all others, and are to be examined on various levels of instrumental differentiation (Chapters XIV, XV, XX) ;
16. The adequate development of the theory of inquiry must await the development of a general theory of language in which form and matter are not separated (p. iv) ;
17. Mathematical forms, and logical forms generally, are properly to be studied in severance from their subjectmatters only when it is recognized that the severance is provisional,

and that their full setting in determinate human action is to be taken into account in the final construction (Chapter XVII) ;

18. The canons of the old logic (including non-contradiction), now entering as forms attained in and with respect to inquiry, lose all their older pretenses to authority as inherent controls or as intuitively evident (pp. 345-6), and, when detached from their place in "the progressive conduct of inquiry," show themselves as "mechanical and arbitrary" survivals (p. 195).

19. "Objects" as determined through inquiry are not determined as existences antecedent to all inquiry, nor as detached products; instead they enter knowledge as conditioned by the processes of their determination (p. 119);

20. No judgments are to be held as *super*-human or as final; organisms and environments alike are known to us in process of transformation; so also are the outcomes in judgment of the logical activities they develop (Chapters I to V; p. 345n).

The other natural approach to logic to be considered is that of J. R. Kantor in his book *Psychology and Logic* (Bloomington, Indiana, 1945). He makes his development upon the basis of his interbehavioral psychology which rates as one of the most important advances in psychological construction since William James. The "natural" characteristic of this psychology is that it undertakes not merely to bring organism and environmental object into juxtaposition, but to investigate their behavioral activities under a form of functional interpretation throughout. Applying his approach to the field of logic Kantor offers eight postulates for a "specificity logic." These follow in his own wordings, and in the main from the first chapter of his book. Two ancillary statements, 2.1 and 4.1, and a few other phrasings, have been supplied from other chapters to compensate compactly for the detachment of the leading postulates from their full contextual exposition.

KANTOR [11]
1. "Logic constitutes primarily a series of operations."

2. "Logical theory is continuous with practice"; the "theory
    . . . constitutes . . . the *study* of operations;" the "prac-
    tice . . . consists of these *operations* themselves."

2.1 "Interbehavioral psychology assumes that organisms and
    objects exist before they become the subjectmatter of the
    various natural sciences."

3. "Logical operations constitute interbehavioral fields."
    "The materials must be regarded as . . . performing op-
    erations co-ordinate with those of the logician."

4. "Logical operations have evolved as techniques for achiev-
    ing systems as products." "No other generalization is pre-
    supposed than that system-building goes on."

4.1 "Not only can the work be separated from the product, but
    each can be given its proper emphasis." "We may inter-
    behave with . . . the objects of our own creation."

5. "Logic is essentially concerned with specific events."

6. "Since logic consists of actual interbehavior it sustains
    unique relations with the human situations in which it
    occurs." "As a human enterprise logic cannot escape cer-
    tain cultural influences."

7. "Logic is inseverably interrelated with psychology." "Logic
    . . . entails a psychological dimension."

8. "Logic is distinct from language." It "is not . . . pri-
    marily concerned with . . . linguistic things." "Contrary
    to logical tradition, for the most part, symbols, sentences,
    or statements are only means for referring to . . . or for
    recording . . . "

The two procedures so outlined resemble each other
in their insistence upon finding their subjectmatter in
concretely observable instances of logical behavior; in their
stress upon *operational* treatment of their subjectmatter;
in their establishment of *natural* and *cultural* settings for
the inquiry; and in their insistence that organism and environment be viewed together as *one system*. Kantor's 1,
2, 4, 5 and 6 follow in close correspondence with Dewey's
2, 8, 4, 7 and 5, while Dewey's 1 and 3 should easily be acceptable to him. Within so similar a framework, however,
marked differences of treatment appear. This, of course,

is as it should be when a live field of fresh research is being developed. Dewey's 6 and Kantor's 3 and 7 might perhaps raise problems of interpretation in their respective contexts. The marked difference, however, is to be found in Kantor's 2.1 and 4.1 as compared with Dewey's 19, and in Kantor's 8 as compared with Dewey's 9 and 16. Kantor treats the system of organism and environment "interactionally," while Dewey makes the "transactional" approach basic. Kantor introduces "pre-logical materials" as requisite for logical activity, distinguishes logical activity sharply from linguistic activity, and offers as outcomes logical products akin in pattern to physical products and serving as stimulants to men in the same manner these latter do. Dewey, in contrast, exhibits inquiry as advancing from indeterminate to determinate situations in full activity throughout, and requires the "objects" determined by inquiry to be held within its system, future as well as past. Where Kantor holds himself to what can be accomplished from a start in which human organisms and environmental objects are presented to logic ready-formed as the base of its research, Dewey brings within his inquiry those very processes of knowledge under which organisms and objects are themselves identified and differentiated in ordinary life and in specific research as components of such a natural world.[12] We have thus within a very similar "natural" background two contrasting routes already indicated for further development.

III

The four other logics which we shall consider retain as presumptively basic various materials and activities derived from the vocabularies and beliefs of pre-Darwinian days. Such items of construction include, among many others, "sense-data," "concepts," "propositions," "intuitions," "apprehensions," "meanings," and a variety of "rationals" and "empiricals" taken either as individually separable "mental existences," as directly present "objects of mind," or as philosophical offspring of terminological interbreeding between them. The question which concerns us is as to how such materials enter into construction and how they behave.[13] In the work of Cohen and Kaufmann we shall find earnest endeavor to smooth them into place in a modern world of knowledge. Thereupon in the light of what these men give us — or, rather, of what they have failed to give us thus far — we shall be able to get a clearer view of the violent struggles of Russell, and the intricate word-searchings of Moore, as they strive to establish and organize logical controls under their ancient forms of presentation.[14]

Professor Cohen's desire to strengthen logical construction had stimulation from Peirce on one side and from the later blossoming of symbolic logic on the other. He has not, however, taken a path which permits him to find Dewey's manner of construction adequate in the direct line from Peirce.[15] The citations we assemble are taken verbatim from his latest book. While they have been removed from their immediate contexts and rearranged, it is hoped that no one of them has been warped from its accurate significance in his construction.

COHEN [16]

1. "Symbols . . . represent . . . only . . . general properties" (p. 8, line 6) ;

2. "Science studies the . . . determinate properties of things" (p. 17, line 18). Physics, e.g., "starts with material assumptions, i.e., assumptions true only of certain objects, namely entities occupying time and space" (p. 16, line 3) ;

3. In the manipulation of symbols . . . "the meaning of our final result follows from our initial assumptions" (p. 8, line 13) ;

4. "The assumption that the objects of physics . . . must conform to logic is necessary in the sense that without it no science at all can be constructed" (p. 16, lines 15-16) ;

5. "The rules according to which . . . symbols can be combined are by hypothesis precisely those according to which

the entities they denote can be combined" (p. 8, lines 8-10) ;
6. "Logically . . . existence and validity are strictly correlative" (p. 15, line 26) .

This reads smoothly enough but it makes science, and apparently logic also, depend for foundations upon a "necessary assumption" — where "necessary" is what we, cannot avoid, and "assumption" what we have to guess at. It separates two great ranges of human attention, one called that of "symbols," the other that of the "determinate properties of things." However modernized their garb, these are little other than the ancient "reason" and "sense." Their organization is by *fiat*, by the flat assertion that they *must* be correlated. Such *fiat* is employed precisely because "system" has *not* been established. If the "entities occupying time and space" make up "nature," then the "symbols" remain "non-natural" in the sense in which we have employed the word, so long as they are not brought within a common system of interpretation, but enter merely by decree.

Professor Kaufmann, as we shall report him, works under a similar severance of certain of man's activities from the environing "nature" upon, within, or with respect to which, these activities are carried on. He develops a far-reaching, intricate, and in his own way powerful, analysis to establish organization for them conjointly. He accepts and admires Dewey's "theory of inquiry" as an outstanding contribution to knowledge but not by itself as an adequate logic. He holds that the theory of deduction must be grounded in intuitional meanings, and that with it must be correlated a theory for the empirical procedures of science in terms of the scientists' *decisions*. Far from regarding himself as severing the logical process and its canons from nature, he holds that what he is doing is to "define inquiry in terms of the canons." [17] This, however, still leaves the contrast with Dewey striking since the latter's undertaking has been to describe the canons along with all other logical activity as inquiry going on, rather than to use canons as criteria of its definition. The following are Professor Kaufmann's "tenets":

KAUFMANN [18]

1. The work of the logic of science is to clarify the rules of scientific procedure.
2. The corpus of science consists of propositions that have been accepted in accordance with such rules.
3. Changes in the corpus of a science, either by acceptance of a proposition into it, or by the elimination of a proposition from it, are called scientific decisions.
4. Scientific decisions are distinguished as correct or incorrect in terms of rules of procedure called *basic*. (Other rules called *preference* rules concern appropriateness of approach.) Basic rules as well as preference rules may be changed. Standards for the correctness of such changes are called rules of the second (or higher) order.
5. Principles governing the scientific acceptance or elimination of propositions, and placing limitation upon the changes of basic rules, are the reversibility of all decisions, the recognition of observational tests, the exclusion of contradictions, and the decidability in principle of all propositions.
6. The two last mentioned principles are called procedural correlates of the principles of contradiction and of excluded middle respectively. The former states that the basic rules of procedure must be such as to foreclose the emergence of contradiction in science. The latter states that the basic rules must be such as not to foreclose the verifiability of any given statement.
7. The correctness of scientific decisions in terms of basic rules depends solely on the knowledge established at the time, i.e., on previously accepted propositions which now serve as *grounds* for the acceptance of new ones.
8. Identifiable propositional meanings are presupposed in scientific decisions.
9. The presupposition of identifiable propositional meanings implies that we take it for granted that for any two given propositions it is determined whether or not one is en-

tailed in the other, and whether or not one contradicts the other.

10. Entailment and contradiction are recognizable either directly in immediate apprehension of meanings or indirectly by deductive process.

11. Deductive processes are autonomous within scientific inquiry and can be described without reference to verification or invalidation.

In his construction Professor Kaufmann rejects the demand for the logical determination of ontological certainty in its older and more brazen form.[19] He is, indeed, unfriendly in many respects to its newer and more insidious forms. However, although he can content himself without the ontological specialized search, he can not content himself without the ontological searcher. He retains the non-natural "mental"—the "ego," "person," "decider," or basic "knower" — if not as existential possessor, then at least as subsistential vehicle or conveyor, of meanings. He sees science as composed of propositions, the propositions as being meanings (i.e., generally as "thoughts," or "concepts"), and the meanings as enjoying some sort of logically superordinate [20] existence over, above, or beyond, their physical, physiological, or behavioral occurrence. He requires decisions to get the propositions, rules to get the decisions, and higher rules to get changes in the lower rules; behind all of which he puts a backlog of invariant (i.e., unchangeable) properties which the rules possess. Underlying all logical procedure he requires the presupposed meanings and the invariant properties; and underlying these he requires the intuition or immediate apprehension which operates them. Deduction is intuition indirectly at work. We are in effect asked to adopt a sort of indirectly immediate apprehension. It feels uncomfortable.

If we compare this with Dewey's "natural" procedure,[21] we find Dewey offering us science, not as a corpus of "propositions" embalmed in "decisions" made in accordance

with prescribed "rules," but as the actual observable ongoing process of human inquiry in the cosmos in which it
takes place. "Propositions," for him, are instruments, not
exhibits. What happens, happens, and no need is found
to insert "intuition" behind it to *make* it happen, or to be
the happening. Meaningful utterance is taken as it comes,
and not as separated from life and language. "Decision"
is the long process of appraisal, often requiring cultural
description; it is never some intermediate act-under-rule.
The outcome in judgment is not a "conception" nor even
a "pronouncement," but the full activity that rounds out
inquiry. Finally the canons are to Dewey outgrowths of
inquiry, not its presuppositions; their high value, when in
active inquiry is fully recognized, but when set off by themselves they are found mechanical, arbitrary, and often
grievously deceptive. This difference is not one of creed or
opinion — Dewey's work is not to be taken on any such
basis as that; it is a difference of practical workmanship,
with the "credal" aspects trailing behind, and with the report we here give furnishing merely the clues to the
practice.

IV

We come now to the struggle of Russell and the subtle-
ties of Moore in their efforts to secure a logic under these
ancient patterns of speech — logical, ontological, psychological, and metaphysical — in which sensings and conceiv-
ings, world and man, body and mind, empiricals and
rationals, enter in opposing camps. Russell offers rich
complexes of such materials, and their kaleidoscopic shiftings are so rapid that it is most of the time difficult to center
one's eye on the spot where the issues are clearest. His
great and everywhere recognized early achievements in
symbolic logic and in planning its organization with mathematics have ended with his efforts in the last half of his
life to find out what actually he has been dealing with. His
view today seems as strong as in his earlier years — perhaps

even stronger — that unless a man adopts some metaphysics and puts it to work, he cannot even make a common statement in everyday language.[22]

To represent Russell we shall establish a base in his Logical Atomism of 1918-1919 and 1924, and supplement this, where it seems desirable, by citations from earlier and later papers. The clumsiness of our report is regrettable, but it is due to overlapping and ever-shifting applications by Russell of such words as "simple," "particular," "entity," and "symbol," which make plain, direct citation often risky, and at times altogether impracticable.[23]

RUSSELL [24]

1. "Ultimate simples," (in theory if not in practical research) are entities "out of which the world is built" (M, 1919, 365). They "have a kind of reality not belonging to anything else" (M, 1919, 365). "Simple" objects are "those objects which it is impossible to symbolize otherwise than by simple symbols" (M, 515).

2. Propositions and facts are complexes. "I do not believe that there are complexes . . . in the same sense in which there are simples" (LA, 374).

3. Complexes are to be dealt with through their component simple entities or simple symbols. "It seems obvious to me that what is complex must be composed of simples" (LA, 375). "Components of a proposition are the symbols . . . ; components of the fact . . . are the meanings [25] of the symbols" (M, 518).

4. Simple symbols are those "not having any parts that are symbols, or any significant structure" (LA, 375. Cf. M, 515).

5. Knowledge is attained through the fixation of the right simples by the right logical proper names, i.e., symbols (the argument of M and LA throughout). "An atomic proposition is one which does . . . actually name . . . actual particulars" (M, 523).[26]

6. As a controlling principle: "Wherever possible, substitute constructions out of known entities for inferences to unknown entities" (LA, 363).[27]

7. Among the simples consider the particulars (M, 497) .[28]
These are "the *terms* of the relation" in atomic facts (M,
522). Proper names properly apply to them and to them
alone (M, 508, 523, 524). "Particulars have this peculiarity . . . in an inventory of the world, that each of
them stands entirely alone and is completely self-subsist-
ent" (M, 525).

8a. Particulars are known by direct acquaintance. "A name
. . . can only be applied to a particular with which the
speaker is acquainted" (M, 524) .[29] "The word 'red' is
a simple symbol . . . and can only be understood through
acquaintance with the object" (M, 517).

8b. "Simples" are not "experienced as such"; they are "known
only inferentially as the limit of analysis" (LA, 375) .[30]

9. For success in attaining knowledge it becomes necessary
to sort propositions into types. "The doctrine of types
leads . . . to a more complete and radical atomism than
any that I conceived to be possible twenty years ago" (LA,
371).

10. In "The Type's Progress," the stages thus far (1945) have
been:
a) The *entities* [31] exist in a variety of types;
b) "The theory of types is really a theory of *symbols,* not
of things" (M, 1919, 362) ;
c) Words (symbols) are all of the *same* type (LA, 369) ;
d) The meanings of the symbols may be of *any* type (I,
44; *see also* LA, 369) ;
e) (when the going seems hard) "Difference of type
means difference of syntactical function" (RC, 692) ;[32]
f) (when the going seems easy) "There is not one relation of meaning between words and what they stand
for, but as many relations of meaning, each of a different logical type, as there are logical types among the
objects for which there are words" (LA, 370) ;
g) (and at any rate) "Some sort of hierarchy is necessary.
I hope that in time, some theory will be developed
which will be simple and adequate, and at the same
time be satisfactory from the point of view of what
might be called logical common sense" (RC, 692) .[33]

Probably the sharpest criticism to be made of Russell's workmanship is to point out his continual confounding of "symbol" and "entity." We have had illustrations of this in the cases, both of the "particular" and of the "type." Fusion of "symbol" and "entity" is what Russell demands, and confusion is what he gets. With an exhibit as prominent as this in the world, it is no wonder that Korzybski has felt it necessary to devote so much of his writings to the insistent declaration that the word is *not* the thing.[34] His continued insistence upon this point will remain a useful public service until, at length, the day comes when a thorough theory of the organization of behavioral word and cosmic fact has been constructed.

Turning now to Moore, we find him using much the same line of materials as does Russell, but he concentrates on the ultimate accuracies of expression in dealing with them. Whether primarily classified as a logician or not, he outlogics the logics in his standards of logical perfection. Where Russell proposes to force the ultimate simples of the world to reveal themselves, Moore takes a frank and open base in the most common-sense, matter-of-fact, personal experiences he can locate, accepting them in the form of "simplest" propositions. He then takes account of sense-data, linguistic expressions, the conceptual and propositional meaningfulness of these latter, man's belief in them, his feelings of certainty about his beliefs, and his assertions of known truth; plus, of course, the presumptive "realities" he takes to be involved. Where Russell finds himself compelled continually to assert that his critics fail to understand him, Moore is frank in his avowal that he is never quite sure that he understands himself.[35] He is as willing to reverse himself as he is to overthrow others. His virtues of acuity and integrity applied to his presuppositions have yielded the following development:

MOORE [36]

1. Start with common sense statements, such as "this is my body," "it was born," "it has grown," "this is a chair,"

"I am sitting in this chair," "here is my hand," "here is another hand." Examine these as propositions, and in all cases under reduction to the simplest expression that can be reached — such, that is to say, as is most secure of ordinary acceptance, and is least liable to arouse conflict (CS, 193-195) .[37]

2. Accept these common-sense propositions as "wholly true" (CS, 197) ; as what "I know with certainty to be true" (CS, 195) .[38]

3. In such a proposition, if it is thus held true, "there is always some *sense-datum* about which the proposition in question is a proposition," i.e., its "subject" is always a sense-datum (CS, 217). Moreover such a proposition is "unambiguous," so that "we understand its meaning" in a way not to be challenged, whether we do or do not "know what it means" in the sense of being able "*to give a correct analysis* of its meaning" (CS, 198) .[39]

4. On the basis of such simplified common sense propositions having sense-data for subjects, very many [40] other instances of knowledge in propositional form can be tested and appraised through Analysis."

5. In Analysis a "concept, or idea, or proposition" is dealt with, "and *not* a verbal expression" (RC, 663, 666) . The word "means" should not be used since that implies a "verbal expression," and therefore gives a "false impression" (RC, 664; this passage is seventeen years later than that in #3 above, where the word "means" is still employed.)

6. To "give an analysis" of a concept you must come across (or, at least, you "must mention") another concept which, like the first, "applies to" an object (though it neither "means" nor "expresses" it) under circumstances such that (a) "nobody can know" that the first concept "applies" without "knowing" that the second applies; (b) "nobody can verify" that the first applies without "verifying" that the second applies; and (c) "any expression which expresses" the first "must be synonymous with any expression which expresses" the second (RC, 663) .[41]

7. Otherwise put, a "correct" analysis in the case of concepts is one which results in showing that two concepts

expressed by different expressions "must, in some sense" be the same concept [42] (RC, 666).

8. To establish itself in firm status for the future, Analysis has two primary tasks, (a) it must make a successful analysis of sense-data (CS, p. 216-222); (b) it must make a successful analysis of Analysis itself (Compare RC, 660-667).

9. Analysis of sense-data has thus far been unsatisfactory. Its present status is best exhibited in a particular case of analysis. Take, for example, "the back of my hand" as "something seen," and seek to establish what, precisely, *is* the sense-datum that enters as subject of the "common sense" and "wholly true" proposition: "This is the back of my hand." In 1925 Moore reported that "no philosopher has hitherto suggested an answer that comes anywhere near to being *certainly* true" (CS, 219). In 1942 his report was "The most fundamental puzzle about the relations of sense-data to physical objects is that there does seem to be some reason to assert . . . paradoxes" (RC, 637).[43]

10. Analysis of Analysis itself also arrives at paradox, so that in the outcome it may be said: "I do not know, at all clearly, *what* I mean by saying that '*x* is a brother' is identical with '*x* is a male sibling,' and that '*x* is a cube' is *not identical* with '*x* is a cube with twelve edges' " (RC, 667).[44]

It may be suggested on the basis of the above display of Moore's techniques and results that his Analysis could reasonably be carried still further. Analysis of "concept" and of "proposition," of "expression" and of "meaning," and of "datum" as well as of "sense," might lead towards solutions. This, however, would involve untrammelled inquiry into "man's analyzing procedures" for whatever such procedures might show themselves operationally to be, in a full naturalistic setting. And this, again, would require throwing off the limitations imposed by the old vocabularies that place "man the analyzer" outside of, or over against the world of his analysis.[45] The differences in spatial and temporal location are huge between what is "sense-datum" and what is "wholly true." The range of the one is a bit of an organism's living in a bit of environment. The range the other seems to claim is all, or even more than all, of space and time. Analysis will surely need to be super-jet, if it is to make this transit, fueled as it is proposed it be by "concept, idea, and proposition," and these alone.

V

The reader who wishes to appraise for himself the situations we have exhibited — and especially the reader who has been accustomed to the use of his hands and eyes on materials such as enter any of the natural sciences — may be interested in an experiment. Let him look on logicians' writings as events taking place in the world. Let him pick out some phase of these events for study. Let him be willing to examine it at least as carefully as he might the markings of a butterfly's wings, remembering also that the present level of inquiry into logic is not much further advanced than that into butterflies was when they were still just museum curiosities, and modern physiology undreamt of. This will mean clearing his work bench of all superfluous terminologies, and "getting down to cases," with the cases under examination, whatever they are, pinned down on the bench and not allowed to squirm themselves out of all decent recognition. Suppose such an inquirer has noticed the word "proposition" frequently present in the text. On the assumption, however rash, that logical terms are supposed to denote, name, designate, point at, or refer to something factually determinate, let him then select the presumptive fact "proposition" for his examination. By way of preliminary orientation, if he should examine the six logicians we have considered he would find that for Dewey a proposition is an instrumental use of language (D9, D10, D15, D16); for Kantor it is a "product" of logical interbehavior; [46] for Cohen "propositions are linguistic forms with meanings that are objective relations between such forms and certain states of fact"; [47] for Kaufmann a proposition is a "meaning" developed from a base in intuition, fundamentally presupposed as such by logic, and not therein to be investigated.[48] For Russell it may be a class of sentences, or the meaning or significance of a sentence, or even at times something he doubts the existence of; [49] for Moore, it is a dweller in a land of thoughts, companion of concepts and of ideas, and to be found midway (or perhaps some other way) between words and objects.[50] Here is surely not merely "food for thought" but much incentive to matter-of-fact research. A few further trails for searchers to follow are mentioned in the footnote.[51]

In the preceding examination I have done my best to be accurate and fair. I hope I have at least in part succeeded. Certainly I have squandered time and effort triple and quadruple what I would have agreed to at the start. I find myself unwilling to close without expressing my personal opinion more definitely than I have heretofore. The procedures of Russell and Moore seem so simple-minded it is remarkable they have survived at all in a modern world. Those of Cohen and Kaufmann are heroic efforts to escape from the old confusions, yet futile because they fail to pick up the adequate weapons. In what may grow from the two other enterprises I have, of course, great hopes.

[1] This chapter is written by Bentley.

[2] Sub-postulations within a wider, tacitly accepted (i.e., unanalysed) postulatory background are common enough. The present viewpoint is that of Morris R. Cohen when he writes: "The philosophic significance of the new logic, the character of its presuppositions, and the directions of its possible application are problems which have attracted relatively little reflective thought." *A Preface to Logic* (New York, 1944), p. ix.

[3] In his very latest publication Bertrand Russell still writes: "From Frege's work it followed that arithmetic, and pure mathematics generally, is nothing but a prolongation of deductive logic," *A History of Western Philosophy*, (New York, 1945), p. 830.

[4] Samples of logicians' linguistic libertinism can be found anywhere, anytime, in current periodicals. Thus, for instance, in a paper just now at hand, we find "principles" of deduction referred to "intuition" for

their justification, and this along with the suggestion that intuition should be "reinforced by such considerations as . . . ingenuity may suggest." A few paragraphs later a set of "principles" containing wholly naïve uses of the word "true" are declared to be "intuitively obvious." Lack of humor here goes hand in hand with inattention to the simpler responsibilities of speech; Max Black, "A New Method of Presentation of the Theory of the Syllogism," *The Journal of Philosophy*, XLII (1945), 450-51.

5 Compare Chapter III where groups of postulations are presented looking towards a natural theory of knowings and knowns.

6 In characterizing these logics as "natural," it is to be understood that the word "natural," as here used, is not to be taken as implying something specifically "material" as contrasted with something specifically "mental." It stands for a single system of inquiry for all knowledge with logic as free to develop in accordance with its own needs as is physics or physiology, and to develop in system with either or both of these as freely as they develop in system with each other. Many logicians rated by us as non-natural would label themselves "naturalistic." Thus Russell declares that he "regards knowledge as a natural fact like any other" (*Sceptical Essays* [New York, 1928] page 70), though our examination of his materials and procedures will give him quite the contrary rating.

7 If Otto Neurath had lived to develop his position further than he did, we could doubtless list him also on the "natural" side. He was from the beginning much further advanced in this respect than others of his more active associates in the projected *International Encyclopedia of Unified Science,* of which he was editor-in-chief. His most recent publication is "Foundations of the Social Sciences," a monograph contributed to the Encyclopedia.

8 "As far as I am aware, he (Peirce) was the first writer on logic to make inquiry and its methods the primary and ultimate source of logical subjectmatter," John Dewey, *Logic, the Theory of Inquiry,* (New York, 1938) p. 9n. The fourth of the postulates for Dewey in the text is frequently called "the postulate of continuity," and perhaps offers the straightest and widest route from Darwin through Peirce to Dewey.

9 All page references are to *Logic, the Theory of Inquiry.* Professor Dewey has made further development since the *Logic* was published, particularly with respect to the organization of language, logical forms, and mathematics. Such advances are intimated, but not expressly set forth, in the numbered paragraphs of the text, since it is desirable, for all logics discussed, to hold the presentation to what can be directly verified by the reader in the pages of the works cited.

10 The radical nature of the advance in postulate 14 over older treatments will be plain when the postulations for Russell are considered. For the equally radical postulate 19 see postulate B-8, and its context, in Chapter III, Section III.

11 All wordings are those of the section-headings of the postulates or of the immediately following text, except as follows: The sentence in 2.1 is from page 140, lines 11-12; the second sentence in 4. is from page 168, lines 13-14; the sentences in 4.1 are from page 294, lines 9-10, and page 7, lines 3-4; the sentence in 5 is from page xiii, lines 2-3; the second sentence in 7 is from page xiii, line 6.

12 This difference is well brought out by a remark of Bridgman's which Kantor quotes in order to sharpen his statement of his own position. Bridgman holds that "from the operational point of view it is meaningless to separate 'nature' from 'knowledge of nature.'" Kantor finds Bridgman's view a departure from correct operational procedure. Dewey, on the contrary, would be in full agreement with Bridgman in this particular respect. P. W. Bridgman, *The Logic of Modern Physics* (New York, 1927), p. 62; Kantor, "The Operational Principle in the Physical and Psychological Sciences," *The Psychological Record*, II (1938), p. 6. For an appraisal of Kantor's work under a point of view sharply contrasted with that taken in the present text see the review by Ernest Nagel, *The Journal of Philosophy*, XLII [1945], 578-80).

13 Typical confusions of logical discussion have been examined from a different point of view in Chapter I. Certain characteristics of the work of Carnap, Cohen and Nagel, Ducasse, Lewis, Morris, and Tarski are there displayed. A thorough overhauling has long been needed of the procedures of Carnap and other logical positivists, both with respect to their logic and their positiveness, and this is now promised us by C. W. Churchman and T. A. Cowan (*Philosophy of Science*, XII [1945], 219). One device many logicians employ to justify them in maintaining the antiquated materials is their insistence that logic and psychology are so sharply different that they must leave each other alone — in other words, that while psychology may be allowed to "go natural," logic may not be so allowed. This argument of the logicians may be all very well as against an overly narrowed psychology of the non-natural type; but by the same token an overly narrowed logic results. The problem is one of full human behavior — how human beings have evolved with all their behaviors — no matter how convenient it has been found in the popular speech of the past to scatter the behaviors among separate departments of inquiry.

14 For an extreme "mentalistic" and hopefully "solipsistic" base for logic, the procedures of C. I. Lewis may be brought into comparison by anyone sufficiently interested. Lewis is represented by the following "postulates," which, from any "natural" point of view, rate as disintegrating and unworkable traditions: (1) Knowledge involves three components, the activity of thought, the concepts which are produced by thought, and the sensuously given; (2) The pure concept and the content of the given are mutually independent; neither limits the other; (3) The concept gives rise to the *a priori* which is definitive or explicative of concepts; (4) Empirical knowledge arises through conceptual interpretation. *See Mind and the World Order* (New York, 1929), pp. 36ff.; "The Pragmatic Element

in Knowledge," *Univ. of California Publications in Philosophy,* VI (1926) ;
A Survey of Symbolic Logic (Berkeley, Calif., 1918) . A characteristic determination arising in such a background is that if "analytic facts" can
"function propositionally," then "they are called. propositions"; so that
"the proposition 'Men exist' is literally one and the same with the fact
that men might exist." (Lewis and Langford, *Symbolic Logic* [New York,
1932] p. 472. For other illustrations of what happens to ordinary integrity
of expression under such a construction see my notes on Lewis' vocabulary,
The Journal of Philosophy (1941) , pp. 634-5. See also Chapter I,
Section VI.

15 See his discussion of Dewey's *Experimental Logic* (1916) reprinted
as an appendix to his book *A Preface to Logic* (New York, 1944) .

16 All citations in the text are from *A Preface to Logic*. Compare the
following from Cohen's essay, "The Faith of a Logician," in *Contemporary
American Philosophy* (New York, 1930) p. 228: "Logical laws are thus
neither physical nor mental, but the laws of all possible significant being."

17 From private correspondence.

18 The book here characterized is Felix Kaufmann's *Methodology of the
Social Sciences* (New York, 1944) . Page references are not given as the
presentation in the text has Professor Kaufmann's endorsement as it stands
with the proviso that "he does not maintain that scientists always consciously apply the rules in their inquiries" but that "he does maintain the
reference to the rules is logically implied when the correctness of scientific
decisions or the appropriateness of the methods applied is judged."
"Formulations of such judgments which do not contain reference to the
rules," he regards as "elliptical." The following citations, which Professor
Kaufmann quite properly insists should be understood in the full context
of the book, are assembled by the present writer who, properly also, he
hopes, believes they are essential to show the manner in which expression
under this procedure develops: "The contrast between deductive reasoning
(in the strict sense) and empirical procedure . . . will be the guiding principle of our analysis and . . . the key to the solution of . . . problems"
(*op. cit.* p. 3) ; "The most general characterization of scientific thinking"
is "that it is *a process of classifying and reclassifying propositions by placing
them into either of two disjunctive classes in accordance with presupposed
rules*" (p. 40) ; "The distinction between the logical order of meanings and
the temporal order of inquiry" is "all important" (p. 39) ; The "temporal
aspect of inquiry does not enter into the timeless logical relations among
propositions" (p. 30) ; "The fundamental properties of the system of rules
are invariable" (p. 232) ; The "genuine logical theory of empirical procedure" is "*a theory of correct scientific decisions in given scientific situations*" (p. 65) ; Language requires "a system of rules that gives to particular
acoustical phenomena the function of symbols for particular thoughts"
(p. 17) ; "Lack of distinction in language is, in most cases, the consequence
of unclear thought." (p. 27) ; "Concepts and propositions *are* meanings"
(p. 18) ; In "problems of empirical science" and "logical analysis" . . . "we
have to presuppose (elementary) meanings" (p. 19) . Kaufmann reiterates

and emphasizes his difference from Dewey in a late paper (*Philosophy and Phenomenological Research*, VI [1945] 63n.) when he states that he cannot follow Dewey when the latter dismisses "intuitive knowledge of meanings" along with "intuitive knowledge of sense-data."

[19] See the two typical marks of distinction between pre-Darwinian and post-Darwinian programs and goals suggested in the opening paragraphs of this chapter. Kaufmann's tenets #5 and #7 mark steps of his advance.

[20] The word "superordinate" is here employed by me as an evasive compromise. Kaufmann would say that "the meanings" are "presupposed in," "essential to," "logically implied by," or "necessary for the definition of" the "inquiry." I would say that what his development actually accomplishes is to retain them as "prior to," "superior to," "independent of," or "in a realm apart from" the "inquiry." He fully satisfies me that my wording is not what he intends, but without affecting my view that I am nevertheless describing what he in effect does.

[21] Direct comparison of particular phrases is not simple, because the whole method of expression — the "linguistic atmosphere" — varies so greatly. However, K2 may be compared with D10 and D15; K4 with D5; K7 with D19; and K10 with D18. In addition the citations about language in footnote 18, taken from Kaufmann's pages 17 and 27 are at the extreme opposite pole, so far as present issues go, from D16.

[22] Or at least this seems to be the purport of such a conclusion as that "the goal of all our discussions" is "that complete metaphysical agnosticism is not compatible with the maintenance of linguistic propositions" (*An Inquiry into Meaning and Truth* [New York, 1940] p. 437).

[23] A specimen of Russell's conflicting phrasings from his book *What I Believe*, is quoted by Cassius J. Keyser in *Scripta Mathematica*, III (1935), 28-29 as follows: (page 1) "Man is a part of nature, not something contrasted with nature"; (p. 16) "We are ourselves the ultimate and irrefutable arbiters of value, and in the world of value Nature is only a part. Thus in this world we are greater than Nature."

[24] The sources of the citations from Russell are indicated as follows:
M. "The Philosophy of Logical Atomism," *Monist*, (1918), 495-527; (1919), 32-63, 190-222, 345-380. Page references are to the 1918 volume unless otherwise indicated.
LA. "Logical Atomism," *Contemporary British Philosophy*, New York, First Series, 1924, pp. 359-383.
RC. "Reply to Criticisms," *The Philosophy of Bertrand Russell*, P. A. Schilpp, editor, (Chicago, 1944), pp. 681-741.
I. *An Inquiry into Meaning and Truth*.

[25] What Russell intends by meaning is, in general, very difficult to determine. It is not that no light is thrown on the question but entirely too many kinds of light from too many points of view, without sifting. Most profitable is an examination of all the passages, a dozen or more, indexed

in the *Inquiry*. See also M, 506-8; LA, 369, and Bertrand Russell, *Mysticism and Logic*, (New York, 1918) , pp. 223-4.

26 For a discussion in terms of "basic propositions" see I, p. 172, p. 362, p. 414. Here the contrast between Russell and Dewey is so sharp (see Dewey, No. 14, preceding) that the extensive discussions between the two men could be reduced to a one-sentence affirmation on this point and a one-page exhibit of the context of discussion, historical and contemporary.

27 An alternative form will be found in a paper in *Scientia*, 1914, reprinted in *Mysticism and Logic*, p. 155: "Wherever possible, logical constructions are to be substituted for inferred entities."

28 These are variously called logical atoms, ultimate constituents, simple entities, etc. "Such ultimate simples I call 'particulars'" *An Analysis of Mind* (New York, 1921), p. 193. They are the hardest of hard facts, and the most resistant to "the solvent influence of critical reflection." They may be sense-data, or entities called "events" (LA, 381) or sometimes point-instants or event-particles. Mathematical-physical expressions sometimes join them among the ultra-safe. If Russell would establish definite usage for at least one or two of these words, his reader might have an easier time doing justice to him. It is particularly disconcerting to find the particulars turning out to be themselves just words, as where (I, 21) he speaks of "egocentric particulars, i.e., words such as 'this,' 'I,' 'now,' which have a meaning relative to the speaker." If "terms" are "words" for Russell (I would not presume to say) then the second sentence in point # 7 in the text also makes particulars out to be symbols rather than entities. For indication of Russell's logical atoms and proper names as of the nature of "cues" and similar primitive behaviors, see Chapter IV, note 11, Chapter VI, Section IV and Chapter VII, Section II.

29 Compare *Problems of Philosophy* (New York, 1912) , p. 91; "On the Nature of Acquaintance," *Monist*, (1914) .

30 If there has been any systematic progress in Russell's work as the years pass by with respect to attitudes 8A and 8B, I have failed to detect it. The difference seems rather one of stress at different stages of argumentation. If the clash as here reported seems incredible, I suggest an examination of a particularly illuminating passage in Professor Nagel's contribution to *The Philosophy of Bertrand Russell*, p. 341, in which, though without directly mentioning the incoherence, he notes (a) that Russell holds that some particulars are perceived, and at least some of their qualities and relations are immediately apprehended; (b) that Russell believes his particulars are simples; and (c) that Russell admits that simples are not directly perceived, but are known only inferentially as the limit of analysis. Further light on the situation may be gained from Nagel's penetrating analysis of *An Inquiry into Meaning and Truth. The Journal of Philosophy*, XXXVIII (1941) , 253-270.

31 RC, 691; *Principles of Mathematics*, (Cambridge, England, 1903) ; *Introduction to Mathematical Philosophy*, (New York, 1919) ; also, off

and on, at any stage of his writings. Note the similar difficulty for "particulars," point #7 and footnote 28.

[32] I, p. 438: "Partly by means of the study of syntax, we can arrive at considerable knowledge concerning the structure of the world."

[33] For the latest illustration of Russell's confusion of statement, pages 829-834 of his *A History of Western Philosophy*, (New York, 1945) may profitably be examined. A passing glance will not suffice since the main characteristic of philosophical language is to make a good appearance. A cold eye, close dissection, and often much hard work is necessary to find out what kind of a skeleton is beneath the outer clothing.

[34] Alfred Korzybski: *Science and Sanity: an Introduction to Non-Aristotelian Systems and General Semantics*, (New York, 1933).

[35] Russell remarked to Professor Schilpp, the editor of the volume *The Philosophy of Bertrand Russell*, that "his greatest surprise, in the reading of the twenty-one contributed essays, had come from the discovery that 'over half of their authors had *not* understood' him (i.e. Russell)." (*Op. cit., p.* xiii). For Moore see No. 9 and No. 10 of the skeleton construction of his logical procedure, which follows:

[36] The sources of the citations from Moore are indicated as follows:
CS. "A Defense of Common Sense," *Contemporary British Philosophy*. Second Series, (New York and London, 1925), pp. 193-223;
RC. "A Reply to my Critics" *The Philosophy of G. E. Moore*, P. A. Schilpp, editor, (Chicago, 1942), pp. 535-677.

[37] See also "Proof of an External World," *Proceedings of the British Academy*, XXV (1939), pp. 273-299. Professor Nagel's comment in his review of *The Philosophy of G. E. Moore* in *Mind*, [1944], 60-75 will be found of interest.

[38] Included are physical objects, perceptive experiences taken as mental, remembered things, and other men's bodies and experiencings. "I think I have nothing better to say than that it seems to me that I *do* know them, with certainty. It is, indeed, obvious that, in the case of most of them, I do not know them *directly*" . . . , but . . . "In the past I have known to be true *other* propositions which were evidence for them" (CS, 206).

[39] "I think I have always both used, and intended to use, "sense-datum' in such a sense that the mere fact that an object is *directly apprehended* is a *sufficient* condition for saying that it is a sense-datum" (RC, 639). A remarkable illustration of his careful expression may be found in the passage on page 181 of his paper, "The Nature of Sensible Appearances" *Aristotelian Society*, Supplementary Vol. VI (1926).

[40] "Very many" is to be understood in the sense in which Moore uses the words (CS, 195), with a trend towards, but not immediate assertion of, "all."

41 Note the confidently reiterated "nobody can" and the "must."

42 In the typical case, however, one concept is opposed to two or more concepts, these latter being accompanied in their consideration by explicit mention of their method of combination (RC, 666).

43 Moore has written: "I define the term (sense-datum) in such a way that it is an open question whether the sense-datum which I now see in looking at my hand and which is a sense-datum of my hand is or is not identical with that part of its surface which I am now actually seeing" (CS, 218). In simplified report his analysis in the case of "the back of my hand" discriminates " a physical object," "a physical surface," and a certain "directly seen" (such as one has in the case of an after-image or double-image). Moore's analysis with respect to the second and third of these has results which indicate to him that at the very time at which he not only feels sure but *knows* that he is seeing the second, he is in a state of doubt whether the third, which also he is seeing (and that *directly* in the indicated sense), is identical with the second or not; recognizing that it may be identical, in which case he is in a position of both "feeling sure of and doubting the very same proposition at the same time" (paradox I); or "so far as I can see," at any rate, "I don't *know* that I'm not" (Paradox II). It is to the second form of the paradox that the comment cited in the text above refers (RC, 627-653, and particularly 636-637, also CS, 217-219).

44 The analysis of Analysis which Moore offers (RC, 664-665) declares equivalence as to concepts between expressions of the form: this "concept" is "identical" with that, this "propositional function" is "identical" with that, and "to say this" is "the same thing" as "to say that." But if we proceed to another form which also we feel we must accept, such as "to be this" is "the same thing" as "to be that," we have, we are told, reached a paradox, which, as between expressions and concepts, remains unresolved.

45 It is significant in this connection that Moore tells us that it is always "things which other philosophers have said" that suggest philosophical problems to him. "I do not think," he remarks, "that the world or the sciences would ever have suggested to me any philosophical problems." *The Philosophy of G. E. Moore*, p. 14.

46 J. R. Kantor, *op. cit.*, p. 223, pp. 282-3; also "An Interbehavioral Analysis of Propositions," *Psychological Record*, 5 (1943) p. 328.

47 M. R. Cohen, *op. cit.*, p. 30. Also: "Acts of judgment, however, are involved in the apprehension of those relations that are called meanings." See also M. R. Cohen and E. Nagel, *An Introduction to Logic and Scientific Method*, (New York, 1934), pp. 27, 28, 392, where facts are made of propositions, and propositions are specifically declared to be neither physical, mental, linguistic, nor communication, and to be identifiable by the sole characteristic that whatever else they are they are "true or false."

48 Felix Kaufmann, *op. cit.*, pp. 18, 19.

49 B. Russell: *An Inquiry into Meaning and Truth*, pp. 208, 210, 217, 237 *et al. Proceedings of the Aristotelian Society*, XI, (1911), 117. *Mysticism and Logic*, p. 219; *Monist* (1918) p. 504.

50 See phrasings in Moore, #1, #3, #5 *et al.* To Moore all such items are as familiar as the tongues of angels, and it is difficult, perhaps even impossible to find a direct cite.

51 Kaplan and Copilowish, *Mind*, (1939), 478-484; Lewis and Langford, *Symbolic Logic*, p. 472; A. P. Ushenko, *The Problems of Logic* (1941) pp. 171, 175, 219; Roy W. Sellars in *Philosophy and Phenomeological Research*, V, (1944) 99-100; G. Ryle, *Proceedings of the Aristotelian Society*, Supplementary Vol. IX (1929) pp. 80-96. An excellent start, and perhaps even a despairing finish, may be made with the Oxford Dictionary, or some other larger dictionary.

CHAPTER NINE

A CONFUSED "SEMIOTIC"[1]

I

CHARLES MORRIS, in *Signs, Language, and Behavior* (New York, 1946) declares himself a semiotician (p. 354) operating in harmony with "behavioristicians" (pp. 182, 250). "Semiotic," he tells us, is "the science of signs," and "semiosis" is that sign-process which semioticians investigate (p. 353). If he is to "lay the foundation for a comprehensive and fruitful science of signs," his task is, he says, "to develop a language in which to talk about signs" (pp. v, 4, 17, 19), and for this, he believes, "the basic terms . . . are statable in terms drawn from the biological and physical sciences" (p. 19). It is possible in this way, he believes, to "suggest connections between signs and the behavior of animals and men in which they occur." (p. 2)

Here is a most laudable enterprise. I wish to examine carefully the technical language Professor Morris develops, find out whether it contains the makings of dependable expression such as we commonly call "scientific," and appraise his own opinion that the terms he adopts are "more precise, interpersonal, and unambiguous" than those favored by previous workers in this field (p. 28). The numerous special features of this book, often of high interest and value, I shall leave to others to discuss.[2]

We are greatly aided in our task by the glossary the author furnishes us. In it he "defines" [3] or otherwise characterizes the main "terms" of semiotic, and stars those which he deems "most important" as "the basis" for the rest. We shall center our attention on a central group of these starred terms, and upon the linguistic material out of which they are constructed. The reader is asked to keep in mind that the problem here is not whether, impressionistically, we can secure a fair idea as to what Professor Morris is talking about and as to what his opinions are, but rather whether his own assertion that he is building a scientific language, and thus creating a science, can be sustained through a close study of his own formulations. The issue will be found to be one of maximum importance for all future research and appraisal of knowings and knowns. Our conclusion will be that his attempt is a failure.

We are somewhat hampered by the fact that, although he builds throughout with respect to behavior, he does not "define" the terms he takes over from "general behavior theory," but says that these "really operate as undefined terms in this system" (p. 345). It is evident that this manner of being "undefined" is not at all the same as the manner we find in a geometrician's postulated "elements." Instead of freeing us from irrelevant questions, it burdens us at almost every step with serious problems as to just how we are to understand the writer's words.

There are other difficulties such as those that arise when we find a term heavily stressed with respect to what it presents, but with no correlated name or names to make clear just what it excludes. The very important term "preparatory-stimulus" is a case in point; the set of variations on the word "disposition," later listed, is another. The difficulty here is that in such instances one is compelled to interpolate other names to make the pattern a bit clearer to oneself, and this always invokes a risk of injustice which one would wish to avoid.

From this point on I shall use the word semiotic to name, and to name only, the contents of the book before us. I shall use the word semiosis to name, and to name only, those ranges of sign-process [4] which semiotic identifies and portrays. It is evident that, so proceeding, the word "semiotician" will name Professor Morris in his characteristic activity in person, and nothing else.

Four none too sharply maintained characteristics of the point of view that underlies semiotical procedure may now be set down for the reader's preliminary guidance:

1. Semiotic "officially" [5] declares the word "behavior" as in use to name, and to name only, the muscular and glandular actions of organisms in goal-seeking (i.e., "purposive") process.[6]

2. Semiosis is expressly envisaged, and semiotic is expressly constructed, with reference to behavior as thus purposive in the muscular-glandular sense. If there exists anywhere any sign-process not immediately thus oriented, it is *technically* excluded from the semiotic which we have before us. (One form of behavioral process which most psychologists regard as involving sign, but which Morris' formulation excludes, is noted in footnote 48 following.) The assurance the semiotician gives us that semiotic provides us with a universal sign-theory does not alter this basic determination; neither does the weft of "sign-signify-significatum" and "sign-denote-denotatum" woven upon this muscular-purposive warp to make a total web.[7]

3. The two other main "factors" of semiotical inquiry — namely, stimulus and disposition to respond — are *not* behavior in the strict sense of the term in semiotic (even though now and then referred to nontechnically as behavioristic or behavioral).

4. With a very few, wholly incidental, exceptions all "official" reports in semiotic are made through the use of such key words as "produce," "direct," "control," "cause," "initiate," "motivate," "seek," and "determine." [8] Semiotic works thus in terms of putative "actors" rather than through direct description and report upon occurrences. This characteristic is so pronounced as to definitely establish the status of the book with respect to the general level of scientific inquiry.

Recall of the above characteristics will be desirable to avoid occasional misunderstandings.

Our primary materials of inquiry are, as has been said, to be found in a central group of the terms that are starred as basic. In fabricating them, the semiotician uses many other words not starred in the glossary, and behind and beyond these certain other words, critical for understanding, though neither starred nor listed. Among the starred terms that we shall examine as most important for our purposes are *sign, *preparatory-stimulus, *response-sequence, *response-disposition, and *significatum. Among unstarred words conveying key materials are behavior, response, stimulus and stimulus-object. Among key words neither starred nor listed are 'reaction,' 'cause,' 'occasion,' 'produce,' 'source,' and 'motivate.' It is interesting to note that *preparatory-stimulus is starred, but stimulus and stimulus-object are not (while "object" is neither indexed nor discussed in any pertinent sense); that *behavior-family is starred but behavior is not; that *response-disposition and *response-sequence are starred but response is not; that *sign and *sign-family are starred but sign-behavior is not. We have thus the "basic" terms deliberately presented in nonbasic settings.

II

Before taking up the terminological organization of semiotic, it will be well to consider two illustrations of the types of statement and interpretation that frequently appear. They serve to illuminate the problems that confront us and the reasons that make necessary the minuteness of our further examination.

Consider the following: "For something to be a sign to an organism . . . does not require that the organism signify that the something in question is a sign, for a sign can exist without there being a sign that it is a sign. There can, of course, be signs that something is a sign, and it is

possible to signify by some signs what another sign signifies." (p. 16).

The general purport of this statement is easy to gather
and some addicts of Gertrude Stein would feel at home
with it, but precision of expression is a different matter.
The word "sign" is used in semiotic in the main to indicate
either a "stimulus" or an "object," [9] but if we try to substitute either of these in the statement we find difficulty in
understanding and may lose comprehension altogether.
Moreover, the verb "signify," closely bound with "sign"
and vital in all semiotical construction, is found strangely
entering with three types of subjects: an "organism" can
signify; a "sign" can signify; and indefinitely "it is possible" to signify.

Try, next, what happens in the development of the following short sentence: "Signs in the different modes of
signifying signify differently, have different significata."
(p. 64).

We have here a single bit of linguistic expression (centering in the word "sign") differentiated with respect to par-
ticipations as subject, verb, or object, and with the three
phases or aspects, or whatever they are, put back together
again into a sentence. What we have before us looks a bit
like a quasi-mathematical organization of sign, signify,
and significatum, the handling of which would require the
firm maintenance of high standards; or else like a pseudo-
physical construction of the general form of "Heat is what
makes something hot." We shall not concern ourself with
the possible difficulties under these respective interpretations, but solely with what happens to the words in the
text.

The sentence in question opens a passage dealing with
criteria for differentiating modes of signifying (pp. 64-67).
I have analyzed the elusive phrasings of its development
half a dozen times, and offer my results for what they may
be worth as a mere matter of report on the text, but with
no great assurance that I have reached the linguistic bottom

of the matter. It appears that the semiotician starts out prepared to group the "modes of signifying" into four types: those answering respectively to queries about "where," "what," "why," and "how" (p. 65, lines 9, 10, 11; p. 72, lines 6-7 from bottom of page). To establish this grouping semiotically, he employs an extensive process of phrase-alternation. He first gives us a rough sketch of a dog seeking food, thereby to "provide us with denotata of the signs which we wish to introduce" (p. 65). Here he lists four types of "stimuli," presents them as "signs," and calls them identifiors, designators, appraisors, and prescriptors. He tells us (p. 65, bottom) that these stimuli "influence" behaviors, "and so" dispositions (although, in his official definition for sign,[10] behaviors do not influence dispositions but instead these latter must be built up independently prior to the behaviors). Next he shifts his phrasings in successive paragraphs from disposition to interpretant, and then from interpretant to significatum, saying what appears to be the same thing over again, but each time under a different name. Finally he revamps his phrasing again into a form in which it is not the stimulus that "disposes" but the interpreter who "is disposed." [11] He then suggests that a new set of names be introduced for four major kinds of significata: namely, *locatum, discriminatum, valuatum,* and *obligatum.* Since there is no official difference between significatum and signification (p. 354) he now has acquired names indicative of the four "modes of signifying" which is what was desiderated.

If the reader will now take these two sets of names and seek to discover what progress in inquiry they achieve, he will at once find himself involved in what I believe to be a typical semiotic uncertainty. This is the problem of verbal and nonverbal signs, their analysis and organization.[13] Taking the case of identifior and *locatum* as developed on pages 64-69, (I am following here the typographical pattern of the text) one finds that both of these words enter without addition of the single quotation marks which are added when it is the word, as a *word,* that is under examination. Now in the case of identifior the lack of single quotation marks corresponds with the use of the word in the text where certain nonverbal facts of life, such as dog, thirst, water, and pond, are introduced. In the case of *locatum*, however, the word enters directly as sign, with indirect reference to it as a term. The italics here are apparently used to stress the status of locatum and its three italicised companions as "special terms for the special kinds of significata involved in signs in the various modes of signifying." (p. 66). The textual introduction of *locatum* in extension from identifior is as follows: "We will use *locatum, discriminatum, valuatum,* and *obligatum* as signs signifying the significata of identifiors, designators, appraisors, and prescriptors." (p. 67). Under this treatment semiotic yields the following exhibits:

a) The identifior has for its significatum location in space and time.

b) *Locatum* is a sign signifying the significatum of identifior.

c) *Locatum* therefore has for its significatum a location in space and time.

d) The significatum of *locatum* thus differentiates one of the great "modes of signifying" which are the subject of investigation — the one, namely, concerning locations.

Here we have an army of words that march up the hill, and then march down again. What is the difference between "location" at the beginning and "location" at the end? How great is the net advance? This can perhaps best be appraised by simplifying the wording. If we drop the word 'significatum' as unproductively reduplicative with respect to 'sign' and 'signify,' we get something as follows:

a) That which a sign of location signifies is location.

b) *Locatum* is a sign used to signify that which a sign of location signifies.

c) *Locatum* thus signifies location.

d) *Locatum* now becomes a special term to name this particular "mode of signifying."

A second approximation to understanding may be

gained by substituting the word 'indicate' for 'signify,' under a promise that no loss of precision will thereby be involved. We get:

a) Signs of location indicate locations (and now my story's begun).

b) *Locatum,* the word, is "used" to indicate what signs of location indicate.

c) *Locatum* thus indicates location.

d) Location, thus indicated by *locatum,* enables the isolation behaviorally (p. 69) of that "mode of signifying" in which signs of location are found to indicate location. (and now my story is done).

In other words the progress made in the development from terms in *or* to terms in *um* is next to nothing.

The semiotician seems himself to have doubts about his terms in "um," for he assures us that he is not "peopling the world with questionable 'entities' " and that the "um" terms "refer only to the properties something must have to be denoted by a sign" (p. 67). But " 'property' is a very general term used to embrace . . . the denotata of signs" (p. 81), and the locatum and its compeers have been before us as significata, not denotata; and signifying and denoting are strikingly different procedures in semiosis, if semiotic is to be believed (pp. 347, 354).[14] The degree of salvation thus achieved for the terms in "um" does not seem adequate.

These and other similar illustrations of semiotical procedure put us on our guard as to wordings. The second of them is important, not only because it provides the foundation for an elaborate descriptive classification of significations which is one of the main developments of semiotic,[15] but further, because it displays the attitude prominent throughout semiotic whereunder subjects, verbs, and objects are arbitrarily severed and made into distinct "things" after which their mechanistic manipulation over against one another is undertaken as the solution of the semiotical problem.

III

With this much of a glimpse at the intricacy of the terminological inquiry ahead of us, we may proceed to examine the semiotician's basic construction line upon line. We shall take his main terminological fixations, dissect their words (roughly "lansigns" in semiotic, p. 350),[16] and see if, after what microscopic attention we can give them, they will feel able to nest down comfortably together again. We shall consider thirty-three such assertions, numbering them consecutively for ease of reference. Only a few of them will be complete as given, but all of them, we hope, will be true-to-assertion, so far as they go, whether they remain in the original wordings or are paraphrased. Paraphrases are employed only where the phrasings of the text involve so much correlated terminology that they are not clear directly and immediately as they stand.

Where first introduced, or where specially stressed, typographical variations will be employed to indicate to the reader whether the term in question is stressed as basic by the semiotician in person, or is selected for special attention by his present student. Stars and italics are used for the basic starred word of the glossary; italics without stars are used for words which the glossary lists unstarred; single quotes are used for unlisted words which semiotic apparently takes for granted as commonly well enough understood for its purposes. Where no page reference is given, the citation or paraphrase will be from the glossary definition for the term in question. Practical use in this way of italics, asterisks, and single quotation marks has already been made in the last paragraph of Section I of this chapter.

We first consider the materials for prospective scientific precision that are offered by the general linguistic approach to the word "sign."

1. Sign (preliminary formulation): "Something" that "controls behavior towards a goal" (p. 7).

2. Sign (roughly): "Something [17] that directs behavior

with respect to something that is not at the moment a stimulus" (p. 354).

3. *Sign* (officially): A kind of "stimulus." [18]

4. *Stimulus:* [19] A "physical energy."

5. *Stimulus-object:* "The 'source' of a stimulus."

6. 'Stimulus-properties': "The 'properties' of the 'object' that produce stimuli" (p. 355).

We have here the presentation of sign on one side as an object or property, and on the other side as an energy or stimulus. We have the unexplained use of such possibly critical words as "source of," "produce," "direct," "control." We are given no definite information as to what organization the words of this latter group have in terms of one another, and so far as one can discover the problems of their organization are of no concern to semiotic. The way is prepared for the semiotician to use the word "sign" for either object or stimulus, when and as convenient, and if and as equivalent.

A second group of words involved in the presentation of the basic "preparatory-stimulus" has to do with impacts upon the organism.

7. 'Reaction': Something that "a stimulus 'causes' . . . in an organism" (p. 355).

8. *Response:* "Any action of a muscle or gland."

9. *Preparatory-stimulus:* "A stimulus that 'influences' a response to some other stimulus." It "necessarily 'causes' . . . a reaction . . . but this reaction need not be a response." [20]

10. Evocative Stimulus (at a guess)[21]: a presumptively primary or standard form of stimulus which is *not* "preparatory", i.e., which, although a stimulus, is not in the semiotic sense a "sign."

To its primarily established "object" or "stimulus" semiotic has now added the effect that the object or stimulus has — that which it (or energy, or property) causes (or produces, or is the source of) — namely, the reaction. One form of reaction it declares to be "any action of a muscle or gland," and it names this form response. Another form (or kind, or variant, or differentiation) of stimulus is one which "influences" some other response by necessarily causing a reaction which is not a response; this form is called "preparatory."

It is important to know what is happening here.[22] Names widely used, but thus far not established in firm dependable construction by the psychologies, are being taken over "as is," with no offer of evidence as to their fitness for semiotical use.[23] "Stimulus" is, of course, the characteristic word of this type. The word "response," although it is much more definitely presented as presumptively a form of reaction, is almost always (I could perhaps venture to say, always) called "action" rather than "reaction" — an attitude which has the effect of pushing it off to a distance and presenting it rather "on its own" than as a phase of semiosical process.[24]

We shall next see that the part of reaction which is *not* response (or, at least, some part of that part) is made into a kind of independent or semi-independent factor or component, viz., disposition; and that a part of that part which *is* response is made into another such factor, viz., behavior. Dispositions and behaviors are thus set over against each other as well as over against stimuli; and the attempt is made to organize all three through various unidentified types of causation without any apparent inquiry into the processes involved.

11. *Response-disposition:* [25] "The state of an organism at a given time such that" (under certain additional conditions) "a given response takes place." "Every preparatory-stimulus causes a disposition to respond" but "there may be dispositions to respond which are not caused by preparatory-stimuli" (p. 9).

12. 'Disposition': Apparently itself a "state of an organism." Described as like being "angry" before "behaving angrily"; or like having typhoid fever before showing the grosser symptoms (p. 15).[26]

13. 'State of an organism': Illustrated by a 'need' (p. 352) or by a brain wave (p. 13). It is a something that can be 'removed' by a goal-object (p. 349), and something "such that" in certain circumstances "a response takes place" (p. 348). (Semiotic rests heavily upon it, but as with 'disposition' there is little it tells us about it.)

14. *Interpretant:* "The disposition in an interpreter to respond because of a sign." "A readiness to act" (p. 304). Perhaps "synonymous" with "idea" (pp. 30, 49).[27]

15. *Interpreter:* "An organism for which something is a sign."

We now have needs, states of the organism, and dispositions, all brought loosely into the formulation. Beyond this some dispositions are response-dispositions, and some response-dispositions are caused by signs. Also as we shall next find (No. 16) some sign-caused responses are purposive, and under the general scheme there must certainly be a special group of sign-caused, purposive dispositions to mediate the procedure, though I have not succeeded in putting a finger clearly upon it. What for the moment is to be observed is that the sign-caused, purposive-or-not, response-disposition gets rebaptized as "interpretant." Now a sharp name-changing *may* be an excellent aid to clarity, but this one needs its clarity examined. Along with being an interpretant, it demands an "interpreter," not professedly in place of the "organism," but still with a considerable air of being promoted to a higher class. While dispositions are mostly "caused," interpretants tend to be "produced" by interpreters and, indeed, the radical differentiation between signals and symbols (Nos. 20 and 21) turns on just this difference. Dispositions have not been listed as "ideas," but interpretants are inclined to be "synonymous" with ideas, while still remaining dispositions. There is also a complex matter of "signification" which runs along plausibly, as we shall later see, in terms of interpretants, but is far from being at home among dispositions directly arising out of stimulant energy. These are matters, not of complaint at the moment, but merely to be kept in mind.

Having developed this much of semiotic — the disposition factor — so as to show, at least partially, its troublesome unclarity, we may now take a look at "response" in semiosis as distinct from stimulus and from disposition; in other words, at behavior, remembering always that the problem that concerns us is one of precision of terminology and of hoped-for accuracy of statement.

16. *Behavior:* "Sequences of . . . actions of muscles and glands" (i.e., of "responses") "by which an organism seeks goal-objects." "Behavior is therefore 'purposive.' "

17. *Behavior-family:* A set of such sequences similar in initiation and termination with respect to objects and needs.[28]

18. *Sign-behavior:* "Behavior in which signs occur." Behavior "in which signs exercise control" (p. 7).

Here we have behavior as strictly muscle-gland action to put alongside of sign as stimulus-energy and of interpretant as nonmuscular, nonglandular reaction. Despite this distinctive status of behavior, it appears that sign-behavior is a kind of behavior that has signs occurring *in* it, or, alternatively, a kind *in which* signs exercise control. In such a rendering sign-behavior becomes approximately equivalent to the very loosely used "sign-process" (No. 25, q.v.) .[29] This is no trifling lapse but is a confusion of expression lying at the very heart of the semiotical treatment of semiosical process.

We know fairly well where to look, not only when we want to find physical "objects" in the environment, but also when we seek the "muscles and glands" that make up "behavior," being in this respect much better off than when comparably we seek to find a locus for a disposition or an interpretant. Nevertheless a variety of problems arise concerning the technical status of behavior which may be left to the reader to answer for himself, reminding him only that precision of statement is what is at stake. Such problems are whether (1) muscle-gland action, set off independently or semi-independently for itself is intelligibly to be considered as itself "purposive"; (2) what muscle-gland action would be as theoretically "purposive," apart from stimulation; and (3) what part the "glands" play in this purposive semiotical construction. Probably only after the semiotical plan of locations for stimuli, signs, and purposes in terms of receptors, muscles, and glands has been worked out, can one face the further problem as to what locations are left over for dispositions and interpretants. On this last point the semiotician is especially cagey.[30]

We are now, perhaps, in a position to consider more precisely what a sign may be in semiotic:

19. *Sign* (officially) [31]: a preparatory-stimulus which,

(*a*) in the absence of certain evocative stimulation,[32]

(*b*) secures a reinvocation of, or replacement for, it, by

(*c*) "causing" in the organism a response-disposition,[33] which is

(*d*) capable of achieving [34] a response-sequence such as the evocative stimulus would have 'caused.'

All this takes place under a general construction that semiosis has its outcomes in purposive behavior, where the words "purposive" and "behavioral" are co-applicable, and where behavior proper in the semiotic sense is an affair of muscles and glands.[35]

It should now be sufficiently well established on the basis of the body of the text that a sign in semiotic is officially a kind of stimulus, produced by an object, which "causes" a disposition (perhaps one named "George") to appear, and which then proceeds to "let George do it," the "it" in question being behavior, that is, muscle-gland action of the "purposive" type. Under this *official formulation*, thunder, apparently, would not semiotically be a sign of storm unless it "caused" a disposition to put muscles and glands into purposive action.[36] Sign, as stimulus, belongs strictly under the first of the three basic, major, operative, relatively independent or semi-independent (as they are variously described) factors: stimulus, disposition, and overt body-action. Not until this is plainly understood will one get the full force and effect of the dominant division of signs in semiotical construction, viz., that signs are divided officially into two groups: those produced by interpreters and all others.

20. *Symbol: "A sign that is produced by its interpreter and that acts as a substitute for some other sign with which it is synonymous."

21. *Signal: "A sign that is not a symbol."

22. *Use of a Sign: "A sign is used . . . if it is produced by an interpreter as a means. . . ." [37] "A sign that is used is thus a means-object."

Certain questions force themselves upon our attention.

If a sign is by official definition a "stimulus" produced by a "property" of an "object" which is its "source," in what sense can the leading branch of signs be said to be produced by "interpreters," rather than by "properties of objects"?

Assuming factual distinctions along the general line indicated by signal and symbol, and especially when such distinctions are presented as of maximum importance, ought not semiotic, as a science stressing the need of terminological strength, be able to give these distinctions plain and clear statement? [38]

What sense, precisely, has the word "use" in semiotic when one compares the definition for "symbol" with that for "use"? [39]

Three other definitions, two of them of starred terms, next need a glance:

23. *Sign-vehicle: "A particular event or object . . . that functions as a sign." "A particular physical event — such as a given sound or mark or movement — which is a sign will be called a sign-vehicle" (p. 20; italics for "is" and "called" not used in Morris' text).

24. *Sign-family: "A set of similar sign-vehicles that for a given interpreter have the same signification."

25. 'Sign-process': "the status of being a sign, the interpretant, the fact of denoting, the significatum" (p. 19). [40]

The peculiarities of expression are great. How is an object that "functions" as a sign different from another object that "stimulates" us as a sign or from one that "is" a sign? Is the word "particular" which modifies "event" the most important feature of the definition, and what is its sense? We are told (p. 20) that the distinction of sign-vehicle and sign-family is often not relevant, but nevertheless is of theoretical importance. Just what can this mean? We hear talk (p. 21) of sign-vehicles that have "significata"; but is not signification the most important characteristic of sign itself rather than of vehicle? If sign is energy is there some sense in which its vehicle is *not* energetic?

On the whole we are left with the impression that the distinction between "sign" and "sign-vehicle," so far as linguistic signs go, is nothing more than the ancient difference between "meaning" and "word," rechristened but still before us in all its ancient unexplored crudity. What this distinction may amount to with respect to non-linguistic signs remains still more in need of clarification.[41]

Our attention has thus far been largely concerned with the semiosis of goal-seeking animals by way of the semiotical vocabulary of object, stimulus, disposition, need, muscle, and gland. We are now to see how there is embroidered upon it the phraseology of the epistemological logics of the past in a hoped-for crystallization of structure for the future.

26. *Signify:* "To act as a sign." "To have signification." "To have a significatum." (The three statements are said to be "synonymous.")

27. 'Signification': "No attempt has been made to differentiate 'signification' and 'significatum'" (p. 354).

28. *Significatum:* "The conditions" for "a denotatum." [42]

29. Sign (on suspicion): The "x" in "x *signifies its significatum*." [43]

30. *Denote:* "A sign that has a denotatum . . . is said to denote its denotatum."

31. *Denotatum:* "Anything that would permit the completion of the response-sequences to which an interpreter is disposed because of a sign." "Food in the place sought . . . is a denotatum" (p. 18). "A poet . . . is a denotatum of 'poet' " (p. 106).

32. Sign (on suspicion:) the "y" in "y *denotes its de-notatum.*"

33. *Goal-object:* "An object that partially or completely removes the state of an organism (the need) which motivates response-sequences."

The above is obviously a set of skeletons of assertions, but skeletonization or some other form of simplification is necessary if any trail is to be blazed through this region of semiotic. If we could be sure whether denotata and goal-objects were, or were not, "the same thing" for semiotic we might have an easier time deciphering the organization.[44] The characterizations of the two are verbally fairly close: "anything" for denotata is much like "an object" for goal-objects; "permitting completion" is much the same as "removing the need"; "is disposed" is akin to "motivates." But I have nowhere come across a definite statement of the status of the two with respect to each other, though, of course, I may have easily overlooked it. The first semiotical requirement for a denotatum is that it be "actual," or "existent" (pp. 17-20, 23, 107, 168; disregarding, perhaps, the case [p. 106] in which the denotatum of a certain ascriptor is "simply a situation such that . . ."). As "actual" the denotatum is that which the significatum is "conditions for." The significatum may remain "conditions" in the form of an "um" component of semiotic even if no denotatum "actually" exists,[45] so that the goal-object would then apparently be neither "actual" nor "existent" (except, perhaps, as present in "the mind of the interpreter" or in some terminological representative of such a "mind"). If goal-object and denotatum could be organized in a common form we might, perhaps, be able to deal more definitely with them. We are in even worse shape when we find, as we do occasionally, that significata may be "properties" as is the case with "formators" (pp. 157-158), or in their coverage of "utilitanda properties" (p. 304; see also p. 67); and that "property" itself is "a very general term used to embrace the denotata (*sic*) of signs . . ." (p. 81). Perhaps all that we can say descriptively as the case stands is that "denotatum" and "goal-object" are two different ways of talking about a situation not very well clarified with respect to either.

IV

I have endeavored to limit myself thus far to an attempt to give what may be called "the facts of the text." I hope the comments that I have interspersed between the numbered assertions have not gone much beyond what has been needed for primary report. In what follows I shall call attention to some of the issues involved, but even now not so much to debate them as to show their presence, their complexities, and the lack of attention given them.

In our preliminary statement of the leading character-istics of semiotic it was noted that the interpretation was largely in terms of causation and control. What this type of statement and of terminology does to the subject-matter at the hands of the semiotician may be interestingly seen if we focus attention upon the verbs made use of in the official accounts of "sign." What we are informed is (1) that if we are provided with a "stimulus-object" possessing "properties," then (2) these properties *produce* a kind of stimulus which (3) *influences* by (4) *causing* a disposition to appear, so that if (5) a state of the organism (a need) *motivates,* and if (6) the right means-objects are in place, then (7) it will come to pass that that which was produced at stage No. 4 proves to *be such that* (8) a response-sequence *takes place* wherein or whereby (9) the stimulus object of stage No. 1 or some other object is *responded* to as a goal-object which (10) in its turn *removes* the state of the or-ganism (the need) that was present in stage No. 5.

What these shifting verbs accomplish is clear enough. Whichever one fits most smoothly, and thus most inconspicuously, into a sentence is the one that is most apt to be used. A certain fluency is gained, but no precision. I have not attempted to make a full list of such wordings but have a few memoranda. "Produce," for example, can be used either for what the organism does, for what a property does, for what an interpreter does, or for what a sign does (pp. 25, 34, 38, 353, 355). It may be voluntary or involuntary (p. 27), though non-humans [46] are said seldom to produce (p. 198). In the use of a comparable verb, "to signify," either organisms or signs may be the actors (p. 16). Among other specimens of such linguistic insecurity are 'because of' (p. 252), 'occasion' (pp. 13, 155), 'substitute for' (p. 34), 'act as' (p. 354), 'determine' (p. 67), 'determine by decision' (p. 18), 'function as' (p. 354), 'be disposed to' (p. 66), 'connects with' (p. 18), 'answers to' (p. 18), 'initiates' (p. 346), 'affects in some way' (p. 9), 'affects or causes' (p. 8), 'controls' (p. 7), 'directs' (p. 354), 'becomes or produces' (p. 25), 'seeks' (p. 346), and 'uses' (p. 356). One can find sentences (as on p. 25) which actually seem to tell us that interpreters produce signs as substitutes for other signs which are synonymous with them and which originally made the interpreter do what they indicated, such that the substitutes which the interpreter himself has produced now make him do what the signs from without originally made him do.[47] The "fact" in question is one of familiar everyday knowledge. Not this fact, but rather the peculiarities of statement introduced by semiotical terminology are what here cause our concern.

V

Though vital to any thorough effort at research and construction, two great problems are left untouched by semiotic. These problems are, first, the factual organization of what men commonly call "stimulus" with that which they commonly call "object"; and, secondly, the corresponding organization of what the semiotician calls "interpreter" with what he calls "interpretant," or, more generally, of the factual status with respect to each other of "actor" and "action." The interpreter-interpretant problem is manifestly a special case of the ancient grammatical-historical program of separating a do-er from his things-done, on the assumption that the do-er is theoretically independent of his things-done, and that the things-done have status in some fairy realm of perfected being in independence of the doing-do. The case of stimulus-object on close inspection involves a quite similar issue. In semiotic the interior organization of disposition, interpretant, and significatum offers a special complexity. We can best show the status of these problems by appraising some of the remarks which the semiotician himself makes about the stepping stones he finds himself using as he passes through the swamps of his inquiry. No systematic treatment will be attempted since the material we have before us simply will not permit it without an enormous amount of complicated linguistic dissection far greater than the present occasion will tolerate.

Semiotic stresses for its development three main components: sign, disposition, and behavior; the first as what comes in; the second as a sort of intervening storage warehouse; the third as what goes out. For none of these, however, despite the semiotician's confidence that he is providing us "with words that are sharpened arrows" (p. 19), can their semiotical operations be definitely set down. Sign, as we have seen, is officially stimulus, practically for the most part object or property, and in the end a glisteningly transmogrified denoter or signifier. Behavior parades itself like a simple fellow, just muscles and glands in action; but while it is evidently a compartment of the organism it doesn't fit in as a compartment of the more highly specialized interpreter, although this interpreter is declared to be the very organism itself in sign action, no more, no less;

moreover, behavior is purposive in its own right, though what purposive muscles and glands all on their own may be is difficult to decipher. As for disposition (or rather response-disposition, since this is the particular case of disposition with which semiotic deals), it is, I shall at least allege, a monstrosity in the form of Siamese triplets, joined at the butts, hard to carve apart, and still harder to keep alive in union. One of these triplets is disposition physiologically speaking, which is just common habit or readiness to act. Another is interpretant which is disposition-in-signing (though why such double naming is needed is not clearly made evident). The third member of the triplet family is significatum, a fellow who rarely refers to his low-life sib but who, since he is not himself either incoming stimulus or outgoing muscle or gland action, has nowhere else to be at home other than as a member of the disposition-triplets — unless, indeed, as suspicion sometimes suggests, he hopes to float forever, aura-like or soul-like, around and above the other two.

The semiotician offers us several phrasings for his tripartite organization of "factors," (of which the central core is, as we have just seen, itself tripartite). "The factors operative in sign-processes are all either stimulus-objects or organic dispositions or actual responses" (p. 19). "Analysis," we are told, yields "the stimulus, response, and organic state terminology of behavioristics" (p. 251). The "three major factors" correspond to the "nature" of the environment, its "relevance" for needs, and the "ways in which the organism must act" (p. 62). The "relative independence of environment, need, and response" is mentioned (pp. 63-64).

Despite this stressed threeness in its various forms, the practical operation of semiotic involves five factors, even if the "disposition-triplets" are seen as fused into one. The two needed additions are object as differentiated from stimulus at one end, and interpreter (or personified organism) as differentiated from interpretant at the other.

(This does not mean that the present narrator wishes to introduce such items. He does not. It merely means that he finds them present and at work in the text, however furbished.) Object and stimulus we have seen all along popping in and out alternatively. "Interpreter" enters in place of interpretant whenever the semiotician wishes to stress the organism as itself the performer, producer, or begetter of what goes on. What this means is that, at both ends, the vital problems of human adaptational living in environments are entirely ignored — the problems, namely, of stimulus-object [48] and of actor-action.

What evidence does the semiotician offer for the presence of a disposition? He feels the need of evidence and makes some suggestions as to how it may be found (pp. 13-15). Each of his remarks exhibits an event of sign-process such that, if one *already believes* in dispositions as particulate existences, then, where sign-process is under way, it will be quite the thing to call a disposition in to help out. None of his exhibits, however, serves to make clear the factual presence of a disposition, whether for itself or as interpretant or as significatum, in any respect whatever as a separate factor located between the stimulation and the action. The only manifest "need" that the introduction of such a disposition seems to satisfy is the need of conforming to verbal tradition.

The issue here is not whether organisms have habits, but whether it is proper semiotically (or any other way) to set up a habit as a thing caused by some other thing and in turn causing a third thing, and use it as a basic factor in construction. Three passages of semiotic let the cat neatly out of the bag. The first says that even though a preparatory stimulus is the 'cause' of a disposition, "logically . . . 'disposition to respond' is the more basic notion" (p. 9). The second tells us that sign-processes "within the general class of processes involving mediation" are "those in which the factor of mediation is an interpretant" (p. 288). The third citation is possibly even more revealing, for we are told that "the merit of this formulation" (i.e., the use of a conventional, naïvely interpolated "disposition") "is that it does not require that the dog or the driver respond to the sign itself" (p. 10); [49] this being very close to saying that the merit of semiotic is that it can evade the study of facts and operate with puppet inserts.

There is another very interesting employment of disposition which should not be overlooked even though it can barely be mentioned here. Semiotic employs a highly specialized sign about signs called a "formator." The signs corresponding to the "modes of signification," at which we took an illustrative glance early in this chapter, are called "lexicators." The formator, however, is not a lexicator. Nevertheless it has to be a "sign," in order to fill out the construction; while to be a sign it has to have a "disposition" (interpretant). This, in the ordinary procedure, it could not attain in ordinary form. It is therefore allotted a "second-order disposition" (p. 157); and this, — since "interpretant" *via* "interpreter" represents the ancient "mind" in semiotic, — is about equivalent to introducing a two-story "mind" for the new "science" to operate with.

As concerns disposition-to-respond and interpretant in joint inspection, all that needs to be said is that if interpretant is simply one species of disposition and can so be dealt with, there is no objection whatever to naming it as a particular species. But, as we have seen in repeated instances, disposition shows itself primarily as a thing seemingly 'caused' from 'without,' while interpretant is very apt to be a thing, or property, or characteristic 'produced' from 'within.' Evading the words 'within' and 'without,' and switching names around does not seem to yield sufficient "science" to cope with this problem.

Consider next the significatum in its status in respect to the interpretant. Remarks upon this topic are rare, except in such a casual form as "a significatum . . . always involves an interpretant (a disposition . . .)" (p. 64-65). At only one point that I have noted is there a definite attempt

at explication. We are told (p. 18) that "the relation between interpretant and significatum is worth noting." Here
we find the significatum as a sort of interpretant turned
inside out. The situation will be well remembered by
many past sufferers from the ambiguity of the word "meaning." In effect, if the interpretant is a disposition with a
certain amount of more or less high-grade "meaning" in-
jected into it, then a significatum is this meaning more or
less referable to the environment rather than to the interpreter. "The interpretant," we are told, "*answers to* the
behavioral side of the behavior-environment complex";
as against this, "the significatum . . . *connects with* the
environmental side of the complex" (p. 18, italics supplied).
Here the interpretant enters "as a disposition," and the
significatum enters "as a set of terminal [50] conditions under
which the response-sequence can be completed," i.e., under
which the "disposition" can make good. What this whole
phase of semiotic most needs is the application to itself
of some of its specialized ascriptors with designators dominant.

As for the organization of significatum with denotatum,
and of both with ordinary muscle action and goal objects,
there seems little that can be said beyond the few problems
of fact that were raised following Assertions No. 26 to 33
in the text above. These comments had to be held to a
minimum because the interior organization lies somewhere behind a blank wall. To be noted is that while to be
"actual" or "existent" is the great duty imposed on the denotatum, the significatum is allotted its own type of actuality [51] and thingness, which is manifestly not of the denotatum type, but yet is never clearly differentiated from
the other. Here is one of the greatest issues of semiotic
— one which may be put in the form of the question "how
comes that conditions are *ums?*" The semiotician could
well afford to keep this question written on his every cuff.[52]
The other great question as to the significata is, of course:
How does it come about that the sign (stimulus) of No. 19

in any of its crude forms, "object," "property," "thing," or "energy," mushrooms into the stratosphere of "the good," "the beautiful," and "the true," with or without the occasional accompanying "denotation" of a few actual goodies, pretties, or verities?

VI

At the start of this chapter it was said that our examination would be expressly limited to an appraisal of the efficiency of the technical terminology which semiotic announced it was establishing as the basis for a future science; we left to others the discussion of the many interesting and valuable contributions which might be offered along specialized lines. The range of our inquiry has thus been approximately that which Professor Morris in a summary and appraisal of his own work (p. 185) styles "the behavioral analysis of signs." The specialized developments which he there further reports as "basic to his argument" are the "modes" of signifying, the "uses" of signs, and the "mode-use" classification of types of discourse, with these all together leading the way to a treatment of logic and mathematics as discourse in the "formative mode" and the "informative use" (pp. 169 ff., 178 ff.).[53] Reminder is made of these specialized developments at this point in order to maintain a proper sense of proportion as to what has here been undertaken. It is, of course, practicable for a reader primarily interested in mode, use, and type to confine himself to these subjects, without concern over the behavioral analysis underlying their treatment.

With respect to the materials which semiotical terminology identifies, we may now summarize. The organism's activities with respect to environments are divided into stimulations, dispositions, and responses. Sign-processes are similarly divided: a certain manner of indirect stimulation is called sign; the sign produces, not a response in muscle-gland action, but a kind of disposition called in-

terpretant; the interpretant, in turn, under proper conditions, produces a particular kind of muscle-gland action —
the "purposive" kind — which is called behavior.[54] Sign
must always be a stimulus; disposition (so far as sign-process
is concerned) always the result of a sign; [55] and behavior
always a purposive muscular or glandular action; if semiotic is to achieve its dependable terminological goal.[56]

With respect to the actualization of this program, we
quickly discover that semiotic presents a leading class of
signs (symbols) which are *not* stimuli in the declared sense,
but instead are "produced by interpreters" (all other signs
being signals). We learn also that many interpretants are
commonly produced by interpreters (by way of symbols)
although they are themselves dispositions, and dispositions
(so far as sign-process goes) are caused by properties of
objects. We discover that significata have been introduced
into the system without any developed connection with the
terminology of goal-objects, purposive behaviors, dispositions, interpretants, or even with that of sign, save as the
word "sign" enters into the declaration that "signs signify
significata." We find also certain interstitial semiotical
appellations called denotata and identified only in the
sense of the declaration that "signs" (sometimes) "denote
denotata." We have the "use" of a sign made distinct from
its behavioral presence; we have denotata declared to be
actual existences in contrast with significata which are
"the conditions" for them; we then have significata gaining a form of actuality while denotata shrink back at times
into something "situational." As a special case of such
terminological confusion we have significata showing themselves up in an emergency as "properties," although "property" is in general the producer of a stimulus (p. 355) and
although it is in particular described as "a very general
term used to embrace . . . denotata" (p. 81); so that the
full life-history of the process property-sign-signify-signi-
ficatum-denote-denotatum-property ought to be well
worth inquiry as an approach to a theory of sign-behavior.[57]

A glance at some of the avowed sources of semiotic may throw some light on the way in which its confusions arise. Its use of the word "interpretant" is taken from Charles Sanders Peirce,[58] and its treatment in terms of "purposive" response is from what Professor Morris calls "behavioristics," more particularly from the work of Edward C. Tolman.[59] The difficulty in semiotic may be fairly well covered by saying that these two sources have been brought into a verbal combination, with Tolman providing the basement and ground floor while Peirce provides the penthouse and the attics, but with the intervening stories nowhere built up through factual inquiry and organization.

Peirce very early in life [60] came to the conclusion that all thought was in signs and required a time. He was under the influence of the then fresh Darwinian discoveries and was striving to see the intellectual processes of men as taking place in this new natural field. His pragmaticism, his theory of signs, and his search for a functional logic all lay in this one line of growth. Peirce introduced the word "interpretant," not in order to maintain the old mentalistic view of thought, but for quite the opposite purpose, as a device, in organization with other terminological devices, to show how "thoughts" or "ideas" as subjects of inquiry were not to be viewed as psychic substances or as psychically substantial, but were actually processes under way in human living. In contrast with this, semiotic uses Peirce's term in accordance with its own notions as an aid to bring back *sub rosa*,[61] the very thing that Peirce — and James and Dewey as well — spent a good part of their lives trying to get rid of.[62]

Tolman has done his work in a specialized field of recognized importance. Along with other psychologists of similar bent he took animals with highly developed yet restricted ranges of behavior, and channelized them as to stock, environment, and activities. He then, after many years, developed a terminology to cover what he had ob-

served. I keep his work close to my table though I may
not use it, perhaps, as often as I should. The fact that the
results which Tolman and his fellow workers have secured
may be usefully reported in terms of stimulus, need, and
response does not, however, suggest to me that this report
can be straightway adopted as a basic formulation for all
procedures of human knowledge. When Tolman, for example, recognizes "utilitanda" one can know very definitely
what he intends; but when Morris takes up Tolman's "utilitanda properties" and includes them, "when signified,
under the term 'significatum' " (p. 304) just as they stand,
intelligibility drops to a much lower level.

Semiotic thus takes goal-seeking psychology at the rat
level, sets it up with little change, and then attempts to
spread the cobwebs of the older logics and philosophies
across it. The failure of Morris' attempt does not mean,
of course, that future extensions of positive research may
not bring the two points of approach together.

Broadening the above orientation from immediate
sources to the wider trends in the development of modern
knowledge, we may report that much of the difficulty
which semiotic has with its terminology lies in its endeavor to conciliate two warring points of view. One point
of view represents the ancient lineage of selves as actors,
in the series souls, minds, persons, brains. The other derives from Newtonian mechanics in which particles are
seen as in causal interaction. The former is today so much
under suspicion that it makes its entries largely under
camouflage. The latter is no longer dominant even in the
physics of its greatest successes. Harnessing together these
two survivors from the past does not seem to yield a live
system which enables sound descriptions of observations
in the manner that modern sciences strive always to attain.

VII

So great are the possibilities of misinterpretation in such
an analysis as the above that I summarize anew as to its

objectives. I have aimed to make plain the "factors" (as purported "facts") which Professor Morris' "terms" introduce, but to reject neither his "factors" nor his "terms" because of my own personal views. I admit them both freely *under hypothesis* which is as far as I care to go with any alternatives which I myself propose. This, manifestly, is not easy to achieve with this subject and in this day, but one may at least do his best at trying. Under this approach his "terms" are required to make good both as between themselves and with respect to the "facts" for which they are introduced to stand. To test their success I take the body of his text for my material and endeavor to ascertain how well his terms achieve their appointed tasks. What standards we adopt and how high we place them depends on the importance of the theory and on the claims made for it. When in his preface Professor Morris names an associate as having done "the editing of the various rewritings," although in the immediately preceding paragraph this same associate had been listed among advisers none of whom "saw the final text," we recognize a very trifling slip. When slips of this kind in which one statement belies another appear in the body of a work in such an intricate field as the present one, we recognize them as unfortunate but as something our poor flesh is heir to. But when such defects are scattered everywhere — in every chapter and almost on every page of a book purported to establish a new science to serve as a guide to many sciences, and when they affect each and every one of the leading terms the book declares "basic" for its construction, then it is time to cry a sharp halt and to ask for a redeployment of the terminological forces. This is the state of the new "semiotic" and the reason for our analysis. Only the radical importance of the inquiry for many branches of knowledge can justify the amount of space and effort that have been expended.

[1] This chapter is written by Bentley.

² A discussion by Max Black under the title "The Limitations of a Behavioristic Semiotic" in *The Philosophical Review*, LVI (1947), 258-272, confirms the attitude of the present examination towards several of Morris' most emphasized names such as "preparatory" "disposition" and "signification." Its discussion is, however, on the conventional lines of yes, no, and maybe so, and does not trace back the difficulty into traditional linguistic fixations as is here attempted. See also reviews by A. F. Smullyan in *The Journal of Symbolic Logic*, XII (1947), 49-51; by Daniel J. Bronstein in *Philosophy and Phenomenological Research*, VII (1947), 643-649; and by George Gentry and Virgil C. Aldrich in *The Journal of Philosophy*, XLIV (1947), 318-329.

³ I shall permit myself in this chapter to use the words "define" and "term" casually and loosely as the author does. This is not as a rule, safe practice, but in the present case it eliminates much incidental qualification of statement, and is, I believe, fairer than would be a continual quibbling as to the rating of his assertions in this respect.

⁴ "Sign-process" is used by Morris in a very general and very loose sense. See Assertion No. 25 following.

⁵ I shall use the word "official" occasionally to indicate the express affirmations of the glossary as to terminology; this in the main only where contrasts suggest themselves between the "official" use and other scattered uses.

⁶ The word "behavioristics" is used loosely for wider ranges of inquiry. The compound "sign-behavior" is sometimes loosely, sometimes narrowly used, so far as the component "behavior" is concerned.

⁷ This statement applies to semiotic as it is now before us and to the range it covers. Professor Morris leaves the way open for other "phenomena" to be entered as "signs" in the future (p. 154, *et passim*). These passages refer in the main, however, to minor, marginal, increments of report, and do not seem to allow for possible variations disruptive of his behavioral construction.

⁸ A longer list of such words with illustration of their application will be given later in this chapter.

⁹ A variety of other ranges of use for the word will be noted later: *see* Assertions No. 1, 2, 3, 19, 29, and 32; also footnote 31.

¹⁰ See Assertion No. 19 later in this paper, and the accompanying comment.

¹¹ Such a shift as this from an assertion that the stimulus (or sign or denotatum) "disposes the dog" to do something to the assertion that "the interpreter (i.e., the dog) is disposed" to do it, is common in semiotic. The trouble is that the "is disposed to" does not enter as a proper passive form of the verb "disposes," but is used practically (even if not categorically) to assert power in an actor; and this produces a radical shift

in the gravamen of construction and expression. As a personal opinion, perhaps prematurely expressed, I find shifts of this type to be a major fault in semiotic. They can be successfully put over, I believe, only with verbs carefully selected *ad hoc*, and their employment amounts to something very much like semiotical (or, perhaps more broadly, philosophical) punning.

12 Elsewhere expressed: "Identifiors *may be said* to signify location in space and time" (p. 66, italics supplied).

13 The words sign, signify, and significatum are employed, often indiscriminately for both language and nonlanguage events. Available typographical marks for differentiation are often omitted, as with the cited matter in the text. Distinction of interpretation in terms of interpreters and their powers to "produce" seems here wholly irrelevant. This situation is high-lighted by almost any page in the Glossary. The glossary entries are at times technically offered as "definitions," at times not, and they are frequently uncertain in this respect. The reports on these entries may begin "A sign . . ."; "A term . . ."; or "A possible term. . . ." But also they may begin: "An object . . ."; "An organism . . ."; "A significatum . . ."; or "The time and place. . . ." Thus the entry for *locatum* reads: "Locatum. . . . A significatum of an identifior." To correspond with the treatment in the text, this should perhaps have been put: Locatum. . . . A sign (word?, name?, term?) for the significatum of an identifior. This form of differentiation is usually unimportant in nontechnical cases, and I do not want to be understood as recommending it or adopting it in any case; it is only for the comprehension of semiotic that it here is mentioned. My report on the cases of identifior and *locatum* as first presented in magazine publication was defective in phrasing in this respect. Reexamination has shown this blind spot in semiotic to be much more serious than I had originally made it out to be.

14 The status of denotation with respect to signification is throughout obscure in semiotic. The practical as distinguished from the theoretical procedure is expressed by the following sentence from p. 18: "Usually we start with signs which denote and then attempt to formulate the significatum of a sign by observing the properties of denotata." Unfortunately before we are finished "properties" will not only have appeared as the source of signs but also as the last refuge of some of the significata. As concerns Morris' "where," "what," "why," and "how" modes of "signifying," comparison with J. S. Mill's five groups (existence, place, time, causation, and resemblance), *A System of Logic* (I, i, Chap. VI, Sec. 1) may have interest, as also the more elaborate classification by Ogden and Richards in connection with their treatment of definition (*The Meaning of Meaning*, [New York, 1923], pp. 217 ff.).

15 Not examined in the present chapter, which is confined to the problem of underlying coherence. See footnote 53.

16 However, "the term 'word' . . . corresponds to no single semiotical term" (p. 222).

[17] For the use of "thing" in "something" compare: "The buzzer is the sign" (p. 17) ; "The words spoken are signs" (p. 18).

[18] For type of stimulus and conditions see Assertion No. 19 following and compare Nos. 29 and 32.

[19] *"Stimulus:* Any physical energy that acts upon a receptor of a living organism" (p. 355).

[20] "If something is a preparatory stimulus of the kind specified in our . . . formulation it is a sign" (p. 17).

[21] "In a sign-process something becomes an evocative stimulus only because of the existence of something else as a preparatory-stimulus" (p. 308). This name does not appear, so far as I have noted, except in this one passage. I insert it here because something of the kind seems necessary to keep open the question as to whether, or in what sense, psychological stimuli are found (as distinct from physiological excitations) which are *not* signs. I do not want to take issue here on either the factual or terminological phases of the question, but merely to keep it from being overlooked. (See p. 252, note D.) The words quoted may, of course, be variously read. They might, perhaps, be intended to indicate, not a kind of stimulus genetically prior to or more general than "preparatory stimulus," but instead a kind that did not come into "existence" at all except following, and as the "product" of, preparatory stimulation.

[22] A little attention to such reports as that of the committee of the British Association for the Advancement of Science which spent seven years considering the possibility of "quantitative estimates of sensory events" would be of value to all free adaptors of psychological experiment and terminology. See S. S. Stevens, "On the Theory of Scales of Measurement," *Science,* CIII (1946), 677-80.

[23] See, however, Morris' appendices No. 6 and 7, and remarks on his relation to Tolman toward the end of the present chapter.

[24] John Dewey's "Reflex Arc" paper of 1896 should have ended this sort of thing forever for persons engaged in the broader tasks of construction. The point of view of recent physiology seems already well in advance of that of semiotic in this respect.

[25] The same as *disposition to respond* (pp. 348, 353). The "additional conditions" are "conditions of need" and "of supporting stimulus-objects" (p. 11). *"Need"* is itself an 'organic state' (p. 352), but no attempt to "probe" it is made (p. 250).

[26] I have noticed nothing more definite in the way of observation or description. Discussion of dispositions and needs (and of producers and interpreters) with respect to expression, emotion, and usage, will be found pp. 67-69.

[27] Semiotic, while not using "mentalist" terms at present, retains mentalist facts and suggests the possibility that "all mentalist terms" may be "incorporable" within semiotic at some later time (p. 30).

[28] This is a very useful verbal device, but not one, so far as I have observed, of any significance in the construction, though it is listed (pp. 8-11) as one of the four prominent "concepts" in semiotic along with stimulus, disposition and response. What it accomplishes is to save much complicated phrasing with respect to similarities absent and present. The typically pleonastic phrasing of the "definition" is as follows: "Any set of response-sequences which are initiated by similar stimulus-objects and which terminate in these objects as similar goal-objects for similar needs."

[29] For loose uses of "sign-behavior" see pp. 15 and 19.

[30] Professor George V. Gentry, in a paper "Some Comments on Morris' 'Class' Conception of the Designatum," *The Journal of Philosophy*, XLI (1944), 383-384, examined the possible status of the interpretant and concluded that a neurocortical locus was indicated, and that Morris did not so much reject this view as show himself to be unaware that any problem was involved. This discussion concerned an earlier monograph by Morris (*Foundations of the Theory of Signs, International Encyclopedia of Unified Science*, I, 2, 1938) and is well worth examining both for the points it makes and for the manner in which Morris has disregarded these points in his later development.

[31] Many other manners of using the word "sign" appear besides those in Assertions No. 1, 2, 3, 29, and 32. A sign may be an activity or product (p. 35). It may be "any feature of any stimulus-object" (p. 15). "An action or state of the interpreter itself becomes (or produces) a sign" (p. 25). "Actions and states and products of the organism . . . may operate as signs" (p. 27). Strictly "a sign is not always a means-object" (p. 305). Thus despite the definitions, formal and informal alike, a sign may be an action, an act, a thing, a feature, a function, an energy, a property, a quality, or a situation; and this whether it is produced by an object (as in the opening statements) or is produced by an organism in its quality as interpreter (as in much later development).

[32] Officially: "in the absence of stimulus-objects initiating response-sequences of a certain behavior-family."

[33] "Causes in some organism a disposition to respond by response-sequences of this behavior-family."

[34] I have found no verb used at this point, or at least do not recall any and so introduce the word "achieve" just by way of carrying on. A form of "delayed causation" is implied but not definitely expressed.

[35] For this background of construction see the nondefinitional statement for 'behavior' in the glossary, as this is factually (though not by explicit naming) carried over into the formal definition of *Behavior-family*.

[36] If a discussion of this arrangement were undertaken, it would need to be stressed that the causation found in semiotic is of the close-up, short-term type, such as is commonly called mechanistic. No provision seems to be made for long-term, intricate interconnection. See also footnote 49 following.

[37] The omitted words in the definition for "use of a sign" cited above are "with respect to some goal." Insert them and the definition seems plausible; remove them and it is not. But they add nothing whatever to the import of the definition, since sign itself by the top definition of all exists only with respect to some goal.

[38] The section on signal and symbol (Chapter I, Sec. 8) has impressed me as one of the most obscure in the book, quite comparable in this respect with the section on modes of significance used earlier for illustration.

[39] The probable explanation of the separation of use from mode can be found by examining the first pages of Chapter IV. Cf. also pp. 92, 96, 97, 104, 125.

[40] The text rejects the word "meaning" as signifying "any and all phases of sign-process" and specifies for "sign-processes" by the wording above. Apparently the ground for rejection of "meaning" would also apply to "sign-process." "Sign-behavior" (No. 18 above) is often used as loosely as is "sign-process." The phrasing cited above is extremely interesting for its implicit differentiation of "status" and "fact" in the cases of sign and denotatum from what would appear by comparison to be an implied actuality for interpretant and significatum.

[41] By way of showing the extreme looseness of expression the following phrasings of types not included in the preceding text may be cited. Although signs are not interpretants or behaviors but stimuli, they "involve behavior, for a sign must have an interpretant" (p. 187), they are "identified within goal-seeking behavior" (p. 7), they are "described and differentiated in terms of dispositions . . . " (p. v). Interpretants, although dispositions, are "sign-produced behavior" (pp. 95, 104) or even "sign-behavior" (p. 166). A fair climax is reached in the blurb on the ᴕover of the book (it is a good blurb in showing, as many others do, which way the book-wind blows), where all the ingredients are mixed together again in a common kettle by the assertion that this "theory of signs" (incidentally here known as semantics rather than as semiotic) "defines signs in terms of 'dispositions to respond'—that is, in terms of behavior." Along with these one may recall one phrasing already cited in which signs were spoken of as influencing behaviors first and dispositions later on in the process.

[42] Significatum: "The conditions such that whatever meets these conditions is a denotatum of a given sign" (p. 354).

[43] "A sign is said to signify its significatum" (p. 354). "Signs in the different modes of signifying signify differently" (p. 64). "Signs signifying the significata of . . . " (p. 67).

⁴⁴ There is also a very interesting question as to means-objects: whether they enter as sign-produced denotata or as directly acting objects which are not denotata at all. But we must pass this one over entirely. Compare Assertion No. 22, and footnote 36.

⁴⁵ "All signs signify, but not all signs denote." "A sign is said to signify (but not denote) its significatum, that is, the conditions under which it denotes" (pp. 347, 354).

⁴⁶ Another interesting remark about animals, considering that semiotic is universal sign-theory, is that "even at the level of animal behavior organisms tend to follow the lead of more reliable signs" (p. 121).

⁴⁷ No wonder that a bit later when the semiotician asks, "Are such words, however, substitutes for other synonymous signs?" he finds himself answering, "This is a complicated issue which would involve a study of the genesis of the signs produced" (p. 34). The "such words" in question are the kind that "are symbols to both communicator and communicatee at least with respect to the criterion of producibility."

⁴⁸ A few references occur in semiotic to modern work on perception (pp. 34, 191, 252, 274), but without showing any significant influence. The phenomenal constancy studies of Katz, Gelb, Bühler, Brunswik, and others on foundations running back to Helmholtz would, if given attention, make a great difference in the probable construction. (For a simple statement in a form directly applicable to the present issues see V. J. McGill, "Subjective and Objective Methods in Philosophy," *The Journal of Philosophy*, XLI [1944], 424-427.) There is little evidence that the developments of Gestalt studies even in the simpler matters of figure and ground have influenced the treatment. The great question is whether "property," as semiotic introduces it, is not itself sign, to start out with. Semiotic holds, for example, that sign-process has nothing to do with a man reaching for a glass of water to drink, unless the glass of water is a sign of something else. The reaching is "simply acting in a certain way to an object which is a source of stimulation," (p. 252) from which it would appear that in semiotic no "response-disposition" is involved in getting water to drink — a position which seems strange enough to that manner of envisionment known as common sense, but which nevertheless will not be objected to in principle by the present writer in the present chapter, if consistently maintained and successfully developed.

⁴⁹ The probable reason why the semiotician is so fearful of getting objects and organisms into direct contact (and he repeatedly touches on it) is that his view of "causation" is of the billiard-ball type, under the rule "once happen, always happen." His "intervening third" is a sort of safety valve for the cases in which his rule does not work. Which is again to say that he makes no direct observation of or report upon behavioral process itself.

⁵⁰ "Terminal" in this use seems much more suggestive of goal-object or denotatum than it is of significatum.

[51] See also the paper by Professor Gentry, previously mentioned, which very competently (and from the philosophical point of view far more broadly than is attempted here) discusses this and various other deficiencies in Morris' sign theory.

[52] Semiotic offers, however, a set of working rules under which it believes difficulties such as those of the theory of types can be readily solved (p. 279). These are: that a sign as sign-vehicle can denote itself; that a sign cannot denote its own significatum; that a sign can neither denote nor signify its interpretant (pp. 19, 220, 279). Herein lies an excellent opening for further inquiries into the fixations of "um."

[53] Something of the manner in which "modes of signifying" were identified was presented in an illustrative way in the earlier part of the present paper. The distinction, and at the same time close relation, of uses and modes is discussed in the book (pp. 96-97). The combination of use and mode for the classification of types of discourse is displayed in tabular form on p. 125. As for "everything else" in the book, Morris composedly writes (p. 185) that "our contention has been merely that it is possible to deal with all sign phenomena in terms of the basic terminology of semiotic, and hence to define any other term signifying sign phenomena in these terms."

[54] The fact that some of these names are starred as basic and others not, and that those not starred are the underlying behavioral names, was noted earlier in this chapter. The attempt is thus made to treat sign authoritatively without establishing preliminary definiteness about the behavior of which sign is a component. It should now, perhaps, be clear that the confusion of terminology is the direct outgrowth of this procedure, as is also the continual uncertainty the reader feels as to what precisely it is that he is being told.

[55] "There may be dispositions to respond which are not caused by preparatory-stimuli" (p. 9).

[56] It is to be understood, of course, that semiotic presents itself as open to future growth. The open question is whether the present terminology will permit such a future growth by further refinement, or whether the primary condition for growth is the eradication of the terminology from the ground up.

[57] The position of the writer of this report is that defects such as we have shown are not to be regarded, in the usual case, as due to the incompetence of the workman, but that they are inherent in the manner of observation and nomenclature employed. Generations of endeavor seem to him to reveal that such components when split apart as "factors" will not remain split. The only way to exhibit the defects of the old approach is upon the actual work of the actual workman. If Professor Morris or any one else can make good upon the lines he is following, the credit to him will be all the greater.

⁵⁸ See Morris, *op cit.*, p. v, and Appendix 2. On page 27 of his text, his analysis of semiotic is "characterized as an attempt to carry out resolutely the insight of Charles Peirce that a sign gives rise to an interpretant and that an interpretant is in the last analysis a 'modification of a person's tendencies toward action'."

⁵⁹ In addition to a citation in the opening paragraph of this chapter see *op. cit.*, p. 2: "A science of signs can be most profitably developed on a biological basis and specifically within the framework of the science of behavior." For Tolman see Appendix 6.

⁶⁰ "Questions Concerning Certain Faculties Claimed for Man," *Journal of Speculative Philosophy*, II (1868) ; Collected Papers, 5.253.

⁶¹ This assertion is made categorically despite Morris's sentence (p. 289) in which he assures us that "The present treatment follows Peirce's emphasis upon behavior rather than his more mentalistic formulations." A typical expression by Peirce (2.666, *circa* 1910) is "I really know no other way of defining a habit than by describing the kind of behavior in which the habit becomes actualized." Dewey's comment (in correspondence) is that it is a complete inversion of Peirce to identify an interpretant with an interpreter. Excellent illustrations of the creation of fictitious "existences" in Morris' manner have recently been displayed by Ernest Nagel (*The Journal of Philosophy*, XLII [1945], 628-630) and by Stephen C. Pepper (*Ibid.*, XLIII [1946], 36) .

⁶² John Dewey in a recent paper "Peirce's Theory of Linguistic Signs, Thought, and Meaning" (*The Journal of Philosophy*, XLIII [1946], 85-95) analysed this and other of Morris' terminological adaptations of Peirce, including especially the issues of pragmatism, and suggested that " 'users' of Peirce's writings should either stick to his basic pattern or leave him alone." In a short reply Morris evaded the issue and again Dewey stressed that Morris' treatment of Peirce offered a "radically new version of the subjectmatter, intent, and method of pragmatic doctrine," for which Peirce should not be called a forerunner. Again replying, Morris again evaded the issue (*ibid.*, pp. 196, 280, 363) . Thus, so far as this discussion is concerned, the issue as to the propriety of Morris' statement that he offers "an attempt to carry out resolutely the insight of Charles Peirce" remains still unresolved. In still another way Morris differs radically from Dewey. This is in regarding his development of semiotic as made "in a way compatible with the framework of Dewey's thought." (*Signs, Language and Behavior*, p. 273.)

CHAPTER TEN

COMMON SENSE AND SCIENCE[1]

THE discussion that follows is appropriately introduced by saying that both common sense and science
are to be treated as transactions.[2] The use of this name has
negative and positive implications. It indicates, negatively, that neither common sense nor science is regarded
as an entity — as something set apart, complete and self-
enclosed; this implication rules out two ways of viewing
them that have been more or less current. One of these
ways treats them as names for mental faculties or processes,
while the other way regards them as "realistic" in the
epistemological sense in which that word is employed to
designate subjects alleged to be knowable entirely apart
from human participation. Positively, it points to the fact
that both are treated as being marked by the traits and
properties which are found in whatever is recognized to be
a transaction: — a trade, or commercial transaction, for
example. This transaction determines one participant to
be a buyer and the other a seller. No one exists as buyer
or seller save *in and because of* a transaction in which each
is engaged. Nor is that all; specific things *become* goods or
commodities because they are engaged in the transaction.
There is no commercial transaction without things which
only are goods, utilities, commodities, in and because of a
transaction. Moreover, because of the exchange or transfer,
both *parties* (the idiomatic name for *participants*) undergo change; and the goods undergo at the very least a
change of *locus* by which they gain and lose certain connective relations or "capacities" previously possessed.

Furthermore, no given transaction of trade stands alone. It is enmeshed in a body of activities in which are included those of *production*, whether in farming, mining, fishing, or manufacture. And this body of transactions (which may be called industrial) is itself enmeshed in transactions that are neither industrial, commercial, nor financial; to which the name "intangible" is often given, but which can be more safely named by means of specifying rules and regulations that proceed from the system of customs in which other transactions exist and operate.

These remarks are introductory. A trade is cited as a transaction in order to call attention to the traits to be found in common sense and science *as* transactions, extending to the fact that human life itself, both severally and collectively, consists of transactions in which human beings partake together with non-human things of the milieu along with other human beings, so that without this togetherness of human and non-human partakers we could not even stay alive, to say nothing of accomplishing anything. From birth to death every human being is a *Party,* so that neither he nor anything done or suffered can possibly be understood when it is separated from the fact of participation in an extensive body of transactions — to which a given human being may contribute and which he modifies, but only in virtue of being a partaker in them.[3]

Considering the dependence of life in even its physical and physiological aspects upon being parties in transactions in which other human beings and "things" are also parties, and considering the dependence of intellectual and moral growth upon being a party in transactions in which cultural conditions partake — of which language is a sufficient instance, — the surprising thing is that any other idea has ever been entertained. But, aside from the matters noted in the last footnote (as in the part played by religion as a cultural institution in formation and spread of the view that soul, mind, consciousness are isolated independent entities), there is the fact that what is

necessarily involved in that process of living gets passed
over without special attention on account of its familiar-
ity. As we do not notice the air in the physiological transaction of breathing till some obstruction occurs, so with
the multitude of cultural and non-human factors that take
part in all we do, say, and think, even in soliloquies and
dreams. What is called *environment* is that in which the
conditions called physical are enmeshed in cultural conditions and thereby are more than "physical" in its technical
sense. "Environment" is not something around and about
human activities in an external sense; it is their *medium,*
or *milieu,* in the sense in which a *medium* is *inter*mediate
in the execution or carrying *out* of human activities, as
well as being the channel *through* which they move and
the vehicle *by* which they go on. Narrowing of the medium is the direct source of all unnecessary impoverish-
ment in human living; the only sense in which "social" is
an honorific term is that in which the medium in which
human living goes on is one by which human life is enriched.

I

I come now to consideration of the bearing of the previous remarks upon the special theme of this paper, beginning with common sense. Only by direct active
participation in the transactions of living does anyone
become *familiarly acquainted* with other human beings
and with "things" which make up the world. While "common sense" includes more than knowledge, this acquaintance knowledge is its distinguishing trait; it demarcates
the frame of reference of common sense by identifying it
with the life actually carried on as it is enjoyed or suffered.
I shall then first state why the expression "common sense"
is a usable and useful name for a body of facts that are so
basic that without systematic attention to them "science"
cannot exist, while philosophy is idly speculative apart

from them because it is then deprived of footing to stand on and of a field of significant application.

Turning to the dictionary we find that the expression "common sense" is used as a name for "the general sense, feeling, judgment, of mankind or of a community." It is highly doubtful whether anything but matters with which actual living is directly concerned could command the attention, and control the speech usage of "mankind," or of an entire community. And we may also be reasonably sure that some features of life are so exigent that they impinge upon the feeling and wit of all mankind — such as need for food and means of acquiring it, the capacity of fire to give warmth and to burn, of weapons for hunting or war, and the need for common customs and rules if a group is to be kept in existence against threats from within and without. As for a community, what can it be but a number of persons having certain beliefs in common and moved by widely shared habits of feeling and judgment? So we need not be surprised to find in the dictionary under the caption "common sense" the following: "Good sound practical sense . . . in dealing with everyday affairs." Put these two usages together and we have an expression that admirably fits the case.[4]

The everyday affairs of a community constitute the *life* characteristic of that community, and only these common life-activities can engage the general or common wits and feelings of its members. And as for the word "sense" joined to "common," we note that the dictionary gives as one usage of that word "intelligence in its bearing on action." This account of sense differs pretty radically from the accounts of "sensation" usually given in books on psychology but nevertheless it tells how colors, sounds, contacts actually function in giving direction to the course of human activity. We may summarize the matters which fall within the common sense frame of reference as those of the uses and enjoyments common to mankind, or to a given community. How, for example, should the *water* of direct and familiar acquaintance (as distinct from H_2O of the scientific frame) be described save as that which quenches thirst, cleanses the body and soiled articles, in which one swims, which may drown us, which supports boats, which as rain furthers growth of crops, which in contemporary community life runs machinery, including locomotives, etc., etc.? One has only to take account of the water of common use and enjoyment to note the absurdity of reducing water to an assemblage of "sensations," even if motor-muscular elements are admitted. Both sensory qualities and motor responses are without place and significance save as they are enmeshed in uses and enjoyments. And it is *the latter* (whether in terms of water or any substance) which is a *thing* for common sense. We have only to pay attention to cases of which this case of water is representative, to learn respect for the way in which children uniformly describe things, — "It's what you do so-and-so with." The dictionary statement in which a thing is specified as *"that* with which one is occupied, engaged, concerned, busied," replaces a particular *"so-and-so"* by the generalized *"that,"* and a particular *you* by the generalized *one.* But it retains of necessity the children's union of self-and-thing.

II

The words "occupied, engaged, concerned, busied," etc., repay consideration in connection with the distinctive subjectmatter of common sense. *Matter* is one of the and-so-forth expressions. Here is what the dictionary says of it: — "A thing, affair, concern, corresponding to the Latin *res,* which it is often used to render." A further statement about the word brings out most definitely the point made about children's way of telling about anything as something in which a human being and environmental conditions co-operate: — "An event, circumstance, state or course of things which is the object of consideration or of practical concern." I do not see how anything could be

more inclusive on the side of what philosophers have regarded as "outer or external" than the words found in the
first part of the statement quoted; while "consideration
and practical concern" are equally inclusive on the side of
the "inner" and "private" component of philosophical
dualisms.[5]

Since, "subject, affair, business" are mentioned as syno-
nyms of matter, we may turn to them to see what the
dictionary says, noting particularly the identification of a
"subject" with *"object of consideration."* *Concern* passed
from an earlier usage (in which it was virtually a synonym
of *dis-cern*) over into an object of care, solicitude, even
anxiety; and then into that "with which one is busied,
occupied," and *about* which one is called upon to act.
And in view of the present tendency to restrict *business* to
financial concern, it is worth while to note that its original sense of force was *care, trouble*. *Care* is highly suggestive in the usage. It ranges from solicitude, through
caring *for* in the sense of fondness, and through being
deeply stirred, over to caring *for* in the sense of *taking*
care, looking after, paying attention systematically, or
minding. *Affair* is derived from the French *faire*. Its
usage has developed through love-intrigues and through
business affairs into "that one has to do with or has ado
with;" a statement which is peculiarly significant in that
ado has changed from its original sense of that which is
a doing over into a doing "that is forced on one, a difficulty, trouble." *Do* and *ado* taken together pretty well
cover the conjoint under*takings* and under*goings* which
constitute that "state and course of things which is the
object of consideration or practical concern." Finally we
come to *thing*. It is so far from being the metaphysical
substance or logical entity of philosophy that is external
and presumably physical, that it is "that with which one
is concerned in action, speech, or thought": — three words
whose scope not only places *things* in the setting of transactions having human beings as partners, but which so

cover the whole range of human activity that we may leave matters here for the present.[6] I can not refrain, however, from adding that the words dealt with convey in idiomatic terms of common sense all that is intended to be conveyed by the technical term *Gestalt,* without the rigid fixity of the latter and with the important addition of emphasis on the human partner.

It does not seem as if comment by way of interpretation were needed to enforce the significance of what has been pointed out. I invite, however, specific attention to two points, both of which have been mentioned in passing. The words "concern," "affair," "care," "matter," "thing," etc., fuse in indissoluble unity senses which when discriminated are called *emotional, intellectual, practical,* the first two being moreover marked traits of the last named. Apart from a given context, it is not even possible to tell which one is uppermost; and when a context of use is present, it is always a question of emphasis, never of separation. The supremacy of subjectmatters of concern, etc., over distinctions usually made in psychology and philosophy, cannot be denied by anyone who attends to the facts. The other consideration is even more significant. What has been completely divided in philosophical discourse into man *and* the world, inner *and* outer, self *and* not-self, subject *and* object, individual *and* social, private *and* public, etc., are in actuality parties in life-transactions. The philosophical "problem" of how to get them together is artificial. On the basis of fact, it needs to be replaced by consideration of the conditions under which they occur as *distinctions,* and of the special uses served by the distinctions.[7]

Distinctions are more than legitimate *in their place.* The trouble is not with making distinctions; life — behavior develops by making two distinctions grow where one — or rather none — grew before. Their place lies in cases of uncertainty with respect to *what* is to be done and *how* to do it. The prevalence of "wishful thinking," of the danger of allowing the emotional to determine what is taken to be a cognitive reference, suffices to prove the need for distinction-making in this respect. And when uncertainty acts to inhibit (suspend) immediate activity so that what otherwise would be *overt* action is converted into an *examination* in which motor energy is channeled through muscles connected with organs of looking, handling, etc., a distinction of the factors which are obstacles from those that are available as resources is decidedly in place. For when the obstacles and the resources are referred, on the one hand, to the self as a factor and, on the other hand, to conditions of the medium-of-action as factors, a distinction between "inner" and "outer," "self" and "world" *with respect to cases of this kind* finds a legitimate place within "the state and course" of life-concerns. Petrifaction of distinctions of this kind, that are pertinent and recurrent in specific conditions of action, into inherent (and hence absolute) separations is the "vicious" affair.

Philosophical discourse is the chief wrong-doer in this matter. Either directly or through psychology as an ally it has torn the intellectual, the emotional, and the practical asunder, erecting each into an entity, and thereby creating the artificial problem of getting them back into working terms with one another. Especially has this taken place in philosophy since the scientific revolution of a few centuries ago. For the assumption that it constituted natural science an entity complete in and of itself necessarily set man and the world, mind and nature as mindless, subject and object, inner and outer, the moral and the physical, fact and value, over against one another as inherent, essential, and therefore *absolute* separations. Thereby, with supreme irony, it renders the very existence of extensive and ever-growing knowledge the source of the "problem" of how knowledge is possible anyway.

This splitting up of things that exist together has brought with it, among other matters, the dissevering of philosophy from human life, relieving it from concern with administration of its affairs and of responsibility for dealing with its troubles. It may seem incredible that human beings as *living* creatures should so deny themselves as alive. In and of itself it is incredible; it has to be accounted for in terms of historic-cultural conditions that made heaven, not the earth; eternity, not the temporal; the supernatural, not the natural, the ultimate worthy concern of mankind.

It is for such reasons as these that what has been said about the affairs and concerns of common sense is a significant matter (in itself as well as in the matter of connections with science to be discussed later) of concern. The attention that has been given to idiomatic, even colloquial, speech accordingly has a bearing upon philosophy. For such speech is closest to the affairs of everyday life; that is, of common (or shared) living. The intellectual enterprise which turns its back upon the matters of common sense, in the connection of the latter with the concerns of living, does so at its peril. It is fatal for an intellectual enterprise to despise the issues reflected in this speech; the more ambitious or pretentious its claims, the *more* fatal the outcome. It is, I submit, the growing tendency of "philosophy" to get so far away from vital issues which render its problems not only technical (to some extent a necessity) but such that the more they are discussed the more controversial are they and the further apart are philosophers among themselves: — a pretty sure sign that somewhere on the route a compass has been lost and a chart thrown away.

III

I come now to consideration of the frame of reference that demarcates the method and subjectmatter of science from that of common sense; and to the questions which issue from this difference. I begin by saying that however the case stands, they are *not* to be distinguished from one another on the ground that science is *not* a human concern, affair, occupation. For that is what it decidedly is. The issue to be discussed is that of the *kind* of concern or care that marks off scientific activity from those forms of human behavior that fall within the scope of common sense; a part of the problem involved (an important part) being how it happened that the scientific revolution which began a few short centuries ago has had as one outcome a general failure to recognize science as itself an important human concern, so that, as already remarked, it is often treated as a peculiar sort of entity on its own account — a fact that has played a central role in determining the course taken by epistemology in setting the themes of distinctively *modern* philosophy.

This fact renders it pertinent, virtually necessary in fact, to go to the otherwise useless pains of calling attention to the various features that identify and demarcate science as a concern. In the first place, it is a *work* and a work carried on by a distinct group or set of human beings constituting a profession having a special vocation, exactly as is the case with those engaged in law or medicine, although its distinction from the latter is becoming more and more shadowy as an increasing number of physicians engage in researches of practically the same kind as those engaged in by the men who rank as scientists; and as the latter increasingly derive their special problems from circumstances brought to the fore in issues arising in connection with the source and treatment of disease. Moreover, scientific inquiry as a particular kind of work is engaged in by a group of persons who have undergone a highly specialized training to fit them for doing that particular kind of work — "job" it would be called were it not for the peculiar aura that clings to pursuits labeled "intellectual." Moreover, the work is done in a special kind of workshop, specifically known as *laboratories* and observatories, fitted out with a particular kind of apparatus for the carrying on of a special kind of occupation — which from the standpoint of the amount of monetary capital invested in it (although not from the side of its distinctive returns) is a business. Just here is a fitting place, probably *the* fitting place to note that not merely the physical equipment of scientific workshops is the net outcome of long centuries of prior *cultural* transformation of physiological processes (themselves developed throughout no one knows how many millions of years), but that the *intellectual* resources with which the work is done indeed, the very problems involved, are but an aspect of a continuing cultural activity: an aspect which, if one wishes to call attention to it *emphatically,* may be called a *passing* phase in view of what the work done *there and then* amounts to in its intimate and indispensable connection with all that has gone before and that is to go on afterwards. For what is done on a given date in a given observatory, laboratory, study (say of a mathematician) is after all but a re-survey of what *has* been going on for a long time and which *will* be incorporated, absorbed, along with it into an activity that will continue as long as the earth harbors man.

The work done could no more be carried out without its special equipment of apparatus and technical operations than could the production of glass or electricity or any one of the great number of industrial enterprises that have taken over as integral parts of *their* especial work processes originating in the laboratory. Lag of popular opinion and repute behind actual practice is perhaps nowhere greater than in the current ignoring of — too often ignorance of — the facts adduced; one of which is the supposition that scientific knowing is something done by the "mind," when in fact science as practiced today began only when the work done (i.e., life activities) by sense and movement was refined and extended by adoption of material devices and technological operations.

I may have overdone the task of indicating how and why "science" is a concern, a care, and an occupation, not a self-enclosed entity. Even if such is the case, what has been said leads directly up to the question: — What is the distinctive concern of science as a concern and occupation by which it is marked off from those of common sense that grow directly out of the conduct of living? In principle the answer is simple. Doing and knowing are both involved in common sense and science — involved so intimately as to be necessary conditions of their existence. Nor does the difference between common sense and science consist in the fact that knowing is the *important* consideration in science but not in common sense. It consists of the position occupied by each member in relation to the other. In the concerns of common sense knowing is as necessary, as important, as in those of science. But knowing there is for the sake of *agenda,* the *what* and the *how* of which have to be studied and to be learned — in short, *known* in order that the necessary affairs of everyday life be carried on. The relation is reversed in science as a concern. As already emphasized, doing and making are as necessarily involved as in any industrial technology. But they are carried on for the sake of advancing the system of knowings and knowns. In each case doing remains doing and knowing continues to be knowing. But the concern or care that is distinctively characteristic of common sense concern and of scientific concern, with respect to *what* is done and known, and *why* it is done and known, renders the subjectmatters that are proper, necessary, in the doings and knowings of the two concerns as different as is H_2O from the water we drink and wash with.

Nevertheless, the first named is *about* the last named, although what one consists of is sharply different from what the other consists *of.* The fact that what science is *of* is *about* what common sense subjectmatter is *of,* is disguised from ready recognition when science becomes so highly developed that the *immediate* subject of inquiry consists of what has *previously* been found out. But careful examination promptly discloses that unless the materials involved can be traced back to the material of common sense concerns there is nothing whatever for scientific concern to be concerned with. What is pertinent here is that science is the example, *par excellence,* of the liberative effect of abstraction. Science is *about* in the sense in which "about" is *away* from; which is *of* in the sense in which "of" is *off* from: — how far off is shown in the case repeatedly used, water as H_2O where use and enjoyment are sweepingly different from the uses and enjoyments which attend laboratory inquiry into the makeup of water. The liberative outcome of the abstraction that is supremely manifested in scientific activity is the transformation of the affairs of common sense concern which has come about through the vast return wave of the methods and conclusions of scientific concern into the uses and enjoyments (and sufferings) of everyday affairs; together with an accompanying transformation of judgment and of the emotional affections, preferences, and aversions of everyday human beings.

The concern of common sense knowing is "practical," that of scientific doing is "theoretical." But *practical* in the first case is not limited to the "utilitarian" in the sense in which that word is disparagingly used. It includes all matters of direct enjoyment that occur in the course of living because of transformation wrought by the fine arts, by friendship, by recreation, by civic affairs, etc. And "theoretical" in the second instance is far away from the *theoria* of pure contemplation of the Aristotelian tradition, and from any sense of the word that excludes elaborate and extensive doings and makings. Scientific knowing is that particular form of *practical* human activity which is concerned with the advancement of *knowing* apart from concern with *other* practical affairs. The adjective often affixed to knowing of this kind is "pure." The adjective is understandable on historic grounds, since it demanded a struggle — often called *warfare* — to free natural inquiry from subordination to institutional concerns that were irrelevant and indeed hostile to the business of inquiry. But the idea that exemption from subjection to considerations extraneous and alien to inquiry as such is inherent in the essence or nature of science *as an entity* is sheer hypostatization. The exemption has itself a *practical* ground. The actual course of scientific inquiry has shown that the best interests of human living in general, as well as those of scientific inquiry in particular, are best served by keeping such inquiry "pure", that is free, from interests that would bend the conduct of inquiry to serve concerns alien (and practically sure to be hostile) to the conduct of knowing as its own end and proper terminus. This end may be called the *ideal* of scientific knowing in the *moral* sense of that word — a guide in conduct. Like other directive moral aims, it is far as yet from having attained complete supremacy: — any more than its present degree of "purity" was attained without a hard struggle against adverse institutional interests which tried to control the methods used and conclusions reached in which was asserted to be science: — as in the well-known instance when an ecclesiastical institution dictated to "science" in the name of particular religious and moral customs. In any case, it is harmful as well as stupid to refuse to note that "purity" of inquiry is something to be striven for and to be sustained by the scrupulous attention that depends upon noting that scientific knowing is one human concern growing out of and returning into other more primary human concerns. For though the existing state of science is *one* of the interests and cares that determine the selection of things to be investigated, it is not the only one. Problems are not self-selecting, and the *direction* taken by inquiry is determined by the human factors of dominant interest and concern that affect the choice of the matters to be specifically inquired into.

The position here taken, namely that science is a matter of concern for the conduct of inquiry *as inquiry* sharply counters such statements as that "science is the means of

obtaining practical mastery over nature through understanding it," especially when this view is expressly placed
in contrast with the view that the business of scientific
knowing is to find out, to *know* in short. There can be no
doubt that an important, a very important *consequence* of
science is to obtain human mastery over nature. That fact
is identical with the "return wave" that is emphasized.
The trouble is that the view back of the quotation ignores
entirely the kind of human *uses* to which "mastery" is put.
It needs little discernment to see that this ignoring is in the
interest of a preconceived dogma — in this particular case
— a Marxist one — of what genuine mastery consists of.
What *"understanding"* nature means is dogmatically assumed to be already known, while in fact anything that
legitimately can be termed *understanding* nature is the
outcome of scientific inquiry, not something established
independent of inquiry and determining the course of
"science." That science is itself a form of doing, of practice, and that it inevitably has reflex consequences upon
other forms of practices, is fully recognized in the account
here given. But this fact is the very reason why scientific
knowing should be conducted without pre-determination
of the practical consequences that are to ensue from it.
That is a question to be considered on its *own* account.

There is, then a problem of high importance in this
matter of the relation of the concerns of science and common sense with each other. It is not that which was taken
up by historic epistemologies in attempting to determine
which of the two is the "truer" representative of "reality."
While a study of the various human interests, religious,
economic, political-military, which have at times determined the direction pursued by scientific inquiry, contrib-
utes to clear vision of the problem, that study is itself historical rather than philosophical. The problem of concern may be introduced (as I see it) by pointing out that
a reference to the *return* of scientific method and conclusions into the concerns of daily life is purely factual, de-

scriptive. It contains no implication of anything honorific or *intrinsically* desirable. There is plenty of evidence that the outcome of the return (which is now going on at an ever-increasing speed and in ever-extending range) is a mixture of things approvable and to be condemned; of the desirable and the undesirable. The *problem,* then, concerns the possibility of giving direction to this return-wave so as to minimize evil consequences and to intensify and extend good consequences, and, if it is possible, to find out how such return is to be accomplished.

Whether the problem is called that of philosophy or not is in some respects a matter of names. But the problem is *here* whatever name be given. And for the future of philosophy the matter of names may prove vital. If philosophy surrenders concern with pursuit of Reality (which it does not seem to be successful in catching), it is hard to see what concern it can take for its distinctive care and occupation save that of an attempt to meet the need just indicated. Meantime, it is in line with the material of the present paper to recur to a suggestion already made: namely, that perhaps the simplest way of getting rid of the isolations, splits, divisions, that now trouble human living, is to take seriously the concerns, cares, affairs, etc., of common sense, as far as they are transactions which (i) are constituted by the indissoluble active union of human and non-human factors; in which (ii) traits and features called intellectual and emotional are so far from being independent of and isolated from practical concerns, things done and to be done, *facta* and *facienda,* that they belong to and are possessed by the one final practical affair — the state and course of life as a body of transactions.[8]

---

[1] This chapter is written by Dewey.

[2] See Chapters IV and V of this volume.

[3] No better illustration of this fact can be found than the fact that it was a pretty extensive set of religious, economic, and political transactions

which led (in the movement named individualism) to the psychological and philosophical theories that set up human beings as "individuals" doing business on their own account.

⁴ Both passages are quoted from the Oxford Dictionary. The first and more general one dates in the illustrative passage cited over one hundred years earlier than the more limited personal usage of the second use. Together they cover what are sometimes spoken of as "objective" and "subjective" uses, thus anticipating in a way the point to be made next.

⁵ This case, reinforced by others to follow, is perhaps a sufficient indication of the need philosophy has to pay heed to words that focus attention upon human activities as transactions in living.

⁶ All passages in quotation marks are from the Oxford Dictionary.

⁷ The list given can be much extended. It includes "pursuit, report, issue, involvement, complication, entanglement, embarrassment; enterprise, undertaking, undergoing," and "experience" as a double-barreled word. As a general thing it would be well to use such words as *concern*, *affairs*, etc., where now the word *experience* is used. They are specific where the latter word is general in the sense of vague. Also they are free from the ambiguity that attends *experience* on account of the controversies that have gathered about it. However, when a name is wanted to emphasize the inter-connectedness of all concerns, affairs, pursuits, etc., and it is made clear that *experience* is used in that way, it may serve the purpose better than any word that is as yet available.

⁸ In the course of consulting the Oxford Dictionary (s.v. Organism) I found the following passage (cited from Tucker, 1705-1774): "When an artist has finished a fiddle to give all the notes in the gamut, but not without a hand to play upon it, this is an organism." Were the word *organism* widely understood as an organization in which a living body and environing conditions cooperate as fiddle and player work together, it would not have been necessary to repeat so often the expression "organic-environmental." The passage may also stand as a typical reminder of what a transaction is. The words "not without" are golden words, whether they are applied to the human or to the environmental partners in a transaction.

CHAPTER ELEVEN

A TRIAL GROUP OF NAMES

UNDERTAKING to find a few firm names for use in
connection with the theory of knowledge — hoping
thereby to promote co-operation among inquirers and
lessen their frequent misinterpretations of one another —
we at once found it essential to safeguard ourselves by
presenting in explicit postulation the main characteristics
of our procedure.[1]

The first aspect of this postulatory procedure to stress is
that the firm namings sought are of that type of firmness
attained by modern science when it aims at ever-increasing
accuracy of specification rather than at exactness (q.v.) of
formulation, thus rejecting the old verbal rigidities and
leaving the paths of inquiry freely open to progress.

An observation which, we believe, any one can make
when the actual procedures of knowledge theorists are examined is that these procedures deal with knowings in
terms of knowns, and with knowns in terms of knowings,
and with neither in itself alone. The epistemologist often
comments casually on this fact, and sometimes discusses it
at length, but rarely makes any deliberate effort to act
upon it. No attempt at all, so far as we are aware, has been
made to concentrate upon it as a dependable base for operations. We accept this observation and report as a sound
basis for an inquiry under which the attainment of firm
names may be anticipated, and we adopt it as our guiding
postulation.

Such a postulation, wherever the inquiry is not limited
to some particular activity of the passing moment but is

viewed broadly in its full scope, will at once bring into the knowing and the known as joint subjectmatter all of their positings of "existence," inclusive of whatever under contrasting manners of approach might be presumed to be "reality" of action or of "being" underlying them. Taking this subjectmatter of inquiry as one single system, the factual support for any theory of knowings is then found to lie within the spatial and temporal operations and conclusions of accredited science. The alternative to this — and the sole alternative — is to make decision as to what is and what is not knowledge rest on dicta taken to be available independent of and prior to these scientific subjectmatters, but such a course is not for us.

Under this postulation we limit our immediate inquiry to knowings through namings, with the further postulation that the namings (as active behaviors of men) are themselves before us as the very knowings under examination. *If* the namings alone are *flatus vocis,* the named alone and apart from naming is *ens fatuum.*

The vague word "knowledge" (q.v.) in its scattered uses covers in an unorganized way much territory besides that of naming-knowing.[2] Especially to remark are the regions of perception-manipulation on the one hand, and the regions of mathematically symbolic knowledge on the other. These remain as recognized fields of specialized study for all inquiry into knowledge. Whether or not the word "knowledge" is to be retained for all of these fields as well as for namings-knowings is not a question of much importance at the present imperfect stage of observation and report.

Some of the words here appraised may be taken as keynames for the postulation employed, and hence as touchstones for the other names. *Fact* is thus used for knowingsknowns in system in that particular range of knowingsknowns, namely, the namings-nameds, which is studied. *Designation* is used as a most general name for the naming phases of the process, and *Existence* as a most general name for the named phases. Attention is called to the distinction between *inter* and *trans* (the former the verbal locus of much serious contemporary confusion), and to the increasingly firm employment of the words "aspect" and "phase" within the transactional framework of inspection.

Certain changes are made from our earlier recommendations.[3] "Existence" replaces "event," since we have come to hope that it may now be safely used. "Event," then, replaces "occurrence." "Definition" has been demoted from its preliminary assignment, since continued studies of its uses in the present literature show it so confused as to rate no higher than a crude characterization. "Symbolization" has been given the duty of covering the territory which, it was earlier hoped, "definition" could cover. "Exact," for symbolization has been substituted for "precise," in correlation with "accurate" for specification. The names "behavior-object" and "behavior-agent" have been dropped, as not needed at the present stage of inquiry, where object and organism suffice.

The reader will understand that what is sought here is clarification rather than insistent recommendation of particular names; that even the most essential postulatory namings serve the purpose of "openers," rather than of "determiners"; that if the distinctions herein made prove to be sound, then the names best to be used to mark them may be expected to adjust themselves in the course of time under attrition of the older verbal abuses; and that every division of subjectmatters through disjunction of names must be taken in terms of the underlying conjunctions that alone make the disjunctions soundly practicable by providing safety against absolutist applications.

Accurate: When specification is held separate from symbolization (q.v.), then separate adjectives are desirable to characterize degrees of achievement in the separate ranges. Accurate is recommended in the case of specification. See *Exact.*

Action, Activity: These words are used by us in characterizations of durational-extensional subjectmatters only. Where a stressed substantive use of them is made, careful specification should be given; otherwise they retain and promote vagueness.

Actor: A confused and confusing word; offering a primitive and usually deceptive organization for the complex behavioral transactions the organism is engaged in. Under present postulation Actor should always be taken as postulationally transactional, and thus as a Trans-actor.

Application: The application of a name to an object may often be spoken of advantageously where other phrasings mislead. See *Reference.*

Aspect: The components of a full transactional situation, being not independents, are aspects. The word is etymologically correct; the verb "aspect" is "to look out." See *Phase.*

Behavior: A behavior is always to be taken transactionally: i.e., never as *of* the organism alone, any more than *of* the environment alone, but always as of the organic-environmental situation, with organisms and environmental objects taken as equally its aspects. Studies of these aspects in provisional separation are essential at many stages of inquiry, and are always legitimate when carried on under the transactional framework, and through an inquiry which is itself recognized as transactional. Transactionally employed, the word "behavior" should do the work that "experience" has sought to do in the past, and should do it free from the shifting, vague, and confused applications which have in the end come to make the latter word so often unserviceable. The phrase "human behavior" would then be short for "behavior with the understanding that is human."

Behavioral: Behavioral inquiry is that level of biological inquiry in which the processes examined are not currently explorable by physical or physiological (q.v.) techniques. To be understood in freedom equally from behavioristic and from mentalistic allusions. Covers equally the ranges called "social" and those called "individual."

Biological: Inquiry in which organic life is the subject-matter, and in which the processes examined are not currently explorable by physical (q.v.) techniques; covers both physiological and behavioral inquiry.

Characterization: The intermediate stage of designation in the evolutionary scale, with cue (q.v.) preceding, and specification (q.v.) following; includes the greater part of the everyday use of words; reasonably adequate for the commoner practical purposes.

Circularity: Its appearance is regarded as a radical defect by non-transactional epistemological inquiries that undertake to organize "independents" as "reals." Normal for inquiry into knowings and knowns in system.

Coherence: Suggests itself for connection (q.v.) as established under specification, in distinction from consistency attained in symbolic process.

Concept, Conception: Conception has two opposed uses: on one side as a "mentalistic entity"; on the other as a current phrasing for subjectmatters designed to be held under steady inspection in inquiry. Only the latter is legitimate under our form of postulation. In any event the hypostatization set up by the word "concept" is to be avoided; and this applies to its appearance in formal logic even more than elsewhere.

Connection: To apply between objects under naming. See *Reference* and *Relation*.

Consciousness: The word has disappeared from nearly all research, but survives under various disguises in knowledge theory. Where substantively used as something other than a synonym of a comparable word, "awareness," we can find under our postulation no value whatever in it, or in its disguises, or in the attitudes of inquiry it implies.

Consistency: To be used exclusively in symbolic ranges. See *Coherence*.

Context: A common word in recent decades carrying many suggestions of transactional treatment. However, where it obscures the issues of naming and the named, i.e., when it swings obscurely between verbal and physical environments, it is more apt to do harm than good.

Cosmos: Commonly presents "universe as system." If the speaking-knowing organism is included in the cosmos, and if inquiry proceeds on that basis, cosmos appears as an alternative name for Fact (q.v.).

Cue: The earliest stage of designation in the evolutionary scale. Some recent psychological construction employs cue where the present study employs signal. Firm expression is needed in some agreed form. If a settled psychologist's use develops, then it, undoubtedly, should govern.

Definition: Most commonly employed for specification (q.v.), though with varied accompanying suggestions of dictionary, syllogistic, or mathematical adaptation. These latter, taken in a group, provide a startling exhibit of epistemological chaos. In recent years a specialized technical application has been under development for the word in formal logic. Establishment in this last use seems desirable, but the confusion is now so great that it is here deemed essential to deprive the word of all terminological status above that of a characterization (q.v.) until a sufficiently large number of experts in the fields of its technical employment can establish and maintain a specific use.[4]

Designation: The knowing-naming phase of fact. To be viewed always transactionally as behavior. The word "name" (q.v.) as a naming may advantageously be substituted wherever one can safely expect to hold it to behavioral understanding. Extends over three levels: cue, characterization, and specification.

Description: Cues organizing characterizations; characterizations developing into specifications. Not to be narrowed as is done when brought too sharply into contrast with narration as temporal. A name is, in effect, a truncated description. Somewhat similarly, with respect to an established name, a description may be called an expanded naming.

Entity: Assumed or implied physical, mental, or logical independence or semi-independence (the "semi" always vague or evasive) in some part of a subjectmatter under inquiry; thus, a tricky word, even when not positively harmful, which should be rejected in all serious inquiry. See *Thing* that, in its idiomatic use, is free from the misleading pretentiousness of entity.

Environment: Situations, events, or objects in connection (q.v.) with organism as object. Subject to inquiry physically, physiologically, and, in full transactional treatment, behaviorally.

Epistemological: As far as this word directly or indirectly assumes separate knowers and knowns (inclusive of to-be-knowns) all epistemological words are ruled out under transactional procedure.

Event: That range of differentiation of the named which is better specified than situation, but less well specified than object. Most commonly employed with respect to durational transition. (In earlier sketches employed where we now employ Existence.)

Exact: The requirement for symbolic procedure as distinguished from the requirement of accuracy (q.v.) for specification.

Excitation: A word suggested for specific use where *physiological* process of environment and organism is concerned and where distinction from behavioral stimulus (q.v.) in the latter's specific use is required.

Existence: The known-named phase of fact, transactionally inspected. Established through designation under an ever-increasing requirement of accuracy in specification. Hence for a given era in man's advance, it covers the established objects in the evolving knowing of that era. Not permitted entry as if at the same time both a "something known" and a "something else" supporting the known. Physical, physiological, and behavioral subjectmatters are here taken as equally existential, however different the technical levels of their treatment in inquiry at a given time may be. Both etymologically and in practical daily uses this application of the word is far better justified than is an extra-behavioral or absolutist rendering (whether physicalist or mentalist) under some form of speculative linguistic manipulation.

Experience: This word has two radically opposed uses in current discussion. These overlap and shift so as to cause continual confusion and unintentional misrepresentation. One stands for short extensive-durational process, an extreme form of which is identification of an isolated sensory event or "sensation" as an ultimate unit of inquiry. The other covers the entire spatially extensive, temporally durational application; and here it is a counterpart for the word "cosmos." The word "experience" should be dropped entirely from discussion unless held strictly to a single definite use: that, namely, of calling attention to the fact that *Existence* has organism and environment as its aspects, and can not be identified with either as an independent isolate.

Fact: The cosmos in course of being known through naming by organisms, themselves among its phases. It is knowings-knowns, durationally and extensionally spread; not what is known to and named by any one organism in any passing moment, nor to any one organism in its lifetime. Fact is under way among organisms advancing in a cosmos, itself under advance as known. The word "fact," etymologically from *factum,* something done, with its temporal implications, is much better fitted for the broad use here suggested than for either of its extreme and less common, though more pretentious applications: on the one hand for an independent "real"; on the other for a "mentally" endorsed report. Whether the word may properly apply to the cosmic presentation of inferior non-communicating animals, or to that of a superior realm of non-naming symbols, is for others to develop at other times and places. *See* Chapter II, Section IV.

Field: On physical analogies this word should have important application in behavioral inquiry. The physicist's uses, however, are still undergoing reconstructions, and the definite correspondence needed for behavioral application can not be established. Too many current projects for the use of the word have been parasitic. Thorough transactional studies of behaviors on their own account are needed to establish behavioral field in its own right.

Firm: As applied to a proposed terminology for knowings and knowns this word indicates the need of accuracy (q.v.) of specification, never that of exactness of symbolization. For the most firm, one is to take that which is least vague, and which at the same time is most free from assumed finality — where professed finality itself, perhaps, is the last word in vagueness.

Idea, Ideal: Underlying differences of employment are so many and wide that, where these words are used, it should be made clear whether they are used behaviorally or as names of presumed existences taken to be strictly mental.

Individual: Abandonment of this word and of all substitutes for it seems essential wherever a positive *general theory* is undertaken or planned. Minor specialized studies in individualized phrasing should expressly name the limits of the application of the word, and beyond that should hold themselves firmly within such limits. The word "behavior" (q.v.) as presented in this vocabulary covers both individual and social (q.v.) on a transactional basis in which the distinction between them is aspectual.

Inquiry: A strictly transactional name. It is an equivalent of knowing, but preferable as a name because of its freedom from "mentalistic" associations.

Inter: This prefix has two sets of applications (see Oxford Dictionary). One is for "between," "in-between," or "between the parts of." The other is for "mutually," "reciprocally." The result of this shifting use as it enters philosophy, logic, and psychology, no matter how inadvertent, is ambiguity and undependability. The habit easily establishes itself of mingling without clarification the two sets of implications. It is here proposed to eliminate ambiguity by confining the prefix *inter* to cases in which "in between" is dominant, and to employ the prefix *trans* where the mutual and reciprocal are intended.

Interaction: This word, because of its prefix, is undoubtedly the source of much of the more serious difficulty in·discussion at the present time. Legitimate and illegitimate uses in various branches of inquiry have been discussed in chapters IV and V. When transactional and interactional treatments come to be explicitly distinguished,[5] progress in construction should be more easily made. For the general theory of knowings and knowns, the interactional approach is entirely rejected under our procedure.

Knowledge: In current employment this word is too wide and vague to be a *name* of anything in particular. The butterfly "knows" how to mate, presumably without learning; the dog "knows" its master through learning; man "knows" through learning how to do an immense number of things in the way of arts or abilities; he also "knows" physics, and "knows" mathematics; he knows *that, what,* and *how.* It should require only a moderate acquaintance with philosophical literature to observe that the vagueness and ambiguity of the word "knowledge" accounts for a large number of the traditional "problems" called *the problem of knowledge.* The issues that must be faced before firm use is gained are: Does the word "knowledge" indicate something the organism possesses or produces? Or does it indicate something the organism confronts or with which it comes into contact? Can either of these viewpoints be coherently maintained? If not, what change iṅ preliminary description must be sought?

Knowings: Organic phases of transactionally observed behaviors. Here considered in the familiar central range of namings-knowings. The correlated organic aspects of signalings and symbolings are in need of transactional systematization with respect to namings-knowings.

Knowns: Environmental phases of transactionally observed behaviors. In the case of namings-knowings the range of the knowns is that of existence within fact or cosmos, not in a limitation to the recognized affirmations of the moment, but in process of advance in long durations.

Language: To be taken as behavior of men (with extensions such as the progress of factual inquiry may show to be advisable into the behaviors of other organisms). Not to be viewed as composed of word-bodies apart from word-meanings, nor as word-meanings apart from word-embodiment. As behavior, it is a region of knowings. Its terminological status with respect to symbolings or other expressive behaviors of men is open for future determination.

Manipulation: See *Perception-manipulation.*

Matter, Material: See *Physical* and *Nature.* If the word "mental" is dropped, the word "material" (in the sense of matter as opposed to mind) falls out also. In every-day use, both "mental" and "material" rate at the best as characterizations." In philosophy and psychology the words are often degraded to "cues."

Mathematics: A behavior developing out of earlier naming activities, which, as it advances, more and more gains independence of namings and specializes on symboling. See *Symbol.*

Meaning: A word so confused that it is best never used at all. More direct expressions can always be found. (Try for example, speaking in terms of "is," or "involves.") The transactional approach does away with that split between disembodied meanings and meaningless bodies for meanings which still enters flagrantly into much discussion.

Mental: This word not used by us. Usually indicates an hypostatization arising from a primitively imperfect view of behavior, and not safe until the splitting of existence into two independent isolates has been generally abandoned. Even in this latter case the word should be limited to service as emphasizing an aspect of existence. See *Behavior* and *Transaction.*

Name, Naming, Named: Language behavior in its central ranges. Itself a form of knowing. Here, at times, temporarily and technically replaced by the word "designation," because of the many traditional, speculatively evolved, applications of the word "name," closely corresponding to the difficulties with the word "concept" (q.v.), many of them still redolent of ancient magic. The word "name" will be preferred to the word "designation," as soon as its use can be assumed in fully transactional form and free from conventional distortions.

Nature: See *Cosmos* and *Fact.* Here used to represent a single system of subjectmatters of inquiry, without implication of predetermined authoritative value such as is usually intended when the word "natural*ism*" is used.

Object: Within fact, and within its existential phase, object is that which acquires firmest specification, and is thus distinguished from situation and event. This holds to the determination of Dewey (*Logic*, p. 119; also pp. 129, 520, *et al.*) that in inquiry object "emerges as a definite constituent of a resolved situation, and is confirmed in the continuity of inquiry," and is "subjectmatter, so far as it has been produced and ordered in settled form."

Objective: A crude characterization which seems easily enough intelligible until one observes that in the behavioral sciences almost every investigator calls his own program objective, regardless of its differences from the many self-styled objective offerings that have gone before. As often employed the word has merely the import of impartial, which might advantageously replace it. Objective is used so frequently to characterize aspects of "subject" rather than of "object," that its own status with respect both to subject and to object should be carefully established before use.

Observation: To be taken as durationally and extensionally transactional, and thus neither separately in terms of the observing, nor separately in terms of the observed. Always to be viewed in the concrete instance but never as substantively stressed "act," nor in any other way as isolated or independent. Always to be postulationally guarded in current technical employment, and always to remain tentative with respect to future observing and knowing. See *Experience.*

Operational: The word "operation" as applied to behavior in recent methodological discussions should be thoroughly overhauled and given the full transactional status that such words as "process" and "activity" (q.v.) require. The military use of the word is suggestive of the way to deal with it.

Organism: Taken as transactionally existent in cosmos. Presentations of it in detachment or quasi-detachment are to be viewed as tentative or partial.

Organization: See *System.*

Percept: To be taken transactionally as phase of signaling behavior. Never to be hypostatized as if itself independently "existing."

Perception-Manipulation: Taken jointly and inseparably as the range of signal behaviors. Differences between perception and manipulation seemed striking in the earlier stages of the development of psychology, but today's specialization of inquiry should not lose sight of their common behavioral status.

Phase: Aspect of fact in sufficiently developed statement to exhibit definite spatial and temporal localizations.

Phenomenon: A word that still has possibilities of convenient use, if deprived of all of those implications commonly called subjective, and used for provisional identifications of situation with no presumptive "phenomenine" behind it for further reference.

Physical: One of the three, at present, outstanding divisions of the subjectmatters of inquiry. Identifiable through technical methods of investigation and report, not through purported differences in material or other forms of purported substance.

Physiological: That portion of biological inquiry which

forms the second outstanding division of the subjectmatter of all inquiry as at present in process; differentiated from the physical by the techniques of inquiry employed more significantly than by mention of its specialized organic locus. See *Behavioral.*

Pragmatic: This word is included here (but no other of its kind except epistemological) solely to permit a warning against its current degradation in making it stand for what is practical to a single organism in limited durational spread — this being a use remote from that of its origin.

Process: To be used aspectually or phasally. See *Activity.*

Proposition: Closely allied to proposal both etymologically and in practical daily use. Widely divorced from this, and greatly confused in its current appearances in the logics. Many efforts in the last two decades to distinguish it clearly from assertion, statement, sentence, and other words of this type upon the basis of the older self-oriented logics, have only served to increase the difficulties. Sufficient light is thrown upon its status by its demand, concealed or open, that its component terms be independent fixities while at the same time it hypostatizes itself into an ultimate fixity. Treated in Dewey's *Logic, the Theory of Inquiry* under radically different construction as an intermediate and instrumental stage in inquiry.

Reaction: To be coupled with excitation in *physiological* reference (q.v.).

Real: Its use to be completely avoided when not as a recognized synonym for genuine as opposed to sham or counterfeit.

Reality: As commonly used, it may rank as the most metaphysical of all words in the most obnoxious sense of metaphysics, since it is supposed to name something which lies underneath and behind all knowing, and yet, as Reality, something incapable of being known in fact and as fact.

Reference: Behavioral application of naming to named. See *Connection* and *Relation.*

Relation: Various current uses, ranging from casual to ostentatious; rarely with any sustained effort at localization of the "named," as is shown by ever-recurrent discussions (and, what is worse, evasions) as to whether relation (assumed to have a certain existence somewhere as itself factual) is "internal" or "external." Suggested by us to name system among words, in correlation with reference and connection (q.v.).[6]

Response: To be coupled with stimulus in the signal range of behavior.

Science, Scientific: Our use of this word is to designate the most advanced stage of specification of our times — the "best knowledge" by the tests of employment and indicated growth.

Self: Open to aspectual examination under transactional construction. Where substantively stressed as itself an object, self should not be permitted also an aura of transactional values, tacitly, and apart from express development.[7]

Self-Action: Used to indicate various primitive treatments of the known, prior in historical development to interactional and transactional treatments. Rarely found today except in philosophical, logical, epistemological, and a few limited psychological regions of inquiry.

Sentence: No basic distinction of sentence from word nor of meaning of sentence from verbal embodiment of sentence remains when language is viewed as transactionally behavioral.

Sign: This name applied transactionally to organic-environmental behavior. To be understood always as sign-process; never with localization of sign either in organism or in environment separately taken. Hence never as if signs were of two kinds: the natural and the artificial. Coterminous with behavioral process, and thus technically characteristic of all behaviors viewed in their knowing-known aspects. Distinctive as technical mark of separation of behavioral from physiological process, with the disjoin-

ture of research in the present day on this borderline more
marked than that on the borderline between physics and
physiology, where biophysics is making strong advance.
Evolutionary stages and contemporary levels differentiated
into signal, name, and symbol.

Sign-Process: Synonym for *Sign*.

Signal: The perceptive-manipulative level and stage of
sign in transactional presentation. Border-regions between
signaling and naming still imperfectly explored, and con-
cise characterizations not yet available.

Situation: The more general, and less clearly specified,
range of the named phase of fact. In our transactional development, the word is not used in the sense of environment; if so used, it should not be allowed to introduce
transactional implications tacitly.

Social: The word in its current uses is defective for all
general inquiry and theory. See *Individual*.

Space-Time: Space and time alike to be taken transactionally and behaviorally — never as fixed or given frames
(formal, absolute, or Newtonian) nor exclusively as physical specializations of the types known since relativity.[8]

Specification: The most highly perfected naming behavior. Best exhibited in modern science. Requires freedom from the defectively realistic application of the form
of syllogism commonly known as Aristotelian.

Stimulus: An unclarified word, even for most of its key-
word uses in psychology. The possibility of an adequate
transactional specification for it will be a critical test of
transactional construction. The indicated method of procedure will be through the thorough-going substitution of
nouns of action such as "stimulation" in place of substantive nouns such as "stimulus" is usually taken to be.

Subject: This word can profitably be dropped, so long
as subjects are presented as in themselves objects. Subject
was object in Greece and remains unclarified today. Might
be properly used, perhaps, in the sense of "topic" as "subjectmatter undergoing inquiry," in differentiation from
"object" as "subjectmatter determined by inquiry."

Subjective: Even less dependable as a word than objective (q.v.).

Subjectmatter: Whatever is before inquiry where inquiry has the range of namings-named. The main divisions in present-day research are into physical, physiological, and behavioral.

Substance: No word of this type has place in the present system of formulation. See *Entity*.

Symbol: A non-naming component of symboling behavior. To be taken transactionally, and not in hypostatization. Thus comparable with name and signal.

Symboling, Symbolization: An advance of sign beyond naming, accompanied by disappearance of specific reference (q.v.) such as naming develops.

System: Perhaps a usable word where transactional inquiry is under way. Thus distinguished from organization which would represent interaction. "Full system" has occasionally been used to direct attention to deliberately comprehensive transactional procedure.

Term: This word has today accurate use as a name only in mathematical formulation where, even permitting it several different applications, no confusion results. The phrase "in terms of" is often convenient and, simply used, is harmless. In the older syllogism term long retained a surface appearance of exactness (q.v.) which it lost when the language-existence issues involved became too prominent. For the most part in current writing it seems to be used loosely for "word carefully employed." It is, however, frequently entangled in the difficulties of concept. Given sufficient agreement among workers, term could perhaps be safely used for the range of specification, and this without complications arising from its mathematical uses. It might, then, be characterized as follows: Term: a firm name as established through inquiry; particularly, a name for the group of all those names that name whatever has acquired technically assured standing as object.

Thing: Most generally used for anything named. This very generality gives it frequent advantage over its pretentious substitutes, Entity and Substance, and more particularly over Object in the common case in which the type of objectivity involved is not specified. Though sometimes facilitating epistemological or logical evasion, its very looseness of application is safer than the insufficiently analyzed rigidities of the other words mentioned. *See* Chapter II, note 3, Chapter IV, note 7, and Chapter X, Section II.

Time: See *Space-time.*

Trans: This prefix has, in older usage, the sense of beyond, but in much recent development it stands for across, from side to side, etc. To be stressed is the radical importance at the present time of a clear differentiation between trans and inter (q.v.).

Transaction: The knowing-known taken as one process in cases in which in older discussions the knowings and knowns are separated and viewed as in interaction. The knowns and the named in their turn taken as phases of a common process in cases in which otherwise they have been viewed as separated components, allotted irregular degrees of independence, and examined in the form of interactions. See *Interaction.*

Transactor: See *Actor.*

True, Truth: These words lack accuracy in modern professedly technical uses, in that the closer they are examined, it frequently happens, the more inaccurate they appear. "Warranted assertion" (Dewey) is one form of replacement. Confinement to "semantic" instances is helpful, so far as "semantic" itself gains accuracy of use. A subjectmatter now in great need of empirical inquiry, with such inquiry apparently wholly futile under traditional approaches.

Vague. This word is itself vaguely used, and this as well in our preceding inquiries as elsewhere. It should be replaced by names specifying the kind and degree of inaccuracy or inexactness implied.

Word: To be used without presumptive separation of its "meaning" as "mental" from its "embodiment" (airwaves, marks on paper, vocal utterances, etc.) as "physical"; in other words, to be taken always as behavioral transaction, and thus as a subjectmatter examined whole as it comes, rather than in clumsily fractured bits.

Some of the above words enter our trial group of names as representative of the postulation we have adopted: The remainder fall into two sub-groups: words, namely, that may probably be clarified and salvaged, and others that show themselves so confused and debased that we unqualifiedly urge their rejection from all technical discourse at the present time. This is as far as we have been able to proceed in terminological systematization under the chaotic state of current discussion.

With respect to our central postulations: first, that knowings-knowns are to be transactionally studied, and secondly, that namings, when transactionally studied, show themselves as directly existential knowings, we renew our repeated reminder and caution. We are all aware that knowings, as behaviors, lie within, or among, wider ranges of behaviors. We are also all aware that the word "knowing" is itself variously applied to phenomena at perhaps every scattered stage of behavior from the earliest and simplest organic orientations to the most complex displays of putatively extrapolated supra-organic pseudocertainties. The range of our own inquiry — the central range of technically transactional fact-determination — will be declared by some readers to demand its own "interpretation" on the basis of behavioral activities taken as antecedent and "causal" to it. By others all inquiry in our range will be declared to be under the control of powers detached from, and presumptively "higher" than, any such behavioral activity. Our own assertion is that, no matter how dogmatically either of these declarations may be made, the passage of time will more and more require an ever broadening and deepening inquiry into the characteristic processes of organization and system they involve. It is our hope that the more naïve fiats will some day cease to be satisfactory even to their most ardent pronouncers. Progress from stylized cue or loose characterization to careful specification becomes thus a compelling need, and it is with the possibilities of such progress under postulation that we have here experimented. Detachable empiricals and detachable rationals are alike rejected.

Finally, both with regard to postulation and to terminology, we are *seeking* the firm (q.v.) and not trying to decree it.

1 See Chapter III.

2 How much territory the word "knowledge" is made to cover may be seen from what is reported of it in Runes' *The Dictionary of Philosophy* (1942). Knowledge appears as: "Relations known. Apprehended truth. Opposite of opinion. Certain knowledge is more than opinion, less than truth. Theory of knowledge, or epistemology (q.v.), is the systematic investigation and exposition of the principles of the possibility of knowledge. In epistemology: the relation between object and subject."

3 Compare especially the tentative list of words suggested at the close of Chapter II.

4 Chapter II, notes 16 and 23; Chapter VI, note 4; and Chapter VII, Section I.

5 Transactions: doings, proceedings, dealings. Interaction: reciprocal action or influence of persons or things on each other (Oxford Dictionary).

6 See Dewey, *Logic, the Theory of Inquiry* (New York, 1938), p. 55, for such a presentation.

7 In illustration: Mead's wide-ranging transactional inquiries are still taken by most of his followers in the sense of interesting comments on an object, namely the "self," in independence.

8 See Bentley, "The Factual Space and Time of Behavior," *The Journal of Philosophy*, XXXVIII (1941), 477-485.

CHAPTER TWELVE

SUMMARY OF PROGRESS MADE

THE research upon which we have made report has exhibited itself in three main phases: at the beginning, an endeavor to secure dependable namings in the chosen field; next, a display of the current linguistic insecurity in activities in those fields; thirdly, an initial development of the transactional approach which becomes necessary, in our view, if reliable namings are to be secured. The first of these phases is presented in Chapters II, III, and XI, and has been allowed to rest with such terminological suggestions as the last of these chapters offers. The second, seen in Chapters I, VII, VIII, and IX, was expanded far beyond preliminary expectation, as it became clear to us that, without increased recognition of the extent of the underlying linguistic incoherence, little attention would be paid to the need for reform. The third was sketched in Chapters IV, V, VI, and X; its further development remains for later presentation in psychological, linguistic, and mathematical ranges corresponding to the levels of Signal, Designation, and Symbol within Behavior.

In most general statement our chosen postulatory approach presents the human organism as a phase of cosmic process along with all of his activities including his knowings and even his own inquiries into his knowings as themselves knowns. The knowings are examined within the ranges of the known, and the knowns within the ranges of the knowing; the word "ranges" being here understood, not as limiting the research in any way, but as vouching for its full freedom and openness. This approach does not imply an absorption of knowing activities into a physical cosmos, any more than it implies an absorption of the physical cosmos into a structure of knowings. It implies neither. This must be most emphatically asserted. Emphasis is all the more necessary because the position of the present writers, whether in their separate inquiries or in the present joint undertaking, is so frequently mis-stated. In illustration, two recent notices of our procedure in the technical journal that we regard as standing closest to our field of inquiry[1] have described us as neglecting a difference, radical in nature, taken to exist between psychological and logical facts: a difference which, they appear to hold, ought to be known to everyone as crucial for all inquiries in this field. One reviewer goes even further, in disregard of our most explicit expression at other points, when from a detached preliminary phrase he infers that we reject "abstraction" from both mathematical and logical operations. This latter opinion will, we feel sure, be dissipated upon even the most hasty survey of our texts. The former is likewise a misunderstanding that cannot maintain itself under study. We may assure all such critics that from early youth we have been aware of an *academic* and *pedagogical* distinction of logical from psychological. We certainly make no attempt to deny it, and we do not disregard it. Quite the contrary. Facing this distinction in the presence of the actual life processes and behaviors of human beings, we deny any rigid *factual* difference such as the academic treatment implies. Moreover, it has been our sustained effort throughout all our inquiry to show the practicability of theoretical construction upon a new basis by offering the beginnings of its development. We have as strong an objection to the assumption of a science of psychology severed from a logic and yet held basic to that logic, as we have to a logic severed from a psychology and proclaimed as if it existed in a realm of its own where it regards itself as basic to the psychology. We regard knowings and reasonings and mathematical and scientific adventurings even up to their highest abstractions, as activities of men — as veritably men's behaviors — and we regard the study of these particular knowing behaviors as lying within the general field of behavioral inquiry; while at the same time we regard psychological inquiry itself and all its facts and conclusions as being presented to us under the limitations and qualifications of their being known. None of this involves any interference with the practical differentiations of inquiry as between logic and psychology, any more than it interferes with differentiations within either of these fields taken separately. Specializations of attention and effort based on methods and on subject-matters methodologically differentiated remain as valid and usable as ever.

The difficulty in mutual understanding in such cases as the above lies, we believe, in the various conventionally frozen sets of implications which many of the crucial words that are employed carry over from the past, and which have not yet been resolved under factual examination. They are like the different focussings of different linguistic spectacles which yield strangely different pictures of presumptive fact. It is this deficiency in communication that calls for the extended examination we have given several of the leading current texts. It is this deficiency also that explains the often clumsy and labored expression we have permitted ourselves to retain in the endeavor to keep the right emphasis upon the intended subjects of our statements. Striking illustration of the dangers of ordinary rhetorical formulation have been provided several times in the course of preliminary publication through the effects that have followed some of the kindly efforts of proofreaders, copyeditors or other good friends to improve our diction by the use of conventional phrasings.

It is often claimed that work in our field of research should be confined to specific problems in limited regions, and that in this way alone can be found safety and escape from metaphysical traps. However we cannot accept this claim. For any reader who regards our procedures and postulations as more general than the present state of inquiry justifies, we suggest consideration of the closing words of Clerk Maxwell in his treatise, *Matter and Motion*, from which we have made earlier citations.[2] Maxwell was discussing the development of material systems, while we are interested in the development of knowledge systems. We cite him strictly upon an issue as to *methods of inquiry* useful in their proper times and places to man, the irrepressible inquirer, and without any implication whatever of preference for material systems over knowledge systems, or *vice versa*. His attention became concentrated upon the use of hypothesis in "molecular science," and he declared that the degree of success in its use "depends on the generality of the hypothesis we begin with." Given the widest generality, then we may safely apply the results we hypothetically secure. But if we frame our hypothesis too specifically and too narrowly then, even if we get resulting constructs agreeable to the phenomena, our chosen hypothesis may still be wrong, unless we can prove that no other hypothesis would account for the phenomena. And finally:

> It is therefore of the greatest importance in all physical inquiries that we should be thoroughly acquainted with the most general properties of material systems, and it is for this reason that in this book I have rather dwelt on these general properties than entered on the more varied and interesting field of the special properties of particular forms of matter.

With the word "behavioral" inserted for the words "physical" and "material," this well expresses our attitude towards our own inquiry. Since it was the mathematics of Clerk Maxwell, dealing with the unparalleled observations of Faraday, that led in the end to the Einsteinian transformation of Newtonian physics, upon one of the highest levels of the use of hypothesis that the world has known, there is much justification for citing Maxwell authoritatively upon this issue. The citation, of course, is not in any way used to give support to our own form of generalization. It applies, instead, to whatever wide-ranging treatment in this field may in the course of time succeed in establishing itself, whosesoever it may be. For the moment the argument is used solely against men of epistemological despair.

We stress once more what has been our theme throughout: namely, that Specification and Transaction, the one on the side of the knowings, the other on the side of the knowns, make common advance. Once under way, once free of the negations and suppressions of ancient verbal lineage, they will be able to make ever more rapidly their joint advances. They make possible at once full spatial-temporal localization, and reference within it to the concrete and specific instance.

Since we have repeatedly said that the recognition of underlying problems and the opening of paths for further construction seems more important to us than the pronouncement of conclusions, we add a memorandum of the places of original publication of our reports for the possible use of anyone desirous of appraising the changes of procedure that came about in the course of the development. The original of Chapter VIII appeared in *Philosophy of Science,* XIII (1946); that of Chapter IX in *Philosophy and Phenomenological Research,* VIII (1947). The publication of the material of the other chapters was in *The Journal of Philosophy,* XLII, XLIII, XLIV, XLV (1945, 1946, 1947, 1948) and, except for that of Chapter X, in the order in which the chapters appear in this volume. The preface and the summary in Chapter XII were later added. The present Introduction accompanied Chapter I in the original publication.

¹ Alonzo Church, Review of three papers by John Dewey and Arthur F. Bentley, *The Journal of Symbolic Logic,* X (1945), pp. 132-133; Arthur

Francis Smullyan, Review of the paper, "Definition," by John Dewey and Arthur F. Bentley, *Ibid*, XII (1947), p. 99.

² J. Clerk Maxwell, *Matter and Motion*, (London, 1894), Articles CXLVIII and CXLIX.

APPENDIX

The following letter was written by John Dewey to a philosopher friend after the chapters of this volume were in type. The friend's questionings that elicited this reply will be found in *The Journal of Philosophy*, XLVI, (1949), pp. 329-342.

I

Discovery Bay,
Jamaica

My dear A——:

In sending you this letter I can not do otherwise than begin with expressing my appreciation of the spirit in which you have written. I also wish to express my gratitude to you for affording me this opportunity to restate the position which, as you suggest, has occasioned difficulties to others as well as to yourself.

When, however, I began to write to you in reply, I found myself in a quandary; in fact, on the horns of a dilemma. On the one hand it seemed obligatory for me to take up each one of your difficulties one by one, and do what I could to clarify each point. The more, however, I contemplated that course, the more I became doubtful of its success in attaining the desired end of clarification. If, I thought, I had not been able to make my position clear in the course of several hundred pages, how can I expect to accomplish that end in the course of a small number of pages devoted to a variety of themes? The other horn of the dilemma was that failure to take up all your points might seem to show a disrespect for your queries and criticism which I am very far from feeling. While I was pondering this matter, I received a letter from a younger fellow student of philosophy. In this letter, written naturally in ignorance of our proposed discussion, he quoted some words written by me some thirty years or more ago. The passage reads: "As philosophers, our disagreements with one another as to conclusions are trivial in comparison with our disagreements as to problems; to see the problem another sees, in the same perspective and at the same angle — that amounts to something. Agreement as to conclusions is in comparison perfunctory."

When I read this sentence it was as if a light dawned. It then occurred to me that I should proceed by trying to show that what is said by me in the book which is the source of your intellectual difficulties, is set forth in a context which is determined, entirely and exclusively, by problems that arise in connection with a development of a Theory of Inquiry; that is, in the context of problems that arise in undertaking an inquiry into the facts of inquiry. Accordingly, I concluded that I might best accede to your request for clarification of the difficulties you have experienced by means of a fresh statement of some of the fundamentals of my position. Since your difficulties and questions hang together, I am sure you will find no disrespect in my treating them as a systematic whole instead of as if they were scattered, independent, and fragmentary. There is also no disrespect in the belief that their systematic nature is due to the fact that you read what was actually written in the context of connection with the conduct of *inquiry* as if it were written in an *ontological* context — especially as this latter context is classic, in comparison with which that set forth in my *Theory of Inquiry* is an upstart.

I hope, accordingly, dear A——, that you will understand why what is here said delays in coming to a direct answer to specific questions you raise. In order to make my position clear as a whole I have to begin at the beginning, which in the present case lies far back of your questions. I think, for example, that the importance in my writings of what is designated by the words "situation" and "problematic" must have escaped you. Whether this be so or not, we have right here at hand what seems to be an excellent example of their meaning. "Situation" stands for something inclusive of a large number of diverse elements existing across wide areas of space and long periods of time, but which, nevertheless, have their own unity. This discussion which we are here and now carrying on is precisely part of a situation. Your letter to me and what I am writing in response are evidently parts of that to which I have given the name "situation"; while these items are conspicuous features of the situation they are far from being the only or even the chief ones. In each case there is prolonged prior study: into this study have entered teachers, books, articles, and all the contacts which have shaped the views that now find themselves in disagreement with each other. It is this complex of fact that determines also the applicability of "problematic" to the present situation. That word stands for the existence of something questionable, and hence provocative of investigation, examination, discussion — in short, inquiry. However, the word "problematic" covers such a great variety of occasions for inquiry that it may be helpful to specify a number of them. It covers the features that are designated by such adjectives as confusing, perplexing, disturbed, unsettled, indecisive; and by such nouns as jars, hitches, breaks, blocks — in short, all incidents occasioning an interruption of the smooth, straightforward course of behavior and that deflect it into the kind of behavior constituting inquiry.

The foregoing, as I quite recognize, my dear friend, is an indirect approach to the questions you raise. Perhaps I can render it somewhat more direct by calling attention to the fact that the unsettled, indecisive character of the situation with which inquiry is compelled to deal affects all of the subjectmatters that enter into all inquiry. It affects, on the one hand, the observed existing facts that are taken to locate and delimit the problem; on the other side, it affects all of the suggestions, surmises, ideas that are entertained as possible solutions of the problem. There is, of course, nothing at all sacred in employing the words "potentiality" and "possibility" to designate the subjectmatters in inquiry that stand for progress made in determining, respectively, the problem and its solution. What is important, and from the standpoint of my position, all important, is that the tentative, on-trial nature of the subjectmatters involved in each case be recognized; while that recognition can hardly be attained unless some names are given. The indecisive and tentative nature of the subjectmatters involved might have been expressed by using either the word "potentiality" or the word "possibility" for the subjectmatters of both the problem and solution. But in that case, it would have been at once necessary to find sub-terms to designate the distinctive places held and the specific offices or functions performed by subjectmatters constituting what is taken during the conduct of inquiry, as on the one hand the problem to be dealt with and on the other hand the solution suggested: both of them, let it be recalled, being tentative on-trial since both are equally implicated in doubt and inquiry.

From the standpoint of conduct of inquiry it directly follows that the nature of the problem as well as of the solution to be reached is *under* inquiry; failure in solution is sure to result if the problem has not been properly located and described. While this fact is not offered as a justification of the use of the particular words "potentiality" and "possibility," given the standpoint of connection with inquiry, it does imperatively demand the use of two different words as *names* and as names for two disparate but complementary uses.

In any case, dear friend, what has been said has a much wider application than simply to the meaning to be assigned to these two words. For it indicates how and why meaning assigned to *any* phase or aspect of my position which puts what is said in an ontological context instead of that of inquiry is sure to go amiss in respect to understanding. And when I say this, I say it in full recognition of the fact that exclusion of the need of ontological backing and reference of any kind may quite readily convert your difficulty and doubt into outright rejection. But, after all, rejection based upon understanding is better than apparent agreement based on misunderstanding. I should be happy indeed, dear A——, to obtain your assent to my view, but failing that, I shall be quite content if I can obtain an understanding of what it is that my theory of inquiry is trying to do if and when it is taken to be, wholly and exclusively, a theory of knowledge.

II

I hardly need remind you that there is nothing new in recognizing that both observed facts and ideas, theories, rational principles, have entered in fundamental ways into historic discussion of philosophical theories of knowledge. There is nothing new to be found in the fact that I have made them the subjectmatter of a problem. Whatever relative novelty may be found in my position consists in regarding the *problem* as belonging in the context of the conduct of inquiry and not in either the traditional ontological or the traditional epistemological context. I shall, accordingly, in the interest of elucidation attempt another line of approach: one in terms of familiar historical materials.

One outstanding problem of modern philosophy of knowledge is found in its long preoccupation with the controversy between empiricism and rationalism. Even today, when the controversy has receded at least temporarily into the background, it can not be denied by one who surveys the course of the historical discussion that important statements were made with respect both to what was called experience and what was called reason, and this in spite of the fact that the controversy never reached the satisfactory conclusion constituted by the two parties arriving at agreement. It is not a mere biographical fact, accordingly, if I call attention to the fact that I am in no way an inventor of the problem in a theory of knowledge of the relation to each other of observed factual material on one side and ideational or theoretical material on the other side. The failure of the controversy to arrive at solution through agreement is an important ground of the idea that it is worth while to take these constituents of controversy out of an ontological context, and note how they look when they are placed in the context of the use they perform and the service they render in the context of *inquiry*. The net product of this way of viewing the two factors in the old controversy is expressed in the phrase "The Autonomy of Inquiry." That phrase does more than merely occur in the book that is the source of the discussion in which we are now engaged, since its use there was intended to serve as a key to understanding its contents. The elimination of ontological reference that at first sight may seem portentous actually amounts to the simple matter of saying that whatever claims to be or to convey knowledge has to be found in the context of inquiry; and that this thesis applies to *every* statement which is put forth in the theory of knowledge, whether the latter deals with its origin, its nature, or its possibility.

III

In approaching the special topic of mathematical subject-matter and mathematical inquiry, I find it necessary, as well as advisable, to begin with the topic of Abstraction. According to the standpoint taken in *The Theory of Inquiry*, something of the nature of abstraction is found in the case of *all* ideas and of all theories. Abstraction from assured and certain existential reference belongs to *every* suggestion of a possible solution; otherwise inquiry comes to an end and positive assertion takes its place. But subjectmatters constituting during the course of inquiry what is taken to be the *problem* are also held in suspense. If they are not so maintained, then, to repeat, inquiry comes automatically to an end. It *terminates* even though the termination is not, with respect to inquiry, a *conclusion*. A flight away from what there and then exists does not of itself accomplish anything. It may take the form of day-dreaming or building castles in the air. But when the flight lands upon what for the purpose of inquiry is an idea, it at once becomes the point of departure for instigating and directing new observations serving to bring to light facts the use of which will develop further use and which thereby develop awareness of the problem to be dealt with, and consequently serve to indicate an improved mode of solution; which in turn instigates and directs new observation of existential material, and so on and on till both problem and solution take on a determinate form. In short, unless it is clearly recognized that in *every* case of obstructed ongoing behavior *"ideas"* are temporary deviations and escapes, what I have called their functional and operational standing will not be understood. Every *idea* is an *escape,* but escapes are saved from being *evasions* so far as they are put to use in evoking and directing observations of further factual material.

I am reasonably confident, dear A——, that in this one point at least we shall find ourselves in agreement. I do not believe that either of us is in sympathy with the wholesale attacks upon abstractions that are now being made in some quarters. Theories as they are used in scientific inquiry are themselves matters of systematic abstraction. Like ideas, they get away from what may be called the immediately given facts in order to be applicable to a much fuller range of relevant facts. A scientific theory differs from the ideas which, as we say, "pop into our heads," only in its vast and systematic range of applicability. The peculiarity of *scientific* abstraction lies in the degree of its freedom from *particular* existential adhesions.

It follows as a matter of course that abstraction is carried on indefinitely further in scientific inquiry than there is occasion for carrying it on in connection with the affairs of everyday life. For, in the latter case, an abstraction loses its serviceability if it is carried beyond applicability to the *specific* difficulty then and there encountered. In the case of scientific inquiry, theory is carried to a point of abstraction which renders it available in dealing with a maximum variety of possible uses. What we call *comprehensiveness* in the case of a theory is not a matter of its own content, but of the serviceability in range of application of that content. It is perhaps worth while to notice that the Newtonian theory was, for a long time, believed to be completely comprehensive in respect to all astronomical subjectmatter; not merely that which had already been observed but to all that ever could possibly be observed. Finally, there occurred what in the case of an everyday affair of life would be called a *hitch* or *block*. Instead of the discrepancy being accepted as a finality it was, however, at once *put to use* in suggesting further development upon the side of theory as abstraction. The outcome constitutes what is known as "The Relativity Theory." Newton had carried *his* abstraction to a point which was shocking to many of his contemporaries. They felt that it took away the reality which gave point and zest to the affairs of life, moral and esthetic as well as practical in a utilitarian sense. In so doing they made the same mistake that professional philosophers made after them. They treated a use, function, and service rendered in conduct of inquiry as if it had ontological reference apart from inquiry.

When viewed from the standpoint of its position in the conduct of inquiry, the relativity theory rendered space and time themselves subjectmatters of inquiry instead of its fixed limits. In the Newtonian theory they had been treated as an *Ultima Thule* beyond which scientific inquiry could not possibly go. These considerations may be used, dear A——, as an example of how submitting inquiry to ontological reference obstructs it. But here they are mentioned on account of their bearing on the question of mathematical subjectmatter. No matter how far physical theory carries its abstractions, it would contradict the very intent of the latter if they went beyond possibility of application to every kind of *observable* existential materials. The privilege of *that* use and office is reserved for mathematical inquiry. The story of the development of mathematical inquiry shows that its advances have usually been occasioned by something which struck some inquirer as a hitch or block in the previous state of its subjectmatter. But in the course of the last one or two generations, mathematicians have arrived at the point at which they see that the heart of the work they are engaged in is the method of free postulation. It is hardly necessary to note how the constructions in which the interior angles of a triangle are, as the case may be, either less or more than two right angles, have removed the ontological obstructions that inhered in Euclidean geometry. While in most respects I am compelled to admit that important features of my position are incompatible with philosophical theories that have received authoritative and, so to say, official formulations, in this matter of mathematics, I believe, Mr. A——, that I am "on the side of the angels." At all events, I did not invent the position that I have taken in the foregoing statements. I took it over almost bodily from what the mathematicians have said who have brought about the recent immense advances in that subject. It is the progress of mathematical inquiry *as* mathematical which has profoundly shaken the ontological rigidity once belonging to the circle and the triangle as their own immutable "essences." I can not, accordingly, refrain from mentioning the rôle that considerations similar to those just mentioned have played in inducing me to undertake an attempt to convert all the *ontological,* as prior to inquiry, into the *logical* as occupied wholly and solely with what takes place in the conduct of inquiry as an evergoing concern.

cf. Kuhn

IV

In the hope that it may further a clarified understanding of my position, I shall now take up another outstanding problem of modern epistemological philosophy. It is a familiar fact that the historical systems of epistemological philosophy did their best to make ontological conclusions depend upon prior investigation of the conditions and nature of knowledge. A fact which is not so familiar, which indeed is often ignored, is that this attempt was itself based upon an ontological assumption of literally tremendous import; for it was assumed that whatever else knowledge is or is not, it is dependent upon the independent existence of a *knower* and of something *to be known;* occurring, that is, between mind and the world; between self and not-self; or, in words made familiar by use, between subject and object. The assumption consisted in holding that the subjectmatters designated by these antithetical terms are separate and independent; hence the problem of problems was to determine some method of harmonizing the status of one with the status of the other with respect to the possibility and nature of knowledge. Controversy on this topic, as is the case with the other historic problem already mentioned, has now receded into the background. It can not be affirmed, however, that the problem is settled by means of reaching an agreed-upon solution. It is rather as if it had been discovered that the competing theories of the various kinds of realism, idealism, and dualism had finally so covered the ground that nothing more could be found to say.

In this matter also it accordingly occurred to me that it might be a good idea to try the experiment of placing in the context of inquiry whatever matters were of moment and weight in what was urged by the various parties to the controversy. For observed and observable facts of inquiry are readily available: there is a mass of fact extending throughout the whole recorded intellectual history of man, in which are manifest for study and investigation both failures and successes — much as is the case in the story of any important human art. In this transfer of matters at issue from their prior ontological setting into a context that is set *wholly and only* by conditions of the conduct of inquiry, what had been taken to be inherent ontological demands were seen to be but arbitrary assumptions from their own standpoint, but important distinctions of use and office in the progressive carrying on of inquiry.

In pursuing this line of inquiry, it proved to be a natural affair to take as a point of departure the physiological connection and distinction of organism and environment as the *most readily observable* instance of the *principle* involved in the matter of the connection and distinction of "subject and object." Consideration of the simpler physiological activities which significantly enough already bore the name "functions" served to indicate that a life-activity is not anything going on *between* one thing, the organism, and another thing, the environment, but that, *as* life-activity, it is a simple event over and across that distinction (not to say separation). Anything that can be entitled to either of these names has first to be located and identified as it is incorporated, engrossed, in life-activity. Hence there was presented in an acute form the following problem: Under what conditions of life-activity and to what consequences in the latter is the distinction relevant?

The issue involved in this question coalesced, almost of itself, with the point of view independently reached in regard to knowing as inquiry with respect to its origin in the event of a hitch, blockage, or break, in the ongoing of an active situation. The coalescence worked both ways. With respect to the distinction within the course of physiological life-activity, the obvious suggestion was that the subjectmatters to which the names "organism" and "environment," respectively, apply are distinguished when some function, say digestion, is disturbed, unsettled, and it is necessary, *in order to do something about it* which will restore the normal activity (in which organs and foods work together in a single unified process) to *locate* the source of the trouble. Is there something wrong inside? Or is the source of the disturbance located in water or in food that has been taken into the system? When such a distinction is once clearly made there are those who devote themselves especially to inquiry into the structures and processes that can be *referred* distinctively to the organisms, (although they could not take place and be capable of such reference without continuous partnership in a single transaction) , while others study the relations of air, climate, foods, water, etc., to the maintenance of health — that is, of unified functionings.

What happens when distinctions which are indispensable to form and use in an efficient conduct of inquiry — that is to say, one which meets its own conditions *as* inquiry — are converted into something ontological, that is to say, into something taken to exist on its own account prior to inquiry and to which inquiry must conform, is exhibited, I submit, my dear questioner, in the epistemological phase of modern philosophy; and yet the new science could not have accomplished its revolution in astronomy, physics, and physiology if it had not *in the course of its own development* of method been able, by means of such distinctions as those to which theory gave the names "subject" and "object," "mind" and "the world," etc., to slough off the vast mass of irrelevant pre-conceptions which kept ancient and medieval cosmology from attaining scientific standing.

It is not implied, however, that what has just been said covers the whole scope of the problem. There remains the question of why at a particular time the distinction between knower and the subjectmatter to be known became so conspicuous and so central as to be for two centuries or more one of *the* outstanding philosophical issues. No such problem was urgent in either ancient or medieval philosophy. The idea that most directly suggests itself as an indication of a solution of this problem is that the rather sudden and certainly striking emergence of the "subject-object" problem is intimately connected with the cultural conditions that mark the transition of the medieval period into that age that is called *modern*. This view of the matter is, I believe, an interesting and even important hypothesis; it is one which in another connection might be followed out with advantage. It is introduced here, however, solely for whatever service it may render in understanding a position which, like that set forth in *The Theory of Inquiry*, transfers what had been taken to be ontological separations into distinctions that serve a useful, indeed necessary, function in conduct of inquiry.

Before leaving this endeavor to clarify my position through reference to well-known events in the history of philosophy, I shall mention a third matter which, unlike the two already mentioned, is still more or less actively pursued in contemporary philosophical discussion. I refer here to the extraordinary contrast that exists beyond peradventure between the subjectmatters that are known in science and those known in the course of our everyday and common living — common not only in the sense of the usual but of that which is shared by large numbers of human beings in the conduct of the affairs of their life. To avoid misunderstanding it should be observed that the word "practical" has a much fuller meaning when used to designate these affairs than it has when it is used in a narrow utilitarian way, since it includes the moral, the political, and the artistic. A simple but fairly typical example of the undeniable contrast between the subjectmatters of this common life and the knowings that are appropriate to it, and the subjectmatter and method of scientific knowing, is found in the radical unlikeness of the water we drink, wash with, sail boats upon, use to extinguish fires, etc., etc., and the H_2O of scientific subjectmatter.

It would appear dogmatic were I to say that the problem involved in this radical unlikeness of subjectmatters is insoluble if its terms are placed in an ontological context. But the differences between, say, a spiritualistic and a materialistic ontological solution remind us how far away we are from any agreed-upon solution. It hardly seems unreasonable to suggest that parties to the controversy are lined up on the basis of preferences which are external to the terms of the issue rather than on grounds which are logically related to it. When the issue pertaining to and derived from this contrast is placed and treated in the context of different types of *problems* demanding different methods of treatment and different types of subjectmatter, the problem involved assumes a very different shape from that which it has when it is taken to concern the ontological "reality." It would be irrelevant to the present issue were I to attempt to tell just what form the problem and its solution assume when they are seen and treated in the context of inquiry. It is relevant, however, to the understanding of the point of view to say that it demands statement on the ground of types of problems so different that they are capable of solution only in terms of types of subjectmatter as unlike one another as are those exemplified in the case of *"water."* I may, however, at least point out that a thirsty man seeking water to drink in a dry land would hardly be furthered in the emergency in which he finds himself by calling upon H_2O as his subjectmatter; while, on the other hand, the physicist engaged in his type of problem and inquiry would soon be brought to a halt if he could not treat water as H_2O. For it is on account of *that* mode of treatment that water is taken out of isolation as a subject of knowledge and brought into vital and intimate connection with an indefinitely extensive range of other matters qualitatively and immediately of radically different kinds from water and from one another.

It seems pertinent at this point, my dear A——, to refer to that aspect of my theory of knowledge to which I gave the name "instrumentalism." For it was intended to deal with the problem just mentioned on the basis of the

idea or hypothesis that scientific subjectmatter grows out
of and returns into the subjectmatter of the everyday kind;
— the kind of subjectmatter to which *on the basis of
ontological interpretation* it is totally and unqualifiedly
opposed. Upon the basis of this view the metaphysical
problem which so divided Berkeley from Sir Isaac Newton,
and which has occupied such a prominent place in philosophy ever since the rise of new physical science, is not
so much resolved as dissolved. Moreover, new construction
accrues to the subjectmatter of physical science just because of its extreme unlikeness to the subjectmatters
which for the sake of brevity may be called those of common sense. There is presented in this unlikeness a striking example of the view of the function of thoroughgoing
abstraction mentioned shortly ago. The extreme remoteness of the subjectmatter of physical science from the subjectmatter of everyday living is precisely that which
renders the former applicable to an immense variety of the
occasions that present themselves in the course of everyday
living. Today there is probably no case of everyday living
in which physical conditions hold a place that is beyond
the reach of being effectively dealt with on the ground of
available *scientific* subjectmatter. A similar statement is
now coming to hold regarding matters which are specifically physiological! Note, in evidence, the revolution that
is taking place in matters relating to illness and health.
Negative illustration, if not confirmation, may be supplied
by the backward state of both knowledge and practice in
matters that are distinctively human and moral. The latter
in my best judgment will continue to be matter of customs
and of conflict of customs until inquiry has found a method of abstraction which, because of its degree of remoteness from established customs, will bring them into a
light in which their nature will be indefinitely more
clearly seen than is now the case.

As I see the matter, what marks the scientific movement
that began a few centuries ago and that has accomplished

a veritable revolution in the methods and the conclusions of natural science are its *experimental* conduct and the fact that even the best established theories retain *hypothetical* status. Moreover, these two traits hang together. Theories as hypotheses are developed and tested through being put to use in the conducting of experimental activities which bring to the light of observation new areas of fact. Before the scientific revolution some theories were taken to be inherently settled beyond question because they dealt with Being that was eternal and immutable. During that period the word "hypothesis" meant that which *was placed under* subjectmatters so firmly as to be beyond the possibility of doubt or question. I do not know how I could better exemplify what I mean to be understood by the functional and operational character of ideational subjectmatter than by the radical change that in the development of scientific inquiry has taken place in the working position now attached to hypothesis, and to *theory* as hypothetical.

Let me say, my friend, that I have engaged in this fairly long, even if condensed, historical exposition solely for the sake of promoting understanding of my position. As I have already indicated, I did not originate the main figures that play their parts in my theory of knowing. I tried the experiment of transferring the old well-known figures from the stage of ontology to the stage of inquiry. As a consequence of this transfer, the scene as it presented itself to me was not only more coherent but indefinitely more instructive and humanly dramatic.

In any event the various factors, ancient and modern, of historical discussion and controversy were precipitated in the book whose subjectmatter is the occasion of this present exchange of views. I am aware that I have not made the kind of reply which in all probability you felt you had a right to anticipate. At the same time, while I have taken advantage of considerations that have occurred to me since the text in question was written, I do not believe that I have departed from its substantial intent and spirit. Yet I am bound to acknowledge that the occasion of precipitating historical materials into the treatise under discussion was the great variety of works on logical theory that appeared during the nineteenth century. As I look back I am led to the conclusion that the attempt conscientiously to do my full duty by these treatises is accountable for a certain cloudiness which obscures clear vision of what the book was trying to do. The force of the word "Logic," in all probability, has overshadowed for the reader the import of what in my intention was the significant expression, *The Theory of Inquiry*. For that source of misapprehension I accept full responsibility. I am, accordingly, the more grateful to you, my dear friendly critic, for affording me this opportunity for restatement, which, I venture to hope, is free from some of the encumbrances that load down the text. I shall be content if I have succeeded in this response to your request for clarification in conveying a better understanding of the *problem* that occupied me. As I reflect upon the historical course of philosophy I am unable to find its course marked by notable successes in the matter of conclusions attained. I yield to none, however, in admiring appreciation of the liberating work it has accomplished in opening new perspectives of vision through its sensitivity to problems it has laid hold of in ways which, over and over again, have loosened the hold upon us exerted by predispositions that owe their strength to conformities which became so habitual as not to be questioned, and which in all probability would still be unquestioned were it not for the debt we owe to philosophers.

Very sincerely yours,

JOHN DEWEY

INDEX

330